John Hampden (1595–1643), c. 1643, attributed to Robert Walker. (By the kind permission of Lady Bianca Eliot, Port Eliot Estate)

John Hampden (1595–1643), copy engraving by S. Freeman, taken from an original painting of John Hampden. (Buckinghamshire Archives – Licence: June22/CDL/157/Lester)

JOHN HAMPDEN AND THE BATTLE OF CHALGROVE 1643

The Political and Military Life of Hampden and His Legacy

Derek Lester

'This is the Century of the Soldier', Fulvio Testi, Poet, 1641

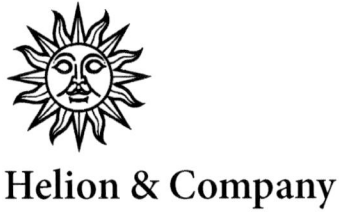

Helion & Company

Helion & Company Limited
Unit 8 Amherst Business Centre
Budbrooke Road
Warwick
CV34 5WE
England
Tel. 01926 499 619
Email: info@helion.co.uk
Website: www.helion.co.uk
Twitter: @helionbooks
Visit our blog http://blog.helion.co.uk/

Published by Helion & Company 2023
Designed and typeset by Serena Jones
Cover designed by Paul Hewitt, Battlefield Design (www.battlefield-design.co.uk)

Text © Derek Lester 2023
Illustrations © as individually credited
Maps drawn by Brigitta Gajdó © Helion & Company 2023
Front cover illustration by Giorgio Albertini © Helion & Company 2023

Every reasonable effort has been made to trace copyright holders and to obtain their permission for the use of copyright material. The author and publisher apologise for any errors or omissions in this work, and would be grateful if notified of any corrections that should be incorporated in future reprints or editions of this book.

ISBN 978-1-804511-96-1

British Library Cataloguing-in-Publication Data.
A catalogue record for this book is available from the British Library.

All rights reserved. No part of this publication may be reproduced, stored in a retrieval system, or transmitted, in any form, or by any means, electronic, mechanical, photocopying, recording or otherwise, without the express written consent of Helion & Company Limited.

For details of other military history titles published by Helion & Company
Limited, contact the above address, or visit our website: http://www.helion.co.uk

We always welcome receiving book proposals from prospective authors.

For Gill, who gave me strength of mind and love to complete each chapter.

For Teddy, who patiently waited by my feet for his walk, ears pricked to hear my glasses being folded away after much typing.

John Hampden's life lived with honour.

Contents

Acknowledgements   viii
Introduction   x

1. John Hampden's Importance   13
2. Let Battle Commence   24
3. Take Oxford or Reading   36
4. Time and Place   49
5. The Battle of Chalgrove   62
6. Aftermath   78
7. Political Aftermath   87
8. Exhumation   97
9. History and Propaganda   111

Appendix I: Book and Journal   129
Appendix II: *The Gentleman's Magazine and Historical Chronicle for May 1815*   132
Appendix III: The John Hampden Club (1812–1822)   134
Appendix IV: The Pye Paper   136
Appendix V: Letter Published in *The Times* (28 July 1828)   138
Appendix VI: Essex's *Two Letters*   143
Appendix VII: James Otis (alias John Hampden)   145
Appendix VIII: *The Sydney Morning Herald*   146
Appendix IX: Collected Letters of Private Correspondence   149
Appendix X: Boulogne and the Brookses: The Live of Reverend. G. W. Brooks   159
Appendix XI: The *Late Beating Up*   161

Bibliography   168

Acknowledgements

The saying 'standing on the shoulders of giants' is an apt quotation. Having stood on a few revered shoulders of the past, it has been discovered that some of these said notable giants were looking in the wrong direction. Many English Civil War historians from then to the present day have recounted with great authority the fiction emanating from these disorientated giants.

The true giants of history are those who listen to evidence presented without the necessity for gymnastics. Dr Simon Townley, editor of the *VCH* (*Victoria County History*), is one and Professor Ian Beckett is another who gave me the honour of citing my research in their publications. These giants, their patience tested with endless questions, gave me their time and expertise. Through their forbearance, *Oxoniensia* published 'The Military and Political Importance of the Battle of Chalgrove (1643)', and the *JSAHR* (*Journal of the Society for Army Historical Research*) published 'Clarendon and History: A Case Study of the Battle of Chalgrove, 18th June 1643'. Acknowledgement is just part of a heartfelt thanks and gigantic debt of gratitude.

Chalgrove Local History Group's support has been consistent from the time English Heritage published and incorporated the 'Battle of Chalgrove' into its Register of English Battlefields. Kevin Poile's expertise as a software engineer enabled my research on the Battle of Chalgrove to be maintained on the internet. His skill in guiding me into the ways of the internet, thus enabling me to glean and post information, is acknowledged with thanks. Keith Hodges, a printer by trade, gave his advice freely, which ensured images were up to the required standard for publication.

The maps capturing the fast-moving cavalry confrontations across Chalgrove's fields that Brigitta Gajdó, a graphic designer, has drawn, are amazing. Brigitta is a joy to watch and I thank her for bringing the battle of Chalgrove into picturesque animation.

Wikipedia's pages made gathering information a joy, and the encyclopaedia is recognised for its contribution. The Internet Archive is amazing. Where else can dozens of differently worded publications of *The History of the Rebellion* be found and word searched? All freely available at the click of a mouse. Internet Archive's contribution to my work is acknowledged with the deepest thanks.

The Bodleian Library is an institution born of another age; its archivists amazing. From an obscure ancient reference, an archivist found in the archive's depths Sir Edward Hyde's account of the Battle of Chalgrove. Hyde's account had been gleaned in the presence of the King from officers

ACKNOWLEDGEMENTS

captured at Chalgrove and written up on the day of the encounter. This find casts Clarendon's imposters' fake accounts of the Civil War to the scrapheap. Thank you is hardly adequate.

The following institutions have, in ways in which they excel, each contributed to the historical accuracy of my book: the *British Library*, *The National Archives*, *British Newspaper Archive*, the *Massachusetts Historical Society* and particularly *The Annotated Newspapers of Harbottle Dorr, Jr.*, the *Wiltshire and Swindon Archives*, *Buckinghamshire Archives* and especially Sally Mason, who diligently searched the records on my behalf, *Buckinghamshire Archaeological Society*, *Abingdon Archaeological Geophysics* and *Oxfordshire History Centre*. For those who freely contributed their expertise and knowledge but are not mentioned, a special thanks.

In 1612, William Webb was commissioned by Magdalen College, which John Hampden attended in 1615, to draw a map of Golder Manor. The Golder Manor map has been reproduced by the kind permission of the president and fellows of Magdalen College, Oxford. John Hampden's image that has pride of place is by courtesy of Port Eliot Estates. Gill, my long-suffering wife, who has stood by me especially in times of frustration when the words in my head refused to be written to the page, a special thanks.

Introduction

The author's craft and understanding of the English Civil War was learnt by leading Colonel John Hampden's Regiment of Foote, part of the English Civil War Society, onto famous battlefields. The regiment fought at Naseby, Marston Moor, Lansdown and Chalgrove, among so many other battles. Before each re-enactment, the history was researched to enable the re-enactors to put on an authentic show. Individuals researched their particular roles in the re-enactment to an academic level. Such was their enthusiasm, and many became authorities on their subject, whether it was the arts and crafts of the period or, as in the author's case, John Hampden's regiment and the Battle of Chalgrove, where Hampden was mortally wounded. Knowledge of seventeenth-century life seeps through the toughest mind or newest recruit when on a muster. What to wear, what is authentic and who will teach the arts of war to this new recruit? Soldiers are trained to be pikemen, musketeers, artillerymen, drummers and ensigns by officers chosen from the ranks for their battlefield skills and knowledge of seventeenth-century life, civilian and military. Officers chosen from the ranks must have the trust of the men when giving orders. Imagine the battlefield scene when the cavalry is bearing down upon your musket block at full gallop – what would be the order to the men? Get that order wrong, and real casualties could be the result. Equally, the officer must have trained his men for them to understand his orders. This engendered a thorough understanding of seventeenth-century military, civilian and political life; the lives of officers and gentlemen were, back then, aloof to those of the lower orders.

John Hampden's Regiment of Foote made the Red Lion, Chalgrove, its headquarters and joined with members of the Chalgrove Local History Group, who met regularly in the Lion. They were keen to show the regiment the History Group's archives relating to John Hampden and the Battle of Chalgrove. The regiment reciprocated by being the star attraction on many occasions for Chalgrove's May Day festival. The History Group had members who owned fields and property in Chalgrove and Warpsgrove and were aware of events that had crossed their land. Some could trace their ancestry back far into the past and were able to relay first-hand accounts of events passed down from the Georgian era. They had played as children in the great hedge, the boundary hedge between Chalgrove and Warpsgrove where Parliament left their reserves by Warpsgrove House.

Bishops of Lincoln, since the thirteenth century, had held the advowson to St James' Church, Warpsgrove. The advowson was passed to St Mary's

Church, Chalgrove, in 1932, but by then any visible traces of St James' were just pegged tiles and pieces of dressed stone dragged up by the plough. During the fourteenth century, plague struck Warpsgrove and devastated the small population, leaving the hamlet deserted. The 1822 Magdalen College estate map states in the gazetteer, 'Death Pit', and it is marked as being in the corner of Solinger field at the confluence of three parishes. Lidar images reveal there is 'something' at the spot marked 'Death Pit', leading to speculation that this plague pit is where those who were killed at the Battle of Chalgrove are buried.

The author was invited on 27 October 1992 to the inaugural meeting of the John Hampden Society in The Great Hall of Hampden House, Great Hampden. The meeting was attended by those who had an interest in 'honouring a great Englishman'. Professor John Adair was appointed president. Adair showed a keen interest in the Honour Guard and praised the soldiers of Hampden's Regiment of Foote on the attention to detail that they had given to their costume. Adair explained that he had raised the first Parliamentarian re-enactment regiment to counter Brigadier Peter Young's Royalist King's Guard. From this humble beginning, the Sealed Knot began its adventure on England's battlefields. Their association, Adair explained, went back to his time in the army being the Brigadier's adjutant. The John Hampden Society, Chalgrove Local History Group and the regiment established a bond of common interest on matters relating to John Hampden. In 1993, Chalgrove Parish Council wanted to celebrate the 350-year anniversary of the Battle of Chalgrove in style. Colonel John Hampden's Regiment of Foote – having previously organised Civil War events for Chalgrove's May Day festival and its association with the History Group – became deeply involved with organising the battle. The Chalgrove Local History Group was keen to dispel the Victorian concept of Chalgrove being a minor encounter. It was recounted that Brigadier Peter Young DSO (Distinguished Service Order), MC (Military Cross) and Two Bars, a notable historian, had come to Chalgrove in the early 1960s to research the battle. Young's papers are held in the archives of the National Army Museum, Chelsea. The term 'skirmish' was the prevailing orthodoxy, with 300 Parliamentarians fighting 2,000 Royalists at Chalgrove. Young asked the question of why the Royalists wrote in a contemporary paper that Parliament had 13 troops and a number of dragoon companies, a total of over 1,100 men. Young's analysis of Chalgrove was cut short when the greater prize of Edgehill was offered for his sharp military mind to investigate.

The anniversary date (Friday, 18 June 1993) began with Colonel John Hampden's Regiment of Foote forming up behind the Colonel's colour. Hampden's plain green standard bears the motto 'Vestigia Nulla Restrorsum', which translates approximately to 'never a backward step'. An American colour party from Upper Heyford followed Hampden's regiment to the monument and paid homage to Colonel John Hampden at a respectful distance while the Earl of Buckinghamshire gave a speech of dedication for John Hampden, his ancestor. Fifty years before, Chalgrove airfield had been commissioned for American airmen to fly reconnaissance missions. Our party stood heads bowed while the colour sergeant read the citation to honour the fallen.

The memorial stone, sourced by John Godfrey of the History Group, was unveiled. The following day, the History Group and John Hampden Society were well represented at the re-enactment of the Battle of Chalgrove held in the estate grounds of Ascott Park. The park was chosen since, on 16 August 1642, John Hampden along with Arthur Goodwin came to Ascott House and arrested the Earl of Berkshire, Sir John Curson, Mr Branthwaite and Mr Hone, who with other Justices were then sitting upon the Commission of Array. They falsely claimed that they were settling the peace of the county at Sir Robert Dormer's house in Ascott to stop him from implementing the commission in Oxfordshire. At the re-enactment of the Battle of Chalgrove, cannons roared, and musketeers stood their ground while firing at their adversaries. Pikeman in armour charged their pikes with aggression, the regiments' ensigns proudly flew their colours, and, with drummers beating out the orders, the armies joined in battle. The re-enactment reignited the villagers' interest in the Battle of Chalgrove.

The writer's research originated from his work for the Chalgrove Battle Group, their earliest success being to make a submission to an independent review panel in the 1990s that compelled English Heritage (with somewhat bad grace) to accept Chalgrove on its Register of English Battlefields, as they had so far classed it only as a skirmish. Subsequently, the *VCH* of Oxfordshire accepted the writer's interpretation of the battle in 2012. With the sponsorship of the *VCH*, the author was then invited to write an article for the journal *Oxoniensia*. Drawing upon previously unused sources, including estate maps and field work, this identified the true site of the battle at Chalgrove.

The Bodleian's catalogue on Clarendon State Papers is accepted by the curator to be very incorrect and the published work said to be by Edward Earl of Clarendon falsely acclaimed. Discussion has begun to find the way to have Clarendon State Papers transcribed and published.

This book not only examines the flawed historiography of the battle but also exposes the myths surrounding Hampden's funeral and burial and the supposed exhumation of his body by Lord Nugent in the nineteenth century. Nugent's work, in particular, is seen to be largely fiction, drawing upon an equally fictional account by 'Edward Clough'. Generally, this book addresses the dubious histories of the English Civil War that surfaced in the nineteenth century, as well as the manipulation of Hampden's political legacy in the eighteenth century, not least in the American colonies. There has been no biography of John Hampden published since that of John Adair in 1976. In short, the author believes that this book is a major contribution (and corrective) to the historiography of John Hampden's role in the English Civil War, as well as to the course and consequence of the Battle of Chalgrove on 18 June 1643. *John Hampden and the Battle of Chalgrove* re-establishes the facts of the English Civil War for historians to enjoy.

1

John Hampden's Importance

The village of Hampden was an Anglo-Saxon settlement. The *Domesday Book* mentions Baldwyn de Hampden as the lord and owner of Hampden. For services to William the Conqueror, Baldwyn de Hampden became Earl of Buckinghamshire and retained the family's estates.[1] By the eleventh century, the Normans had lost power in England. The monarchy had the ultimate power to rule, but descendants of William the Conqueror's appointed great barons had rights over the land inherited from their forefathers. These great barons had to attend the King's Council each year to receive the Monarch's orders. King John raised huge revenues from the barons to maintain an army, which caused them to rebel. The barons forced the King into signing the Magna Carta, which gave them a collective power over the monarchy. The King's Council evolved into a Parliament and later the House of Lords. Lords of the manor, other gentry and wealthy merchants fought for the right of representation into this elite band. The Lower House beneath the King's chamber evolved into the House of Commons, or Commoners' chamber, where the gentry could voice an opinion. The landed gentry's power derived from withholding taxes until the King's counsellors conceded to its demands, and these rights accumulated. The Commoners could not make law; they could only recommend items to the House of Lords. These items on occasions were bargained for against subsidies, which if the King gave a Royal Seal of Approval became Common Law. Commons representatives were elected by their peers, but who was selected led to candidates being bought or placed. It was the Monarch's prerogative whether to call or prorogue the House of Commons. The King had the power to arrest, incarcerate or order the death penalty on whoever he chose. The right of free speech in the House of Commons had been hard won, but those who questioned the King outside of the Commons could be subject to arbitrary arrest. By 1640, there had been 19 members of the Hampden family who had been High Sheriff of Buckinghamshire, and several had been MPs (Members of Parliament) from the fourteenth century onwards. John's father, William, had been MP for East Looe. Sir Edmund Hampden (1398–1471), Sheriff of Buckinghamshire,

---

1 Ann Williams, *Domesday Book* (London: Folio Society, 2003), vol. I, p.408.

was an ardent supporter of the House of Lancaster in the Wars of the Roses and died in the battle at Tewkesbury in May 1471. This was the House of Commons and attendant 400 years of history that John Hampden was elected to on becoming the member for Grampound in 1621.

Hampdens in America

Hampdens may have been in the Americas long before the *Mayflower* sailed from Plymouth in 1620. There are hints that Hampdens financed and manned privateers to capture Spanish galleons in the late 1500s. The John Hampden in the story below, apparently being more acquainted with the area and local 'Indian' customs than the brethren, was asked to be an escort or consort. Edward Winslow, a 'Saint' on the *Mayflower*, relayed the following story:

> The English, hearing of Massasoit's illness, and bearing in mind the Indian custom of visiting the sick, sent a delegation to his village. Governor Carter of Plymouth chose Edward Winslow, who had come with him on the *Mayflower*, as an emissary. Winslow knew the way, having been there before. The governor gave him medicinal cordials for Massasoit and provided him with a consort: 'one master John Hamden, [sic] a gentleman of London (who then wintered with us, and desired much to see the country) …'[2]

The name 'John' is common in the Hampden lineage. It is certain that the John Hampden mentioned above is not *the* John Hampden, for his whereabouts in 1622 are known and he was yet to become famous. In 1626, Charles I imprisoned Hampden and Sir John Eliot in the Gatehouse Goal, and 75 other gentlemen were similarly incarcerated for refusing to pay forced loans. The Providence Island Company was formed in 1629 on an island off the coast of what is now Nicaragua as a place for God-fearing people to grow tobacco and cotton. With the tacit approval of King Charles, the islanders engaged in privateering. John Hampden was not a shareholder but was cousin to one who had shares. Providence Island was an excellent stronghold for the privateers. The overladen Spanish ships were easy pickings for boats slipping out of Providence Island to intercept the galleons. Although Hampden was not a shareholder, he arbitrated between them and the company's London agents. An opposition party to King Charles' arbitrary rule coalesced around a group of Providence Island Company shareholders. They met to discuss company business at Brook House, Gray's Inn Road, Holborn, but party business was on the agenda.[3] Finally, after many attempts, in 1641, the Spanish overran Providence Island and dispersed the privateers.

---

2   Maija Jansson, 'Shared Memory: John Hampden, New World and Old', *Journal for Eighteenth-Century Studies*, 32:2 (2009), pp.157–71.

3   Arthur P. Newton, *The Colonising Activities of the English Puritans: The Last Phase of the Elizabethan Struggle with Spain* (New Haven, CT: Yale University Press, 1914), p.240.

The Massachusetts Bay Colony was founded in 1628 by the Massachusetts Bay Company, which included investors from the short-lived Dorchester Company of Cape Ann that had failed in 1623. In 1629, John Winthrop Sr was elected to be governor of the Massachusetts Bay Colony, a post he held for 20 years. Charles I prorogued Parliament in 1629 and began to persecute and suppress nonconformists. He was to rule by the Divine Right of Kings for the next 11 years. Winthrop Jr left Groton, Suffolk, for Massachusetts Bay with a large group of Puritan colonists. Through the 1630s, Massachusetts Bay Colony's success drew in 20,000 migrants, largely of Puritan persuasion. The colony was governed by a small group of Puritan leaders elected by designated freemen who had been admitted into the local church. Little tolerance was shown to Quakers, Anglicans or others of Baptist theology. Hampden became deeply involved in having the Petition of Right (1628) passed by both Houses. Throughout the 1628–1629 Parliament, the King endeavoured to impose Ship Money on all counties but was thwarted by Parliament. In the same year, Charles granted the Massachusetts Bay Colony a Royal Charter. The Massachusetts Bay Company agreed upon terms that became known as the 'Cambridge Agreement' in August 1629. The terms stipulated that the Massachusetts Bay Company would operate under local control in New England and would be answerable only to the English Crown.

In 1635, Saybrook Colony was formed in present-day Connecticut, headed by Lord Saye and Lord Brook. John Hampden was a founding investor in Saybrook. Trade between Saybrook and the Providence Island Company, through its association with John Hampden and Lord Brook, bolstered both companies. John Winthrop Jr (1606–1676) was the first governor of Saybrook, which he helped to build. Rector Robert Lenthall Sr (1565–1640) and Rector Robert Lenthall Jr (1600–1658) were from Great Missenden, Buckinghamshire, a small town just three miles from Great Hampden. They were jointly rectors of St Peter and St Paul's Church in Great Missenden through the benefice of the Fleetwood family. Through the church, John Hampden was well acquainted with the Lenthall family. A number of Great Missenden's puritanical residents left Great Missenden for Weymouth, Massachusetts, in the early 1630s. The Missenden colonists sent an invite to Robert Lenthall Jr to come to Weymouth, demanding that he write down a covenant for a new church.[4]

In 1635, the King imposed Ship Money on all English counties, and Hampden was assessed at 20 shillings on Stoke Mandeville – a sum that, on principle, he refused to pay. In the subsequent trial in 1637, the court found Hampden guilty by seven votes to five, but it was a guilty verdict that later was to establish the principle of 'no taxation without representation'. The Ship Money trial became his defining moment. When the case against Hampden was declared null and void by the Short Parliament, the cause of 'no taxation without representation' by an arbitrary court was invoked. Lenthall Jr set out for Weymouth into the stormy Atlantic in the winter of

---

[4] Patricia W. Claus, *Conscience is my Crown: A Family's Heroic Witness in an Age of Intolerance* (Leominster: Gracewing, 2017), p.70. Patricia Claus is a descendant of Rector Robert Lenthall.

JOHN HAMPDEN AND THE BATTLE OF CHALGROVE

The Hampden Monument, at Great Hampden.

1637–1638 with his wife, Susanna, and two children.[5] Lenthall brought the news that John Hampden had lost the High Court case against the King. At this juncture, the Ship Money trial did not have the sobriquet of 'no taxation without representation'. On 10 February 1638, Lenthall was forced to justify his beliefs before a conference of ministers in Dorchester, Massachusetts.[6] Robert Lenthall Jr was hounded out of the colonies, and, sometime around late spring of 1643, he set sail for home and a living at Great Hampden.[7]

The Ship Money trial may not have been so contentious following the guilty verdict. John Hampden paid the £8.4s.0d levied on Great Hampden but refused to pay the £1.0s.0d levied on Stoke Mandeville. By a quirk of how the ancient parish system operated, Honorend was technically in Stoke Mandeville although it formed part of the Great Hampden estate – a genuine reason to question the payment? Whether there was reason for his default of payment on the £1.11s.6d for Great Kimble is an open question. Hampden was found guilty of default of payment, yet – if, as history states, the stand at court was to challenge the King's authority – it begs the question: why he did not end up in front of the Star Chamber? The actual phrase of 'no taxation without representation' was first used in 1768 by Lord Camden. *The London Magazine* (February 1768) published Lord Camden's Speech on the Declaratory Bill of the Sovereignty of Great Britain with the headline 'No Taxation without Representation'.

Two hundred and fifty-seven years after the Ship Money trial, a monument was raised on Hampden's estate at Great Hampden, although the plot of land on which it stood was technically in Stoke Mandeville, on which the assessment for Ship Money was made. From August through September 1863, newspapers across the land recorded in a press release, 'Memorial to John Hampden – Several gentlemen interested in preserving the memory of the great patriot, and among them Lord Chief Justice Erle, have resolved to erect a monument by public subscription in the field in Stoke Mandeville in which the levy for ship money was made which led to a contest ending in Civil War'. This trumpeted event appears not to have happened in 1863. Lord

---

5   Claus, *Conscience is my Crown*, p.69.
6   Claus, *Conscience is my Crown*, p.68.
7   Claus, *Conscience is my Crown*, p.78.

Chief Justice William Erle (1793–1880) is accredited with having a Celtic cross raised at Honorend, as the dedication reads:

> For these lands in Stoke Mandeville, John Hampden was assessed in twenty shillings Ship Money, levied by command of the King, without authority of law, the 4 August 1635. By resisting the claim of the King in legal strife he upheld the rights of the people under the law, and became entitled to grateful remembrance. His work on earth ended after the conflict of Chalgrove Field, the 18 June 1643, and he rests in Great Hampden Church. W.E. 1863.

The monogram 'W.E. 1863' is that of William Erle.

The *Bucks Herald* (16 September 1865) ran an article titled 'Through Bucks', and the writer described part of his walk as, 'the Chiltern beech woods where Great Hampden lies so secluded that John Hampden's grandfather had to cut an avenue when Queen Elizabeth came to visit him'. The Ship Money monument is situated near Queen Elizabeth's avenue and is unmissable. Had the monument been erected when the writer passed by, he would have noted its presence. The *Bucks Herald* (12 November 1870) later ran an article titled 'Great Hampden – Restoration of the Church'. The article describes the church's setting in the Chiltern Hills in intimate detail, remarking on the farmsteads and cottages set amongst the extensive beech woods. Had the Ship Money monument been erected at the time, it would have been described in the detail afforded to the farmsteads and cottages.

Robert Gibbs (1816–1893), editor of the *Bucks Advertiser and Aylesbury News* (1878–1882), published in 1882 *Buckinghamshire: A Record of Local Occurrences and General Events, Chronologically Arranged*. In one of the volumes, Gibbs related that, on 11 September 1863, 'a monument was erected at Priestwood in Stoke Mandeville'.[8] 'Priestwood', an ancient name for Prestwood, had not been used for up to 100 years prior to 1882. *Record of Local Occurrences* was of limited edition and for general readership. Who would have been bothered to report and to whom – presuming the person was sufficiently knowledgeable to know the area of land on which Hampden refused to pay the Ship Money tax and had read Gibbs' article – that a monument did not exist? An assumption is easily made that, being the editor of the *Bucks Advertiser*, Gibbs had access to his newspaper's archive. A meticulous search had been made of the *Bucks Advertiser and Aylesbury News* dated 12 and 19 September 1863 for mention of the Ship Money monument; none was found. None of the multitude of newspapers, the *Bucks Herald* included, that received the press release that stated a monument 'is to be erected' and that gave the wording for the dedication that Gibbs had accessed mentioned the date of monument's erection.

The *Bucks Herald* (18 November 1882) published an article titled 'Local Intelligence' of erudite gentlemen strolling amongst the Chilterns and to Great Hampden. They wrote, 'At Stoke Mandeville they found the very

---

8   Robert Gibbs, *Buckinghamshire: A Record of Local Occurrences and General Events, Chronologically Arranged* (Aylesbury: Bucks Advertiser and Aylesbury News, 1882), vol. IV, p.181.

piece of land for which John Hampden refused to pay 40s. Ship money'. It is reasonable to assume that, had the monument been in evidence, the reporter would have described it in detail. The *Bucks Herald* (17 June 1893) then reported that 64 gentlemen from the prestigious Norwood Athenaeum Society visited the Earl of Buckinghamshire at Great Hampden, who showed them around his estate. The Earl personally escorted these gentlemen around his estate, eulogising about John Hampden and his stand against King Charles. The subsequent account in the society's journal by G. H. Lindsey-Renton, who organised the visit, makes it clear that he was well aware of the history of the Ship Money case.[9] It also indicates that the group looked up the Queen's Gap towards Hampden House from Honorend. There is no mention, however, of any monument, and it seems unlikely in the extreme that such a distinguished group would not have recorded its existence. Two years later, the *Bucks Herald* (25 May 1895) reported that photographs of an outing to Prestwood by the binding department of the Aylesbury printers, Hazell, Watson, and Viney, were taken of them standing by John Hampden's Ship Money monument. This begs the question: did Robert Gibbs, when writing *Record of Local Occurrences* in 1882, make the assumption that the monument had to have been erected in September 1863 and thus created the date 11 September 1863? The erected monument's dedication is as advertised in the newspapers of 1863. The press release stated that the monument was to be raised by public subscription. It was customary to engrave the names of leading subscribers into the stone, but, on the Ship Money monument, none are found. It is therefore safe to assume that the monument was carved and engraved in 1863 but never paid for; hence, there is no list of subscribers engraved on the stone. The evidence suggests it was erected at a later date. The writer conjectures that the Maltese cross monument (complete with inscription) was found in a stonemason's yard 30 years after being carved, possibly when the business moved to a new premises. The stonemason may have offered the monument to the Earl of Buckinghamshire at a knocked-down price. The Earl – conscious that purchasing or being given a 'second-hand' monument that had not been properly paid for could affect his reputation – determined that it would be erected on the site at Prestwood without ceremony or being reported to a newspaper. Taking the evidence that the monument was not evident in June 1893 but in May 1895 there is a report of photographs being taken of the obelisk it is reasonable to assume that it had been erected sometime between these dates.

Ordnance Survey has map 'Buckinghamshire sheet XXXVIII Surveyed: 1874 to 1877, Published: 1883' and has this map published on vellum. This map shows a monument at Honorend Farm on the Hampden Estate. The evidence is compelling on what is said to be the first published map of Great Hampden. The Ship Money monument is clearly depicted. But all is not as it

---

9   Lambeth Archive (LA) Stanley and W. F. Harradence (eds), '[visit] No 4 June 10th 1893 (Led by) Mr G. H. Lindsay-Renton – Great Hampden, Halton and Wendover', in *Upper Norwood Athenaeum: An Account of the Winter Meetings and Summer Excursions of 1892–3* (Privately published, n.d. [1893]), pp.47–54.

seems, as later confirmed by Ordnance Survey. Stoke Mandeville is written in bold letters, and under it is stated, 'Included since 1886 in the Civil Parish of Great and Little Hampden'. It follows that the original map published in 1883 was regularly updated and added to up to the second edition published in 1899. Thus, the Ship Money monument, as the evidence suggests, was not erected until after the visit by the Norwood Athenaeum Society in June 1893, and the writer's conjecture holds true.

In 1645, it was recorded that a 'John Hampden' settled in Christchurch, Barbados. How this Hampden got to Barbados is not known, but it is possible that he escaped from Providence Island. The family's history is told through an unbroken genealogy except for the period 1645 to 1674. Hurricanes are rife in the Caribbean, and, in 1674, one of tremendous ferocity hit Christchurch, and Hampden's possessions and records were lost. Hampden's genealogical record is confirmed by documentation from 1674 onwards. Earlier records from 1645 to 1674 were recorded from living memory of those who had suffered the hurricane's devastation.[10] The Hampdens' lineage is traced returning to England after a 200-year odyssey. Charles I's 11 years without a Parliament came to an abrupt end when the King recalled Parliament. Ship Money was an unpopular tax that a significant number had refused to pay until forced. By 1640, only a third of the tax had been collected, and, after the first Bishops' War, the King had to recall Parliament. The King's demand for subsidies to finance the second Bishops' War (1639–1640) was met with howls of protest from MPs. Oliver St John's address to the Ship Money judges at the trial had been profound. He had argued that the ancient rights of the Magna Carta and the 1628 Petition of Right gave Parliament alone the right to raise money beyond the normal revenue of the Crown. The legal definition of 'no taxation without representation' was established but not spoken when the King agreed to a bill in mid 1640 that declared Hampden's case null and void and Ship Money illegal. John Hampden had truly earned the title of '*Patriae Pater*' – 'father of the people'. When and by whom this phrase was first coined and published is open to question. The earliest mention of '*Patriae Pater*' so far found is in the 1702 first edition of *The History of the Rebellion and Civil Wars in England*.[11] Clarendon's original manuscripts are yet to be transcribed and published. Whether the '*Patriae Pater*' phrase said to have been coined by Edward Hyde in 1641 will be found in his private journal is an open question.

Oliver St John's move in Parliament to overturn the legality of Ship Money may have been the last straw. Unable to secure subsidies from Parliament to continue the fight against the Scots, the King dissolved the Short Parliament on 5 May 1640. Undaunted, the King assembled an army to fight the Scots in what became known as the second Bishops' War. The ill-supplied and reluctant army led by the King, with the Earl of Essex as his lieutenant general,

---

10 *Family tree of an unbroken line of Barbadian Hampden's 1645–1950 who returned to England in early 1800s* (private collection, unpublished).

11 Edward Hyde, *The History of the Rebellion and Civil Wars in England* (Oxford: Printed at Theater, 1702–1704), vol. II, book VII, pp.202–205.

marched slowly north to confront the Covenanters. Desertions were rife. In August 1640, the Earl of Strafford was appointed captain general of the Irish Army. His orders from the King were to invade Scotland to suppress the Covenanters. Following Strafford's appointment, the Earl of Argyll besieged Dumbarton Castle then raised an army through the power of the Committee of Estates for a pre-emptive invasion of England. The Covenanters' rout of the English Army at the Battle of Newburn (28 August 1640) wrecked the King's designs to subdue them. This military disaster caused the King's financial backers and Gentlemen of note to convene a Magnum Concilium, an ancient Great Council. The Concilium advised that the King should engage with Parliament. On the same day, a petition drafted by John Pym called for a new Parliament in England. The King then retired to York, opening the way for the Covenanters to march farther into England. By the end of September 1640, the King conceded to the Covenanters' demands, and, in consequence, Parliament was recalled. The King signed the Treaty of Ripon, which ended the Bishops' Wars, but the Scots demanded against an indemnity that a final settlement had to be agreed by the English Parliament. The King issued writs summoning Parliament to reconvene on 3 November 1640. The Scottish reformers occupied Westmoreland and Northumberland and referred to Durham and Newcastle as the 'Bishoprick'. The Scots held the North of England in pawn until February 1641 when the agreed settlement was paid. 'Yet the hearty giving of it to us, as to their brethren, refreshed us as much as the money itself', a preacher stated. A note following this statement and taken from Letters and Journals added, 'This money was charged by the Parliament to the King's account. – Hobbes'. The English Parliament was subsidising the Scots to do their work.[12]

The Earl of Strafford returned to England in August 1640 because of his failing health. It was said, however, that he was to join with the King at York. In November 1640, Strafford was sent to London by the King but was promptly arrested and charged with raising an army against England. Strafford was imprisoned in the Tower to languish there before being brought to the House of Lords to hear the charges against him. The arms, ammunition and supplies held by the King's Army of the North was, on its gradual disbanding throughout the summer of 1641, directed to the magazine at Hull under the King's order. The fact that Hull was an open port to the continent with easy and defendable access by way of the Humber had not gone unnoticed by Parliament. Parliament was aware that Charles had given his trusted servant, the Earl of Newcastle, a private commission to be governor of Hull.[13] The illegal imposition of Ship Money was strongly debated in the 'Long Parliament' during November and December 1641, which ended with the publication of the 'Grand Remonstrance'. Analyses

---

12   Eliot Warburton, *Memoirs of Prince Rupert, and the Cavaliers. Including their Private Correspondence, Now First Published from the Original Manuscripts* (London: Bentley, 1849), vol. I, p.176.

13   Edward Hyde, *The History of the Rebellion and Civil Wars in England* (Oxford: Printed at Theater, 1717), vol. I, p.509.

of the debates fail to find mention of 'no taxation without representation', although Ship Money was declared to be illegal.[14] King Charles I famously entered the House of Commons on 4 January 1642 to arrest John Hampden, Denzil Holles, Sir Arthur Hasilrigg, John Pym and William Strode. This act of folly effectively declared civil war. The King – with Queen Henrietta Maria and the Royalist entourage – left London for Hampton Court, arriving on 10 January 1642. Two days later, they left Hampton Court for the more defendable Windsor Castle. Queen Henrietta's closest servants were relaying her innermost secrets and the King's private instructions to Parliament. The Queen's plan to escape England through Dover, taking the Crown Jewels with her, was known to Parliament before she left Windsor. The King escorted Henrietta to Dover, and maybe Parliament hoped that he would go into exile with his Queen. While the Queen waited for a fair wind, the King's nephew, Prince Rupert, recently released from arrest by Holy Roman Emperor Ferdinand, came to Dover after a rough crossing. The King bade fond farewell to Henrietta as she boarded *The Lyon*, commanded by Captain Fox. The Queen – with the Crown Jewels on board and escorted by Prince Rupert – landed at Helvoetsluys on 28 February 1642. This royal entourage made their way to the Court of Prince Frederic Henry at The Hague. Charles would not see Henrietta again until mid July 1643.[15]

The Militia Ordinance was passed by the House of Lords on 5 March 1642. The news was taken by Lords Holland and Pembroke to the King, who, by 9 March, was in Newmarket. The King's grip on power ebbed away – his control of both Houses lost to the Acts of Parliament that he, by circumstance, was forced to sign. The King was pursued by Parliament's courtiers, who demanded that he sign over control of the Tower and that he give his consent to the Militia Bill. He refused, and, with protestations from Parliament following him, the King travelled north to York. Parliament petitioned the King to allow them to remove the arsenal from Hull to the Tower of London. Within days, the King was before the gates of Hull, but his demand for entry was refused by Sir John Hotham.[16] Without a garrison port in which to store an arsenal, supplies from the Low Countries could not be landed in England, even if they could be procured. Around this time, Charles received a letter from his Queen, and she wrote, 'the Dutch bargained like Turks [Barbary pirates]', which meant that no deal for arms and supplies could be made for the foreseeable future.

Edward Hyde MP – the great writer better known as 'Clarendon' – slipped away from London in May 1642 and joined the King at York. Edward Hyde was knighted and became Charles' Privy Counsellor and close advisor. Hyde had been keeping a private journal of events of the looming Civil War as

---

14 John Forster, *The Debates on the Grand Remonstrance, November and December, 1641. With an Introductory Essay on English Freedom under Plantagenet & Tudor Sovereigns* (London: John Murray, 1860).

15 Edward Hyde, *The History of the Rebellion and Civil Wars in England*, 1969 edn (Oxford: Clarendon Press, 1888), vol. I, pp.482–577.

16 Hyde, *The History of the Rebellion* (1888), vol. II, pp.48–49.

they happened since becoming an MP. The King's only chance of holding onto power was to get supplies from the Low Countries. At York Castle, in early June 1642, the King received 'Nineteen Propositions' from both Houses. These demands of Parliament would sequester the King's powers. Without the chance of a shipment of arms from the continent and rejecting Parliament's terms, the King was desperate. Clarendon wrote, 'The King had not at that time one barrel of powder nor one musket, nor any other provision necessary for an army.' Then 'Providence', stated Hyde, a small boat, set sail from Holland for Hull loaded with 200 barrels of powder, 3,000 muskets and eight field pieces. It was God's 'Providence' that had taken the Queen to Holland, although this ship was named *The Lyon*, and this little ship laden with supplies for the King was discovered heading for Hull. Ships under Parliament's command corralled *The Lyon* into the Humber, from which there was no escape – or so they thought. *The Lyon* slipped up a narrow creek in which the big boats could not follow and somehow, according to Clarendon, 'run the *The Lyon* ashore near Burlington'. The supplies were taken to York Castle. *The Lyon* only carried, as stated by Clarendon, 'in truth of cannon, powder, and bullet, with eight hundred muskets, which was all the King's magazine'. The audacious ruse had worked, but the Queen was powerless and in danger of capture by agents in Holland loyal to Parliament.[17]

The King's position appeared hopeless, but, with exaggeration of his supply of arms and money from his Queen, he granted commissions to loyal men of quality to raise regiments. The Earl of Lindsay was declared general of the army, Sir Jacob Ashley became major general of the foot, and Prince Rupert general of the horse. Rupert was trapped with the Queen in Holland and, with every port in England in Parliament's control, was unable to find a way to England. The King raised regiments of horse by subscription from persons of quality. The officers and troopers were the sons of lords and gentry who used horses from their own stables. In response to the Nineteen Propositions, the King gave an order to Parliament for the return of Hull or he would take it by force.[18] The King treated with the Earl of Essex, which allowed time for Princes Rupert and Maurice to come from Holland to witness the raising of the Royal Standard at Nottingham Castle. He demanded that Parliament attend him at Beverley on 16 July 1642 with its reply to his order. The King set out from York and went to Newark, where he was rapturously received. His progress continued to Lincoln to ensure the people supported the Royalist cause. On the appointed hour, the Royalists entered Beverley to meet the Parliamentarian retinue that had arrived from London. The Royalists visited counties that had shown dissent to the King and, for their 'safety', emptied their magazines of their contents. The King sent the lords and gentlemen who had attended him in York to go to their counties with a Commission of Array. In the name of the King, Royalist groups implemented the Commission of Array in towns and cities across the country.

---

17 Hyde, *The History of the Rebellion* (1888), vol. II, pp.213–14.
18 Hyde, *The History of the Rebellion* (1888), vol. II, pp.230–40.

JOHN HAMPDEN'S IMPORTANCE

The Militia Ordinance was passed by Parliament on 15 March 1642 without Royal Assent. Parliament's commanders were quick to secure the county militias. The Commons appointed William, Lord Paget (1609–1678), in February 1641 lord lieutenant of Buckinghamshire. Lord Paget had been one of the peers – including Bedford, Warwick and Essex – to sign the petition of 12 peers in September 1640. Buckinghamshire was the first to implement an ordinance, an important symbol of loyalty to Parliament. In March 1642, Lord Paget was ordained to assemble the men of Buckinghamshire and to have them arrayed to train them in the exercise of arms. On 23 May 1642, Paget reported that 10 deputy lieutenants, which included John Hampden, had mustered about a quarter of Buckinghamshire's militia. Lord Paget set 10 June 1642 to muster a county militia. A parliamentary ordinance appealing for plate, money and horses was enthusiastically subscribed by gentlemen of Buckinghamshire, with John Hampden's donation being the most generous among his peers.[19] On 14 June 1642, John Hampden reported to the House of Commons that Lord Paget had gone over to the King. Hampden requested that, in order for the Buckinghamshire general muster (arranged for the following Friday) to go ahead, a new lord lieutenant be appointed or leave be given for the deputy lieutenants (including Hampden) to proceed with the Militia Ordinance. This request was backed up on 17 June 1642; a petition from the Buckinghamshire Trained Bands and nearly 1,000 volunteers called for a lord lieutenant in which they could confide. Lord Wharton was appointed. Hampden went to Aylesbury on that Friday, where 32 deputy lieutenants assembled to read the ordinance.

The Earl of Essex received his commission as captain general of the army on 15 July 1642. This empowered him to raise an army and to issue commissions to officers. The 20 colonels he commissioned included John Hampden.[20] 'Once John Hampden withdrew his sword, he threw away the scabbard', said an apocryphal story, and, with a commission in hand, left London for Aylesbury to raise a regiment of 'Greencoats'.

---

19 Ian F. W. Beckett, *Wanton Troopers: Buckinghamshire in the Civil Wars, 1640–1660* (Barnsley: Pen and Sword, 2015), pp.42–43.

20 Michael J. Pearson, *The History of a Regiment of Foot in the Earl of Essex's Army, 1642–1645*. 1997. Unpublished. University of Wales, Certificate in Local History, Recruitment, pp.29–40.

2

Let Battle Commence

Hampden left London with Colonel Goodwin on 9 August 1642 to raise troops in Buckinghamshire. Evidence from within state papers show that at least three of Hampden's captains received their commissions between the time Hampden set forth from London and the arrival of Hollis' regiment in Aylesbury.[1] Robert Farrington was commissioned captain 'ye 9th of Augt. 1642'.[2] Captain Hercules Arnett received his commission 'ye 11th of August 1642'. Ralph Nicholls received his commission as captain on 11 August 1642 and 'recd of Wagstaffe [Lieutenant Colonel to Colonel Hampden] in Alesbury feilds entertainment mony £05.00.00'. In fact, Captain Nicholls had spent £15.17.04 'for 68 men from the 3rd. of August to the 10th' and '£13-12 for exercising [sic] his men in before he had his comser [commission]'.[3] This means that recruitment had been going on before Hampden arrived in Aylesbury.[4] The Earl of Essex, the captain general, began a recruiting drive in early August 1642 centred on the Guildhall, London. Twenty colonels were commissioned by Essex to raise regiments. Arthur Goodwin's regiment was formed on 8 August 1642 with four troops, which equates to approximately 240 men.[5] Colonel John Hampden received information that the Earl of Berkshire was at Ascott (in Oxfordshire), intending to execute the King's Commission of Array. (In reply to Parliament passing the Militia Ordinance, the King recruited through issuing Commissions of Array.) So, on Monday, 16 August 1642, Hampden, accompanied by 100 horses and 400 musketeers, marched from Aylesbury to Ascott and 'without much ceremony, entered the house and apprehended the Earl, who affirmed that he was innocent and had done nothing; to whom Mr Hampden replied he was therefore sent to protect him'.[6]

---

1 The National Archives (TNA) SP 28/252 Part 1 and SP 28/140 Part 6.
2 TNA: SP 28/252 Part 1; The National Archives (TNA) SP 28/39, ff. 571r–72.
3 The National Archives (TNA) SP 28/1D Part 2, f. 477.
4 Pearson, *History of a Regiment of Foot*, Recruitment, pp.29–40.
5 The National Archives (TNA) SP 28/1C, f. 226.
6 John Adair, *A Life of John Hampden, The Patriot, 1594–1643* (London: Macdonald and Jane's, 1976), pp.181–82.

LET BATTLE COMMENCE

It is suggested that, in early August 1642, Robert Pye Jr assumed a knighthood as a snub to King Charles and his father. He took the title 'Captain Sir Robert Pye' and raised a troop of horse from in and around Faringdon. Faringdon House is 20 miles from Ascott, where Anne Hampden, John Hampden's 16-year-old daughter, was enjoying married life with 19-year-old Robert Pye Jr. Circumstantial evidence suggests that Sir Robert Pye Jr, with a troop of horse, joined his father-in-law and Arthur Goodwin at Ascott for the arrest of the Earl of Berkshire. Leaving Ascott, Captain Sir Robert Pye's troop marched with his father-in-law's brigade back through Oxford to Banbury where the royal commissioners were in possession, under arms. Lord Saye and Colonel Hampden prepared for a siege, but the commissioners fled, and Hampden returned to Buckinghamshire.[7] On 22 August 1642, Colonel John Hampden's regiment – with Lords Brookes, Saye, Sele and Grey – came to Southam, Warwickshire. On the night of 22 August 1642, 'We had an Alarm which kept us all upon our Guard the whole Night … In the morning early they were called to their Arms, being placed in complete Battell, Colonell Hampden placing himself like a noble and valiant Champion with his Regiment in the forefront of the Battell'.[8]

> At which time [eight o'clock in the morning] came into the Field the Earle of Northampton with his forces, were standing opposite, expecting each minute the word of command to give fire, but none being on his part, the word was given by the Lord Brookes, and Colonel Hampden his Regiment discharged with such courage, as the enemy at the first onset were stricken with feare and terrour.[9]

The Royal Standard was raised at Nottingham Castle on 22 August 1642 – a declaration of war. Clarendon reported that the standard had blown down and was raised again on 23 and 24 August 1642. The Banner Royal (as it was more properly called) was entrusted to Sir Edmund Verney of Claydon, whom Hampden of course well knew as a fellow Buckinghamshire resident and MP. The call to arms failed to recruit sufficient men to fight Parliament's army. Parliament controlled the navy, the ports and all the arsenals that allowed its troops to be supplied to take the war to the Royalists. The King travelled to the Welsh borders, gaining support or raiding towns sympathetic to Parliament for much needed men, arms and supplies. At Powick Bridge, a sharp encounter led by Prince Rupert routed Parliament's cavalry. Warburton related that Colonel Sandys reported to Essex that Prince Rupert had received a dangerous wound in the head.[10] Lord Falkland, in an over-enthusiastic letter to the Earl of Cumberland, stated that 400 had been slain – among them, Colonel Sandys, Major Gunter and Captain Austin. Gunter and Austin were at the Battle of Chalgrove in June 1643. Lord Falkland continued, 'Prince Maurice hath

---

7   Pearson, *History of a Regiment of Foot*, Wanderings, pp.2–3.
8   British History Online (BHO) *Journal of the House of Lords*, vol. 5, 1642–1643, p.321.
9   British Library (BrL) Thomason Tracts (TT), E 114 (25): *A True and Perfect Relation of the first and victorious skirmish*.
10 Warburton, *Memoirs of Prince Rupert*, vol. I, pp.401–09.

received two or three scars of honour on his head, but is abroad and merry'.[11] The story is told that a troop of Parliament's horse were snooping around Pitchford, and inside Pitchford Hall was the wounded Prince. The Prince was bundled into a priest hole and remained so until the troops had left. On the wall of Pitchford Hall is a picture of Sir Francis Otley, the owner of the house; with it is believed to be Prince Maurice. The owner of Pitchford Hall, Francis Ottley, was knighted and made governor of Shrewsbury while the King was in town. Having been brought to Pitchford Hall on 24 September 1642, Prince Maurice was well cared for and was able to join with the King when the Royalists left Shrewsbury on 12 October 1642. The anecdote was told to the author by the owner of Pitchford Hall, a descendant of Sir Francis Ottley. The picture was taken off the wall and examined. Sir Francis Ottley is standing by the side of a seventeenth-century officer. The brass badge states, 'Prince Rupert with Sir Francis Ottley'. Prince Maurice was injured at Powick Bridge, and the anecdote more likely refers to him. Upon leaving Shrewsbury, the Royalists' stated intention was to threaten London to draw Essex into a battle.

Battles were customarily 'pitched' by agreement to the time, date and location where the armies would meet. Armies rarely came together to face each other for a major battle by accident. Within the terms, there was room for manoeuvre to gain an advantage. It is inconceivable that Essex would allow the Royalists to range their artillery from the top of Edgehill and deploy the foot on the steep slopes leading down towards the flat plain. On 22 October 1642, Essex's artillery and 2,000 or 3,000 of his finest troops were over a day's march away from Kineton. The artillery's escort was Colonel John Hampden's Regiment of Foote, Colonel Grantham's Regiment of Foote and Colonel Willoughby's Horse. Lord Rochford's regiment was in Coventry, and the Earl of Stamford's regiment was in Hereford. Sir John Merrick's regiment and Lord St John's regiments were in Worcester. The Earl of Peterborough's regiment – probably augmented by two companies from Meldrum's regiment – was in Banbury.[12] In the knowledge that important elements of the army would not arrive until late 23 October 1642, Essex would have never agreed to a battle on that date. Warburton remarked in a footnote, 'of Ludlow who was on the spot, that Hampden's brigade did not arrive until four o'clock on the following morning'. There are many other equally incompatible accounts.[13] Ludlow's supposed account that Hampden arrived 'about Day-light' or gone seven in morning on 24 October 1642 is too absurd to countenance. The battle ended as darkness fell on the evening of 23 October 1642, and in the morning the dead, dying and wounded were being attended to some 12 hours after hostilities ended. Contrary to those who published fictitious eulogies of Ludlow's Civil War memoirs, Hampden – with the artillery – never made it to Edgehill.[14] In the early hours of 23 October 1642, the King wrote to Prince

---

11   Warburton, *Memoirs of Prince Rupert*, vol. I, pp.405–09.
12   Christopher L. Scott, Alan Turton, and Eric Gruber von Arni, *Edgehill: The Battle Reinterpreted* (Barnsley: Pen and Sword, 2004), p.57.
13   Warburton, *Memoirs of Prince Rupert*, vol. II, pp.30–31, footnote 2.
14   Edmund Ludlow, *Memoirs of Edmund Ludlow Esq; Lieutenant General of the Horse, Commander in Chief of the forces in Ireland, one of the Council of State, and a Member of the Parliament which*

Rupert, 'NEPHEU I have given order as you have desired ; so as I doubt not but all the foot and cannon will be at Eggehill betymes this morning, where you will also find Your loving uncle & Faithful friend, Charles R, 4 o'clock this Sunday morning.'[15] Had the King reneged on his word, or was this a brilliant tactical move by Rupert to wrong foot Essex? The King had assembled an impressive army, but they were ill equipped and probably had insufficient gunpowder for fierce, all-day battle. On 22 October 1642, Essex had his tent erected in Great King's field, an area well to the rear of a flat plain ideally suited for a battle. Three miles in the distance from where Essex pitched his tent, the steep slopes rise up to Edgehill. Some of Essex's troops were quartered around Kineton, but others were in villages three or four miles away and unprepared for battle. Essex was on his way to Kineton Church at around eight o'clock Sunday morning when he was informed of significant numbers of Royalist horse on Edgehill at Knoll End: 'This news came as a surprise as he [Essex] and his officers intended to rest the Sabbath-day, and the rather, that our Artillery and the Forces left with it might come up to us.'[16]

It is clear that Essex had pitched the battle on the flat plain close to Kineton for that Monday. At eight in the morning, 23 October 1642, Prince Rupert ranged the Royalist cavalry along Edgehill. He let it be known that he was there and surveyed the scene before him. Was Rupert's action a breach of terms if the battle was pitched for the following day? Essex's tent was a mile short of the flat plain and had surveyed the scene. Essex had brought some of his men close to the proposed battlefield, and others (including the artillery) were making haste to Kineton. The Royalists' troops and artillery were also making haste to Edgehill. Had Rupert calculated that Essex could not ignore the threat his cavalry posed? Had a battle been planned for that day, Essex's troops would have been dressed and ready to march the short distance to the battlefield. Essex sounded the alarm, but it was early afternoon before his troops were deployed. The Royalists deployed their forces high on the slopes under Edgehill. Essex held back, refusing to move forward until the Royalists came off Edgehill. There is no flat ground under Edgehill towards Kineton – only places that are less steep. A gentle slope gives the infantry a tremendous advantage to those on the higher ground. As in a game of chess, Rupert had forced Essex to respond to his moves. The King and Rupert rode up and down the troops to embolden them to shout huzzas and send insults echoing down the valley at the enemy. Was this Rupert's master plan? Goad Essex's troops into responding to the cheers and insults echoing down the valley to come to them? According to Brigadier Peter Young, founder of the Sealed Knot re-enactment group and noted military historian, 'It may be that it was this royal progress and storm of cheering that provoked Essex to open fire.' Young spoke from experience on how to provoke an enemy into reckless behaviour.[17]

---

began on November 3, 1640 (Switzerland: Printed at Vivay in the Canton of Bern, 1698), vol. I, p.51.
15 Warburton, *Memoirs of Prince Rupert*, vol. II, p.12.
16 Scott, Turton, and Gruber von Arni, *Edgehill*, p.56, The Official Parliamentary Account.
17 Scott, Turton, and Gruber von Arni, *Edgehill*, p.79.

A lone artillery piece of Parliament's opened fire, and, such had been the hurried order of deployment, this was taken to be the signal to advance. At first, Essex had refused to advance, but then came the fateful cannon shot, and his battle plan was in disarray. Essex had fallen into the Royalists' trap. The battle was fierce, with many casualties on both sides, including Verney, the King's standard bearer. *Edgehill: The Battle Reinterpreted* recounts how Robert Walsh, captain lieutenant of Lord Wilmot's own troop, 'kept his command intact' and was instrumental, along with Captain Smith, in the recapture of the King's Banner Royal.[18] In the evening after the battle, Captain Smith was made a knight banneret, Warburton quoted (Sir Richard) Bulstrode (1610–1711).[19] Warburton found in the archives a manuscript referring to the taking of the King's banner. In the margin of a page is 'Robert Wal: Pye who was an Enemy', which is in juxtaposition with text referring to the taking and retaking of the King's banner.[20] It is reasonable to presume that 'Robert Wal' is Robert Walsh, and it was he who stated, 'Pye who was an Enemy'.[21] How Walsh recognised the self-styled Captain Sir Robert Pye is open to question, but it suggests that he was flying a guidon and leading a troop under his command into the battle at Edgehill.

The battle came to a stuttering halt as darkness fell. Soldiers fled the scene of carnage in all directions and carried the news that all was lost. Upon hearing the news that the battle had ended, Hampden would not have risked such a prize of the big guns to fall into enemy hands and would have distanced the artillery trayne from the battlefield. It is inconceivable that the artillery trayne would have continued to Kineton to arrive in the early evening after the battle had ended, as suggested in the most recent interpretation of Edgehill.[22] The report of regiments coming from 'over miles away and as a result, arrived at various stages during the action and had to find their own way into the line' underlines that Essex had been blundered into a battle on the King's terms.[23] Once the armies had formed up on the battlefield and were ready to engage, it was too late to deploy heavy artillery. Runners between Essex's general staff and the slow-moving artillery trayne would have been able to inform Essex of its location. At midday, when battle lines were drawn, the artillery trayne may have been two miles away. A messenger on a fast horse would have found the trayne within minutes. The slower-moving trayne would, in the same scenario, have been two hours away.

Eliot Warburton appears to have become disillusioned, stating politely:

> Clarendon's Rebellion, iii. 389. This battle is a very debatable subject of description. We have the testimony of Lord Clarendon, Warwick, and (Sir Richard) Bulstrode on the King's side … We have likewise the report of Ludlow on the other side … Lord Wharton's 'Speech to the Mayor and Council of London,' and a report to Pym,

---

18 Scott, Turton, and Gruber von Arni, *Edgehill*, p.142.
19 Warburton, *Memoirs of Prince Rupert*, vol. II, pp.25–26, footnote 3.
20 Wiltshire and Swindon Record Office (WSRO) 413/444 Personal 11.
21 WSRO: 413/444 Personal 11.
22 Scott, Turton, and Gruber von Arni, *Edgehill*, p.58.
23 Scott, Turton, and Gruber von Arni, *Edgehill*, p.58.

signed by Holles, Balfour, Meldrum and other leaders. Besides these, we have many inflated and passionate reports in the publications of the day. Nevertheless, it is impossible to make any two accounts agree on the whole. I have only given what appears to me to be the most uncontroverted, I will not say incontrovertible facts.[24]

Warburton, by definition, was not a historian but was tasked with collating the history of the English Civil War. Warburton's contemporaries, Lord Macaulay and Lord Nugent, were the living authorities on the English Civil War – their knowledge of the war's events gained from those dismissed by Warburton. Warburton overturned or incorporated Nugent's, Macaulay's and Clarendon's fictional narratives by inventing *Prince Rupert's Diaries*.[25] Warburton's source for *Prince Rupert's Diaries* will be examined in a later chapter. Warburton remarked that (Sir Richard) Bulstrode's account was contrary to Ludlow's, in that he reported Hampden and the artillery-guard beat back Prince Rupert's regiment when scattered in the chase. The sound of battle would be echoing around the countryside for miles. (Sir Richard) Bulstrode suggested by his statement that the artillery trayne was close by when the opening cannonade signalled the start of the battle. Upon learning that the battle had begun, the trayne at the very least would have gone to ground or turned about to take them away from the danger of being captured. Horse from Hampden's artillery-guard may have engaged with Rupert's regiment at Kineton, which could account for his regiment's reported seven casualties. Colonel John Hampden, it is conjectured, did not bring the artillery trayne into Kineton. Lord Nugent embellished (Sir Richard) Bulstrode's account into a 'picturesque description (according to his wont), that Hampden and the artillery-guard beat back Prince Rupert's regiment when scattered in the chase'.[26] Nugent's improbable account upon further inquiry will find that, as with the Battle of Chalgrove, he endowed Hampden with heroic deeds. Nugent's description that Hampden's and Grantham's regiments raced through the night from Stratford with five artillery pieces is fiction. As they came to Kineton, Nugent wrote that they met Prince Rupert, who had just charged through Parliament's left flank. Hampden, he reported, set up the cannons and drove Prince Rupert away from the baggage train.[27] The artillery pieces that Hampden was escorting were likely to be culverins, each of which weigh two tons. Each of these five artillery pieces required up to 40 horses to haul them and numerous carts to bring up the gunpowder, cannonballs and equipment necessary to fire them. Culverins, once ranged and unlike field pieces that could be moved around the battlefield, remained static.

The Battle of Edgehill was said to have been something of a draw, which may be true regarding the number of casualties suffered by each side. The King was hailed by the Royalists as the hero of the hour. He had overcome

---

24 Warburton, *Memoirs of Prince Rupert*, vol. II, pp.30–31, footnote 2.
25 WSRO: 413/444 Personal 11.
26 Warburton, *Memoirs of Prince Rupert*, vol. II, pp.30–31, footnote 2.
27 Lord George Nugent, *Some Memorials of John Hampden, His Party and His Times* (London: John Murray, 1832), vol. II, p.296.

JOHN HAMPDEN AND THE BATTLE OF CHALGROVE

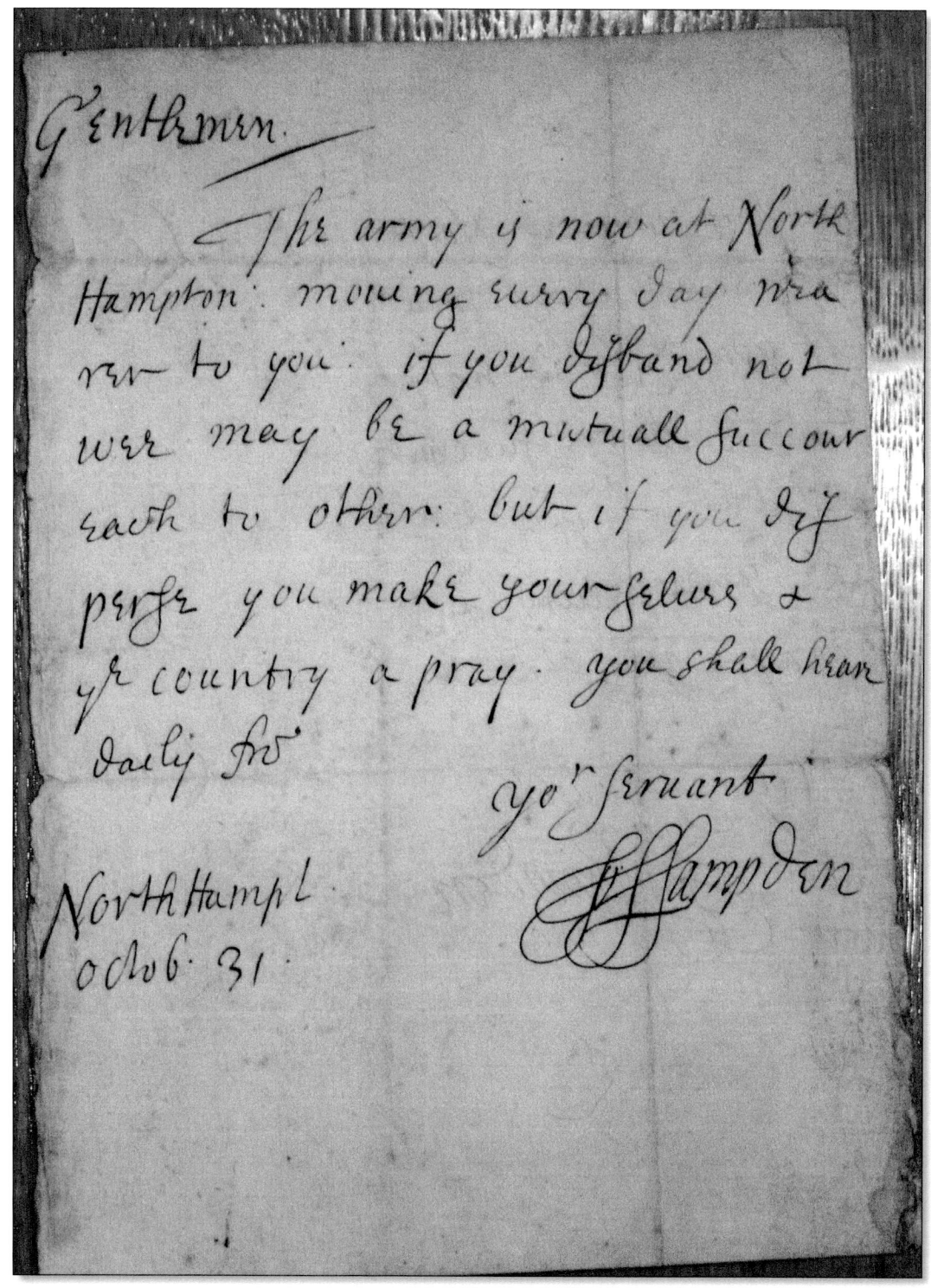

An eighteenth-century copy of Hampden's letter. The letter reads, 'Gentlemen, The army is now at Northampton moving every day nearer to you: if you disband not wee may be a mutual succour each to other: but if you disperse you make yourselves & your country a pray. You shall hear daily fro' Your Servant John Hampden. Northampt. Octob. 31'. (Penelope Benson-Wright)

impossible odds to raise an army. At every turn, he outmanoeuvred the Earl of Essex, and, had his cavalry regained its order after wiping out Essex's left flank and charged the rear of the right flank, peace terms could have been agreed upon by Christmas. Darkness of the night stopped the battle, and the armies withdrew, leaving the wounded to their fate. Charles slept in his coach up on Edgehill and, in the morning after the battle, came down to the battlefield. Charles, along with his officers, were masters of the battlefield, for Essex had left the scene. Essex left the dead and wounded to the mercy of the Royalists and raced back to London to prepare them for attack. Essex's officers and men knew that Essex had been outsmarted by the King and that it was he to be blamed for their suffering. Dissent from his officers and the ranks grew. Essex knew that his army had suffered a devastating mauling under his command. On 29 October 1642, the King marched into the city of Oxford to a hero's welcome. The King consolidated his position, making Christchurch College his headquarters. Essex had lost the respect of the men, for at Edgehill, they were not fighting to win but battling to stay alive.

On 31 October 1642, Hampden was at Northampton. He addressed a letter to Colonel (Henry) Bulstrode, Captain Grenville, Captain Tyrell and Captain West. All four are identified in the House of Lords Journal as members of the Commission of the Deputy Lieutenancy for Buckinghamshire on 12 August 1642.[28] The said named, except Edmund West, were also identified as being on the Committee for Buckinghamshire. The tenor of the letter is a plea to the leaders of Buckinghamshire not to disband but to stay together and continue the fight.

Battle of Aylesbury

A parliamentary broadsheet titled *Good and Joyfull Newes out of Buckinghamshire* reports that 10,000 men commanded by Prince Rupert were beaten out of Aylesbury, suffering 600 dead, with a further 200 taken prisoner.[29] Evidence for the 'battle' is lacking. Besides, Prince Rupert is documented to be in Abingdon on the day.[30] *Abingdons and Ailisburies Present Miseries*, dating from 19 December 1642, states that Aylesbury was raided four days before Abingdon by Royalists under Henry, with Lord Wilmot acting under the general direction of Rupert, 'who was not there in person'.[31] Following the Battle of Edgehill, the King marched into Oxford on 29 October 1642. That day, Prince Rupert secured the town of Abingdon for

---

28   BHO: *Journal of the House of Lords*, vol. 5, 1642–1643, p.286.
29   British Library (BrL) Thomason Tracts (TT), E 126 (9): *Good and Joyfull Newes out of Buckinghamshire, Being an exact relation of a battle stricken between Prince Robert and Sir William Balforth, Lieut-General to his Excellency the Earl of Essex, near Aylesbury, in this County on Tuesday last, 1 Nov' when the said Sir William obtained a happy and glorious Victory* (London: Francis Wright, 1642).
30   Beckett, *Wanton Troopers*, pp.137–39.
31   Bodleian Library (BoL) 249: E, 128, no. 33: *Abingdons and Ailisburies Present Miseries*, 19 December 1642.

the King: 'Well, thither they came, and billeted themselves for that night in the best innes … honest matrons and beautiful virgins defended themselves with knives and spits until the trained bands arrived and put the raiders to flight'.[32] If the raid described in *Abingdons and Ailisburies Present Miseries* happened four days previously, then it occurred on 25 October 1642. On the morning of 24 October 1642, following the Battle of Aylesbury, the Royalists set out in pursuit of Parliament's soldiers fleeing from Edgehill. Aylesbury was a day's ride away from Edgehill and was virtually unguarded. Aylesbury's garrison was returning from Edgehill. The quote 'Well, thither they came, and billeted themselves for that night …' describes classic rape and pillage.

John Hampden's 31 October 1642 letter describes, between the lines, that Parliament's army is a rabble and calls upon his officers to regroup. His officers – with 1,500 men – were most likely those who dislodged the Royalists out of Aylesbury four days after they arrived (1 November 1642). Lord Nugent blended the story from the *Good and Joyful Newes* with a raid reported in a parliamentary broadsheet, *Abingdons and Ailisburies Present Miseries*, to conjure the story of the Battle of Aylesbury.[33] Lord Nugent recounted in *Some Memorials of John Hampden, His Party and His Times* that:

> Thither Prince Rupert marched with a force of some thousands of horse and foot, and, after some days, passed in securing for the King's use much of the produce of the vale and despoiling and laying waste much more than he secured, entered and possessed himself of the town. Here, after one day more of free-quarter in Aylesbury, during which the inhabitants were made to suffer all sorts of outrage from his soldiers …[34]

The Gentleman's Magazine and Historical Chronicle for January 1820 published a letter dated 12 October 1819 from 'An Old Correspondent'. The writer described a scene of work in progress where skeletons had been found while extracting gravel. The writer commented that 38 skeletons had been found prior to his visit, stating, 'it seems probable that many more [skeletons] may be hereafter discovered'. The writer continued that, upon close examination of the bones, 'some locks of hair were observable still hanging to one or two of the skulls'. Visitors, 'attracted by the curiosity', speculated on the reason for so many bodies to be buried in one location. The writer commented, after speculating upon other causes for their death, 'The most probable account is … that these were bodies of soldiers slain during the civil wars of Cromwell'. He continued, 'The spot in which they have been found is about a mile Northward of the parish church.' A particular mention was made about these skeletons being found buried in oak-tree clay: a type of soil not found in the area around Holman's Bridge.

---

32 BoL: 249: E, 128, no. 33: *Abingdons and Ailisburies Present Miseries*, 19 December 1642.
33 BoL: 249: E, 128, no. 33: *Abingdons and Ailisburies Present Miseries*, 19 December 1642.
34 Nugent, *Some Memorials* (1832), vol. II, pp.320–21.

The Chronicle (12 November 1825), published at Aylesbury, had an article that, in the writing and claims made, had the hallmarks of Lord Nugent's persuasive prose and inaccurate statements. The article begins with the words:

> About seven years ago, many of our readers will recollect that in a field within half a mile betwixt Aylesbury, on the road to Buckingham, there was discovered, on digging for gravel, such a large quantity of human bones, buried together, and in such a condition, as to show that they were the remains of men who had fallen in battle, and that the battle was not of very ancient date … In all civil contests, the imagination, as well as passions, become extravagant ; and, as to exaggeration, though the number of skeletons accidentally found on the spot is not half that stated in this account of the slain, it may not be all that were underground ; and if, even then, the statement were overruled, a large allowance is due to a narrator who gives an account in the heat of battle – Voltaire says 'All gazettes of Battles are Liars … the English, perhaps, the least of any.'

Perhaps Nugent should have added to Voltaire's quote that historians with egotistic intent to claim authority of a battle are the greater liars.

Also within the article's text is:

> The bones having been collected and deposited in a safe tomb in the churchyard of Hardwick, near Aylesbury, at the instance of a noble personage of that neighbourhood, the following inscription was, on the authority above stated, engraved on the incumbent tablet:- 'Within are deposited the bones of 247 Persons who were discovered A.D. 1818, buried in a field adjoining to Holman's Bridge, near Aylesbury.'

The Earl of Essex, following the Battle of Chalgrove, retreated out of Thame on 1 July 1643 and made camp at Bierton on 4 July 1643. The Earl of Essex's letter to the Master Speaker dated 9 July 1643 details Prince Rupert's harassment of Parliament's troops on their retreat to Great Brickhill.[35] Significant engagements around Boarstall House and Aylesbury happened in the summer of 1644, but the writer of *The Chronicle*'s article, clearly Lord Nugent, centred on the false account of a supposed Battle of Aylesbury. In St Mary's Church, Hardwick, on the south side of the tower, is a sarcophagus memorial, on which Nugent engraved:

> Within are deposited the bones of 247 Persons who were discovered A.D. 1818, buried in a field adjoining to Holman's Bridge, near Aylesbury. From the History and appearances of the place where they were found, they were considered to be the bones of those officers and men who perished in an engagement fought A.D. 1642, between the troops of K. Charles I., under the command of Prince Rupert, and the Garrison who held Aylesbury for the Parliament. Enemies from their attachment to opposite leaders and to opposite Standards, in the sanguinary

---

35 British Library (BrL) Thomason Tracts (TT), E 64 (3): The Earle of Essex His Letter to Master Speaker, 9 July 1643.

conflicts of that Civil War, they were together victims to its fury. United in one common slaughter, they were buried in one common grave, close to the spot where they had lately stood in arms against each other. After the lapse of more than a century and a half their bones were collected, and deposited still in consecrated ground. May the memory of brave men be respected, and may our country never again be compelled to take part in a conflict such as that which this tablet records.

In 1832, *Some Memorials of John Hampden* was published, and it has in a footnote:

> *Good and Joyful Newes out of Buckinghamshire – Dr. Mundell's Letter, Some of the remains of this skirmish were discovered a few years ago, by labourers who were digging pits for gravel, in a field at Holman's Bridge, near the old ford. More than two hundred skeletons were found buried in the small space which was opened; among which, many appeared, from the manner in which they were laid, to have been those officers.[36]

Use of unverifiable or fictitious sources such as 'Dr. Mundell's Letter' is a feature of Nugent's research. The contrived statements 'in a field at Holman's Bridge' and 'More than two hundred skeletons' were taken from the plaque on the side on the sarcophagus memorial. The plaque, it is conjectured, was erected in 1825, and the article in *The Chronicle* was placed with the editor by the authority of the Grenville cartel. It therefore follows that Lord Nugent did not remove 247 skeletons from Holman's Bridge in 1818. Neither did he reinter them in a sarcophagus memorial that he had erected in consecrated ground on the south side of St Mary's Church, Hardwick. The sarcophagus is as vacuous as the words Nugent used to describe the disinterment and the Battle of Aylesbury.

The Royalists marched on towards London to press home their advantage. The King's forces 20 miles to the west threatened to take London by storm. The King demanded peace talks, which were accepted under terms, and they marched towards London. On 12 November 1642, Brentford was attacked with devastating force, and Parliament suffered a great loss.[37] John Hampden's eldest son, John, said to have been with Denzil Holles' regiment in Brentford, may have been a casualty. John Hampden's Regiment of Foote marched on Brentford and forced the Royalists to disengage. The Battle of Turnham Green took place the following day, during which Hampden's regiment pressed towards the Royalists, forcing them to retreat. Essex is said to have refused to send reinforcements to Hampden and ordered his regiment to cease fighting. The fading light, which may have caused the Royalists to begin to withdraw, was sufficient for Essex to claim victory.[38] Essex was rebuked for losing the day and for allowing the Royalists to take

---

36 Nugent, *Some Memorials* (1832), vol. II, p.323.
37 Stephen Porter and Simon Marsh, *The Battle for London* (Stroud: Amberley Publishing, 2010), p.70.
38 Porter and Marsh, *The Battle for London*, pp.99–100.

Reading as they retreated to Oxford. Once again, Essex had been fooled into allowing the King sufficient licence to allow him to gain a tactical advantage on the battlefield. John Hampden's military reputation grew, but was this at the price of losing his eldest son? Upon their retreat to the King's new headquarters at Oxford, they left a garrison at Reading as an outpost, which effectively blocked the trade routes from the West Country to London. Both armies retired to winter quarters.

Whether Essex wanted to prolong the war for his own aggrandisement or preferred a political peace treaty is open to question. Essex's incompetence on the battlefield led many to give importance to John Hampden to take command. As the King's army withdrew from London towards Oxford after the Battle of Turnham Green, they occupied Reading. The garrison of 3,000 soldiers, commanded by Sir Arthur Aston, was hosted by around 3,000 reluctant residents. The town's walls were strengthened during the winter with stone obtained from Reading Abbey, and the town's defences were further reinforced by a system of ditches, earthworks and fortified outposts. It was customary for an army to retire to winter quarters. Essex chose Windsor Castle, and the King selected Christchurch College, Oxford. Throughout the winter of 1642–1643, local commanders continued the fight, and Hampden did what he could to encourage action in the south. John Hampden had become the go-between for the Lord General and the House of Commons and journeyed so frequently to and from Windsor and Westminster that he was lampooned by Sir John Denham:

Have I so often passed between
Windsor and Westminster, unseen,
And did myself divide,
To keep His Excellencie in awe'
And give the Parliament the law?
For they knew none beside.[39]

John Hampden's importance to the cause became significant as colonels came to him to seek Essex's permission for them to carry out a particular action. Effectively, Hampden had become second-in-command of the army, Essex's voice in Parliament and his representative in the Committee of Safety. Hampden wrote to Goodwin thanking him for his attack on Brill and confirming that he had attempted an assault on Reading in the last week of January. The postscript reads, 'I thank you for your favour to Robert Pye, to whom I beseech you to continue it and add your own counsel'.[40] The postscript gives credence to the argument that Captain Sir Robert Pye, Hampden's son-in-law, joined Goodwin's regiment at Edgehill then kept with them through to Thame and the Battle of Chalgrove.

---

39 Adair, *A Life of John Hampden*, p.214.
40 Adair, *A Life of John Hampden*, p.210, Postscript of a letter from John Hampden to Arthur Goodwin.

3

Take Oxford or Reading

Peace negotiations began in Oxford on 1 February 1643, with Parliament adding clauses to proposals that closely followed the terms of the Nineteen Propositions that the King had refused to accept the previous June at Beverley. The King prevaricated, asking for terms that directly challenged Parliament's offer of peace. Charles was aware that Queen Henrietta Maria had procured a vast armoury of supplies and had sailed from Holland in mid January.[1] Queen Henrietta landed a huge shipment of arms from the continent at Bridlington on 13 February 1643.[2] The Queen was met by the Earl of Newcastle and taken with the supplies to the safety of York Castle. The Queen was desperate, as was the King, to get this arms shipment to Oxford. Sir Ferdinando Fairfax, leading Parliament's Army of the North, was a constant threat, and his army was too strong for the Royalists to attempt moving the convoy to Oxford however much the King desired to be reunited with his Queen. Letters flowed between Henrietta Maria, Charles and Prince Rupert from the moment the Queen landed until she paraded in triumph through Oxford.[3] Peace negotiations continued into April, but, on the first of the month, Prince Rupert slipped out of Oxford and headed north through Banbury with 1,200 horse and dragoons, accompanied by 600 foot.[4] He razed Birmingham to the ground on 3 April 1643 and, following his letter to the King informing him of his intention, headed for York. The King received Rupert's letter on 6 April 1643, and the reply was back to Rupert on Sunday, 9 April. The King wrote, 'I recommend to you to do that which you shall find to conduce most to my wife's coming hither'.[5] On 8 April 1643,

---

1 Mary Anne Everett Green (ed.), *Letters of Queen Henrietta Maria, Including Her Private Correspondence with Charles the First. Collected from the Public Archives and Private Libraries of France and England* (London: Richard Bentley, 1857), pp.163–64.
2 Green (ed.), *Letters of Queen Henrietta Maria*, pp.172–73, '22 Feb 1643 – I have already been here nine days'.
3 Green (ed.), *Letters of Queen Henrietta Maria*, pp.162–223.
4 Warburton, *Memoirs of Prince Rupert*, vol. II, pp.148–49, Taken from 'Special Passages' no. xliii (King's Collection).
5 Warburton, *Memoirs of Prince Rupert*, vol. II, pp.155–56, Letter from Charles R to Rupert.

Rupert sent a summons to the Lichfield garrison, but Governor Russell (or Rousewell) answered with a peal of the cathedral's bells to show defiance.[6] Rupert's intention was to take Lichfield then fight his way through to York and escort the Queen and convoy of arms to Oxford. Lichfield Cathedral was defended as strongly as a castle with a moat and walls that easily withstood the battering that small artillery pieces could inflict.

The peace negotiations that had begun in February were being kept alive by the King offering terms to Parliament's peace commissioners. Oxford's magazine was near empty, and the King could not withstand an attack on the city. It was imperative the convoy of arms that was at York Castle was brought to Oxford without delay. It was reported that Rupert's march north to be effective must be rapid, and it was important to leave a clear route for his return with the Queen. Edward Nicholas, the King's private secretary, wrote to Prince Rupert on 6 April 1643 that Essex's army was making preparation to 'march towards our quarters'. Nicholas recommended agreement to two propositions being offered by Parliament's peace committee to save the negotiations from collapse. While negotiations continued, Nicholas reasoned 'the Earl of Essex's will not come this way [to Oxford]'.[7] The King received news on 6 April 1643 of Essex's advance on Reading with an army of 16,000 foot, 3,000 horse and a train of artillery. On 10 April 1643, Edward Nicholas wrote to the King reporting that Sir Arthur Aston had informed him that Parliament's troops were at Oakingham. He wrote, 'there are very many sick and the carts of that country are called in to carry them to London'.[8] Fresh troops had arrived at Windsor and, almost certainly, would have been in contact with those who were sick and being sent to London, the fittest being asked to lift the sick onto the carts. The incubation period for typhoid is 10 to 14 days. Epidemic typhus, also known as louse-borne typhus, is a form of typhus so named because the disease often causes epidemics. Civil War soldiers were often lousy with fleas, and, once typhus was among soldiers, an epidemic was inevitable. Essex may have realised that, as the siege progressed, his army was being decimated by disease and would soon be unable to defend itself from an attack. Nicholas continued that both Houses had agreed to give the peace commissioners a further seven days to conclude a peace treaty: 'The truth is, Parliament is not willing to treat, but would gladly have the people believe they could not obtain peace'.[9]

Both sides were aware that Oxford had little means to defend the city and brought into question on whose side John Pym's, leader of the Committee of Safety, loyalty lay. Adair stated, 'as Mr Hampden and all they who desired still to strike at the root very earnestly insisted upon, without doubt they had put

---

6   Warburton, *Memoirs of Prince Rupert*, vol. II, p.161.
7   Warburton, *Memoirs of Prince Rupert*, vol. II, pp.159–60, Letter from Edward Nicholas to Prince Rupert.
8   Warburton, *Memoirs of Prince Rupert*, vol. II, pp.160–61, Letter from Edward Nicholas to the King 10 April 1643.
9   Warburton, *Memoirs of Prince Rupert*, vol. II, pp.160–61, Letter from Edward Nicholas to the King 10 April 1643.

the King's affairs into great confusion. For Oxford lacked proper fortifications and a well-founded garrison'.[10] The Committee of Safety ordered Essex to continue his march towards Reading. The weather, it was reported, was cold, and the rain incessant. On 14 April 1643, Essex appeared before Reading at the head of a large army of foot, horse and a train of artillery capable of overwhelming its occupants. Essex demanded Reading's surrender, but Sir Arthur Aston defiantly declared that 'he would keep the town or starve in it' rather than lay down his arms.[11] Parliamentarian troops swept around the northern outskirts of the town and seized Caversham Bridge to guard against the possibility of reinforcements arriving from Oxford. Gun batteries were set up, and Essex established his headquarters at the old moated manor house of Sir John Blagrave at Southcote. On the night of 16 April 1643, the cannons of both armies' artillery roared. The barrage was incessant, continuing for two days until, on Tuesday, 18 April 1643, the guns fell silent. On that day, Parliament's peace commissioners left Oxford with the treaty unsigned, probably unaware that, once again, the King had outwitted his enemy. Edward Nicholas sent a letter to Prince Rupert at Lichfield dated 11 April 1643 that underlined the discontent in Parliament and that of his colonels towards the Earl of Essex's leadership: 'We hear that the two Houses have sent to the Earl of Essex to deliver up his commission, and they will give him an honourable recompence, and that they intend to make Mr. Hampden their general.'[12] John Hampden's importance to the cause was laid bare. The King had outwitted the Earl of Essex at every turn, leaving Hampden to resolve the colonels' discontent at the lack of leadership. The Committee of Safety were, at best, ambivalent about prosecuting the war – an attitude that Hampden had to reconcile with the colonels. Though Essex's army was before the gates of Reading, they could not trouble nor stop Prince Rupert from escorting the Queen and convoy from York. Reading's defenders were reinforced by 600 musketeers and a supply of ammunition, which arrived by boat from Sonning. On 19 April 1643, Sir Arthur Aston was struck on the head by a falling brick. The wound apparently rendered him unable to speak, so his deputy, Colonel Richard Fielding, took command. King Charles sent urgent orders to Prince Rupert, who was at Lichfield, for him to return immediately to Oxford.[13] The King wrote to his nephew on 16 April 1643 and again the next day, ordering him again to return to Oxford.[14] The King expected Essex, with such an overpowering force, to take Reading and march on Oxford. With the moat around Lichfield Cathedral emptied and

---

10 Adair, *A Life of John Hampden*, pp.215–16.

11 M. C. Barrès-Baker, *The Siege of Reading, April 1643: The Failure of the Earl of Essex's 1643 Spring Offensive* (Ottawa: eBooksLib, 2004), p.65.

12 Warburton, *Memoirs of Prince Rupert*, vol. II, pp.176–77, Letter from Edward Nicholas to the King 26 April 1643.

13 Warburton, *Memoirs of Prince Rupert*, vol. II, p.164, Letter from Edward Nicholas to Rupert at Lichfield 11 April 1643.

14 Warburton, *Memoirs of Prince Rupert*, vol. II, pp.171–72, Letter from Charles R to his Nephew 16 April 1643 – Footnote 1 of the second letter to same recipient.

the walls undermined, a mine was detonated, causing a huge breach. After some further resistance, Colonel Russell (or Rousewell) was offered quarter, and in the morning Parliament's men surrendered. Before Rupert could consolidate his position, he received another desperate message from the King ordering him to return to Oxford.[15]

Colonel Richard Fielding's spies, many of whom were ladies, were able to come and go between Essex's camps and Reading town. While going about their business in the camp, the ladies had learnt that many of the soldiers were sick and dying. Typhus, which was evident when Essex left Windsor with supposedly healthy fresh troops, had, after the incubation period, become endemic. Fielding's position appeared hopeless. Totally surrounded and without hope of relief from Oxford, he considered his options. On 25 April 1643, Fielding raised a flag of truce, and, after a few cannon shots of discontent, a drummer was sent out to call Parliament to parley to discuss terms to surrender the town.[16] A parley at a siege could last for days, the terms refused by the dominant side until an acceptable agreement was reached. Fielding's terms of surrender were of the most advantageous to the beleaguered town. Essex appeared to have been negotiating from a position of weakness, which may well have been the case. Camp fever, once endemic, leaves an army unable to defend itself, of which the experienced Essex would have been aware. Essex agreed to Fielding's terms on the proviso that the soldiers in Reading leave the town without delay. Terms for surrender were agreed on 26 April 1643, and the ink on the signed articles was barely dry when a Royalist relief force led by the King and Prince Rupert arrived from Oxford. They attacked Caversham Bridge and tried to break into the town, hoping that Fielding would sally out. Fielding refused to break the truce and would not send troops from the town to help. The rain was incessant, which made the firing of muskets and pistols near impossible, and the relief force was driven back. Heavy rain deluged from the heavens above, and, like divine providence, a tremendous thunderstorm broke over the attackers' heads, which sent them scurrying for cover. The King and Prince Rupert retreated to the safety of Wallingford. On 27 April 1643, the Royalists marched out of Reading with ensigns flying, drums beating, match light and muskets loaded and with as much bounty as they could carry.[17] The generous terms of surrender were much to the chagrin of the Parliamentarian soldiers, especially as their promised money was still to be paid. With the threat that Essex's soldiers would pillage the town regardless, each soldier was promised 12 shillings to abide by the terms of surrender.[18] The King expected Essex to follow his troops back to Oxford and take the city by storm. Essex's soldiers occupied Reading, which they plundered for two days before order was restored. Upon his arrival at Oxford, Colonel Fielding was court-martialled

---

15 Warburton, *Memoirs of Prince Rupert*, vol. II, p.174, footnote 1, Letter to Nephew from Charles R. 21 April 1643.
16 Barrès-Baker, *Siege of Reading, April 1643*, p.126.
17 Adair, *A Life of John Hampden*, p.220.
18 Barrès-Baker, *Siege of Reading, April 1643*, p.152.

for surrendering the town and was sentenced to death. However, Fielding was reprieved at the last minute by the intercession of the Prince of Wales and the prompting of Prince Rupert.

Essex had 'won' the siege of Reading and had retaken the town, but his troops had contracted camp fever. Clarendon wrote, 'But that which troubled the earl of Essex more than these discourses [political debate], was the ill condition his army was in; they had contracted in this short siege so great a sickness, and such an indisposition to action, and so many killed and run away, that he was in no posture to pursue his advantage.'[19] The immediate result of the fall of Reading was panic among the multitude of Royalist nobility, ladies and gentry in Oxford. The city was ill prepared to withstand an attack, and a siege was too intolerable for the nobility to contemplate. The Royalists, desperately short of powder, threw up earthworks as a last-ditch attempt to defend themselves from the expected onslaught. The Royalists in Oxford perceived Essex as a threat who would soon be sighting his artillery pieces on Oxford. The mere threat of such action prompted the King to send an express message to his Queen in York. He ordered that, at whatever the risk, a convoy be immediately sent to Oxford with men, arms and gunpowder. However, an assault on Oxford never came because Essex's army had contracted camp fever and were unable to move. Essex's forces were so racked with disease that they were unable to march or fight. Sir William Waller, who was expected to meet up with Essex at Oxford, was 'entertained' by Sir Ralph Hopton's Army of the West, which prevented a planned rendezvous. The dead and dying were being loaded onto barges while the sick remained in camp at Reading for over a month – desertions were rife, others turning coat.[20] Essex's army was too ill to mount an attack, and Oxford was spared. John Hampden's regiment had avoided the ravages of camp fever possibly because John Hampden cared for his men's welfare. His regiment garrisoned Reading and, being as it appeared from pay warrants to be unaffected by camp fever, became the rearguard when the army made its way to Thame.

The Earl of Newcastle had been attending Queen Henrietta Maria in York Castle for over two months, waiting for the order to send the arms shipment to Oxford. The Queen was aware that the King's arsenal at Oxford was near empty and that Essex had amassed a vast, well-equipped army. The Queen was mindful that Essex's army had been diverted from attacking Oxford and was glad that Rupert had returned to Oxford to help the Reading garrison. Her letter from York dated 23 April 1643 has, 'I hope, too that we shall be strong enough to make our way. The powder that you desire sets out to-day, and the match, although my lord Newcastle not be here.' In the same letter, Henrietta wrote, 'A ship has just now arrived at Scarborough, with arms for us; I know not what proportion', and in the postscript wrote, 'News is this

---

19 Hyde, *The History of the Rebellion* (1888), vol. III, p.32, footnote extract from *The Hist*. p.438.
20 Warburton, *Memoirs of Prince Rupert*, vol. II, p.202, Letter from Lewis Dives to Prince Rupert 6 June 1643 – 'four hundred of them were sent this day in barges for London'.

instant brought me, that another vessel of arms is arriving at Newcastle.'[21] Parliament's Army of the North was in need of money and supplies, which allowed the Royalists an advantage to take the fight to the enemy. Parliament's troops had besieged Pontefract but fled to Leeds to join Fairfax's forces when confronted by Royalist reinforcements. The Royalists followed the enemy to Leeds and resolved to besiege the town. Leeds was a big town, and the Royalists 'were not enough to make lines of circumvallation'. Goring suggested to his fellow officers that negotiation with Fairfax was a better option than either mounting an all-out attack or laying siege. Goring learnt that Fairfax wanted 'a cessation arms for four days, during which they wished to treat'. Henrietta proposed sending a large detachment into Lancashire 'to clear out that country [sic], which I hope can be done ten to twelve days and thus come to rejoin me at Newark'.[22] The Queen had received a letter from Parliament informing her that 'the lords Say, Salis[bury], Manchester, Pym, Hampden … whether I am willing to listen to a peace'. She added, 'they promised this bearer that till his return, the army of Essex should not advance. I judged that to be for your service, since by this delay the convoy may arrive'.[23]

The convoy of arms that left York on 23 April 1643 was a small part of the supplies held in the castle. John Hampden was perceived to be a lord by the Queen and his name linked to both factions in Parliament. This recognition gives further indication of John Hampden's importance. The extent of how depleted Oxford's arsenal had become is revealed in a letter from the Queen dated 11 May 1643. Had Parliament advanced on Oxford instead of Reading, the King would have immediately fled north. Henrietta wrote, 'I hope that the ammunition is arrived, and that you will be able to stay on the defensive, till my army go to you, which I hope to send word in ten or twelve days'.[24]

The convoy made slow progress, the heavy carts sinking into the rain-soaked tracks, making just eight or nine miles a day. The convoy arrived in Oxford on 15 or 16 May 1643 with, according to the *Mercurius Aulicus*'s probably exaggerated claim, '300 barrels of powder, 1,500 muskets, 1,500, bandoliers, proportionate quantity of match, and some corslets, helmets and other armes'.[25] Other sources claim that 'on 16 May 1643 Colonel Thomas Pinchbeck arrived in Oxford from York with 136 barrels of gunpowder and 1,000 fresh troops to the King's blessed relief'.[26] With Essex's army still in Reading and unable to move, the Royalists, with their replenished arsenal,

---

21 Green (ed.), *Letters of Queen Henrietta Maria*, pp.188–93, Letter 23 April 1643 from Henrietta to the King at Oxford.
22 Green (ed.), *Letters of Queen Henrietta Maria*, pp.188–93, Letter 23 April 1643 from Henrietta to the King at Oxford.
23 Green (ed.), *Letters of Queen Henrietta Maria*, pp.193–94, Letter 5 May 1643 from Henrietta to the King at Oxford.
24 Green (ed.), *Letters of Queen Henrietta Maria*, pp.197–99, Letter 11 May 1643 from Henrietta to the King at Oxford.
25 Barrès-Baker, *Siege of Reading, April 1643*, p.169.
26 Keith Roberts and Graham Turner, *First Newbury 1643: The Turning Point* (Oxford: Osprey Publishing 2003), pp.11–12.

went on the rampage. The Parliamentarian counties of Buckinghamshire, Hertfordshire and Middlesex were defenceless to the Royalist attack. Vast stores of pillaged goods were brought back to Oxford, and large sums were raised by ransoming important Parliamentarians. Towns ever closer to London were coming under attack, which prompted the Committee of Safety to order Essex into action.

The Queen reported in a letter dated 27 May 1643 that Goring and Ramsey were taken prisoner and that 500 or 600 were lost at Wakefield. She wrote, 'The rebels are grown strong, and we have weakened since our loss; but I hope that, if we take Leeds, all will yet go well'.[27] The Queen wrote to the Earl of Newcastle, her cousin, on 28 May 1643 stating that 'I have news from the king, that his army is as strong as Essex's, and that Essex does not advance'.[28] She pressed her cousin to get the troops ready for the convoy to leave York. On 3 June 1643, she told Newcastle in a letter, 'It will not be needful for you to come this evening to the place where I am to sleep; for, if it please God, to-morrow I shall pass by Tadcaster to go to Pontefract'.[29] On 4 June 1643, Queen Henrietta Maria left York Castle with the convoy of arms and supplies. She and the convoy arrived at Newark Castle on 16 June 1643 in great triumph. By the beginning of June, Essex's army was in a most ragged state. Death stalked Essex's army, desertions were rife, and regiments – for want of provisions – refused to obey orders. In this confusion, Essex was ordered to put his army between Oxford and London and made ready to march to Thame. On 6 June 1643, Lewis Dives reported in a letter to Prince Rupert that the Earl of Essex's army, that morning, had marched away from Reading towards Henley.[30]

Advance to Thame

Before leaving Reading, Essex wrote on 27 May 1643 to Colonel Nathaniel Fiennes, the commander at Bristol, but the letter was intercepted. Essex had loaned four regiments of horse to the Bristol garrison to bolster its defence. Essex wrote that, when Sir William Waller would go to Devonshire, 'our want of horse is so great that it is my desire that they be forthwith sent to the army'.[31] The information that Essex's army was in great need of horses was, it seems, exploited by the Royalists from then on to deprive them of this means to conduct the war. Essex's horse were active around Reading,

---

27 Green (ed.), *Letters of Queen Henrietta Maria*, pp.208–13, Letter 27 May 1643 from Henrietta to the King at Oxford.
28 Green (ed.), *Letters of Queen Henrietta Maria*, pp.214–16, Letter 28 May 1643 from Henrietta to the Earl of Newcastle.
29 Green (ed.), *Letters of Queen Henrietta Maria*, p.218, Letter 3 June 1643 from Henrietta to the Earl of Newcastle.
30 Warburton, *Memoirs of Prince Rupert*, vol. II, p.202, Letter Lewis Dives to Prince Rupert 6 June 1643.
31 Warburton, *Memoirs of Prince Rupert*, vol. II, p.196, Letter to Colonel Nathaniel Fiennes from Essex 27 May 1643.

beating up poorly protected quarters then rounding up horses to carry away the plunder.[32] The Royalists were less constrained: the adjacent counties to the eastward and towards London were mainly of Parliamentarian principle and undefended. The Royalists' guerrilla tactics included crashing into a town in the dead of night, waking the burghers from their midnight sleep and bringing them in a confused state before the commanding officer. The burghers were obliged to sign over to the King whatever was demanded. Throughout May, the Royalists' adventures were getting ever more numerous and closer to London.[33] Essex was powerless to intervene. After seven weeks of sitting around Reading, many animals that would have been used to pull carts had probably ended up in the stew pot. On 7 June 1643, Lord Grey of Werke was at Nettlebed, having marched just eight short miles from Reading on the way to Thame. An artillery trayne travelling across rough or waterlogged terrain was expected to cover eight miles a day in such circumstances. Lord Grey, in a letter to the Gentlemen Householders of Essex, in reply to misconduct allegations, remarked that Essex's regiment conducted by Major Dawkins refused to take orders to march to Cawsham (Caversham) and stayed in their quarters at Maidenhead.[34] Essex's logistical problem of controlling and manoeuvring his army, even before camp fever became endemic, was probably a factor for why he agreed to such favourable terms to the Royalists for lifting the siege.

Ewelme church is resplendent in medieval paintings and icons that have survived intact from the ravages of the Protestant Reformation and the Puritans' ideology of the English Civil War. The building's royal connection to Henry VIII ensured that the church survived the Reformation. Ewelme church must be blessed to have survived the Earl of Essex's puritanical army. The story is still told of how one man, Francis Martyn, gallantly fought off a mob of Puritans who were hell bent on defacing and destroying the paintings, windows and icons in Ewelme church. The story seemed apocryphal, but detailed analysis of historical events concerning the movements of the Earl of Essex's army between 6–9 June 1643 reveal that Lieutenant Colonel Francis Martyn, commanding officer of Colonel Thomas Ballard's Regiment of Foot, was at the siege of Reading. Ewelme is on the shortest route between Reading and Thame. Francis Martyn may have been friends with Bartholomew Hone, who lived in Wace Court, Ewelme. In 1650, Francis Martyn purchased the mortgage from Hone's widow, making Wace Court his principal residence. Lieutenant Colonel Francis Martyn had the power of life and death, as did every officer, over a common soldier. Should a fanatical Puritan mob decide to ransack Ewelme church, Martyn's order to have them stopped would have been sufficient. Lieutenant Colonel Martyn's order would have been passed

---

32 Warburton, *Memoirs of Prince Rupert*, vol. II, p.184, Letter to the King from the Earl of Crauford 5 May 1643.

33 Warburton, *Memoirs of Prince Rupert*, vol. II, pp.183–95, describes the guerrilla warfare in some detail.

34 British Library (BrL) MS Egerton 2646, f. 259: Grey of Werke, Letter sent from Nettlebed, Oxon, 7 June 1643.

to fellow officers to keep their men in order. Ewelme was saved, and the army passed through to make camp at Thame. The Battle of Chalgrove was such a disaster for Essex that he had to take his army out of Oxfordshire, leaving Ewelme church in the safe hands of the Royalists until 1646. The first Sunday of June is a fitting day to celebrate the salvation of Ewelme church, as Wednesday, 7 June 1643, is a likely date that Francis Martyn fended off the puritanical mob.

On 9 June 1643, Essex stopped at Stokenchurch and was most prolific with his pen. The Earl wrote from Stokenchurch to the deputy lieutenants of Essex, calling for money and supplies. He also said that he would send colonels to assist them in the work.[35] Essex sent another letter to the Gentlemen Householders of Essex that said in as many words that, if they did not send money and men to the army, their estates may be overrun with malignants.[36] Colonel John Hampden wrote from Stokenchurch on 9 June 1643 – his last known letter – to his cousin Sir Thomas Barrington, pleading for money and men.[37] Essex made his headquarters at Thame House, Thame, on 10 June 1643. His beleaguered foot soldiers were loosely quartered in the villages around Thame to help contain the spread of disease. The troops were in want of pay; many in rags and, so weak, were barely able to move.[38] Cavalry troopers were more likely to be paid for fear that they could be better rewarded by the enemy. Being recruited from the upper class, many had their own means and were generally fitter and better dressed. The cavalry distanced themselves from dragoons and the foot soldiers, for they were a class apart. The cavalry were mainly quartered away from the foot in villages a distance from Essex's headquarters. Essex pleaded with the Committee of Safety for money, supplies and fresh troops. Within days, the New Bedfordshire Levies, a dragoon regiment, were settled into Chinnor, three miles away from the diseased troops. Essex was told to expect the pay convoy sometime in the next few days. All the while, Scout Master General Sir Samuel Luke was bringing in reports. He told of hundreds of the King's troops being at Rycote, three miles from Thame, and of a vast army camped at Shotover.[39] Essex had no answer to the Royalists' threat except to wait for them to march into Thame. The Committee of Safety's decision to attack Reading rather than Oxford was either a monumental blunder or a deliberate act to undermine Parliament's cause. Whatever Parliament's motivation, the Royalists were poised to bring the Civil War to a close.

---

35 British Library (BrL) Thomason Tracts (TT), E 55 (19): Second letter of *Two Letters* from the Earl of Essex, 'For my worthy friends the Deputy Lieutenants of Essex', Stokenchurch, 9 June 1643.

36 British Library (BrL) MS Egerton 2646, f. 263: Letter from the Earl of Essex, 'For my worthy friends the Gentlemen Householders and other well affected in the County of Essex', Stokenchurch, 9 June 1643.

37 British Library (BrL) MS Egerton 2643, f. 7: Col. John Hampden's last known letter, 9 June 1643, from Stokenchurch, Oxon, to Sir Thomas Barrington.

38 Derek and Gill Lester, 'The Military and Political Importance of the Battle of Chalgrove (1643)', *Oxoniensia*, 80 (2015), <https://johnhampdensregiment.org.uk/oxoniensia/#p=1>, p.32.

39 Bodleian Library (BoL) MS. Eng. Hist. c. 53: Parliamentary scout reports of Royalist forces at Rycote, 14 June 1643 during the first English Civil War, fol. 46r. – fol. 47r., 16 June 1643.

Raid on Chinnor

After the fall of Reading, it was expected that Parliament's army would be at the gates of Oxford within a couple of days. Oxford, desperately short of gunpowder, threw up earthworks as a last-ditch attempt to defend itself from Essex's expected onslaught. The southern and westerly approaches to Oxford City were protected by Port Meadow and the River Thames. Prince Rupert further secured Oxford by fortifying the bridges that crossed the River Thames and Thame. Marshy, boggy ground was a feature of large areas of Oxfordshire, which Rupert utilised to his advantage. Bridges were strategic points that could be easily defended and, because of the nature of the terrain, could not be easily circumvented. The Committee of Safety blundered by ordering Essex to take Reading before Oxford. The natural defences around Oxford City determined that a siege with the threat of a heavy bombardment would cause the King to yield. The London-to-Oxford road that crossed Wheatley Bridge and continued towards Headington was the route to haul heavy guns. Cannon ranged on the high ground of South Park that overlooks the city would have caused the noble lords of the King's entourage to encourage Charles to yield. The shortest route from Reading to Oxford was via Wallingford, but the natural defences precluded hauling heavy artillery to Oxford. The long narrow bridge across the Thames at Wallingford was defended by a strongly garrisoned Royalist-held castle. On route to Oxford, Essex's army had no necessity to cross Wallingford Bridge but would not have been able to ignore the possibility that Royalist forces out of Wallingford Castle could harass their rear. The River Thame flowed into the River Thames at Dorchester, and the town was reached by means of a narrow bridge. Once Parliament's army had crossed the bridge at Dorchester and continued towards Oxford, there was no going back. From Dorchester, the Thames loops round in a wide arc to Abingdon.

The town is strategically placed and protected from direct attack by the confluence of a number of rivers and streams. Prince Rupert placed a large garrison in the town, and, although on the opposite side of the Thames, its location afforded Oxford protection. Parliament's army, had it crossed Dorchester Bridge and continued on the direct route towards Oxford, gave licence to the Royalists' army to cross Abingdon Bridge and come up behind Essex's troops. With no way forward, except to the confront troops out of Oxford, left no option but to retreat back over Dorchester Bridge. Surrender was inevitable if the Royalists manned the bridge. At Dorchester, a decision on whether to continue towards Oxford had to be made. If the judgement was that to continue was too risky, then the only option would be to head eastward and follow the River Thame. The slow-flowing River Thame meanders its way across to Drayton St Leonards, a small village surrounded by deep marshy land. The river continues across the flat marshy plain to the Royalist-held and easily defendable Chiselhampton Bridge. Had Parliament taken this option, troops no longer needed at Abingdon could track Parliament's progress and be ready to bolster the defenders' position against an assault wherever it was needed. The River Thame meanders its way to Wheatley Bridge, the main river being joined by many tributaries that spring up from the ground. An attack on Oxford's eastern flank was a better option to take the city, although Magdalen Bridge afforded a formidable defence into the city. This medieval ancient structure was a bridge of 20 arches some 1,500 feet in length that did not allow for two carts to pass.[40] Heavy artillery ranged on South Park was the key to Oxford's gates. The resupplied King's army had access to the shires east of Oxford and were threatening to take London.

Primarily on the Committee of Safety's order, in early June, Essex put his army between Oxford and London to help contain the threat of incursions on the Home Counties.

The weakened Parliamentarian army made its way to Thame without heavy ordnance. Any chance of taking Oxford was absolutely lost, compounded by Prince Rupert's brilliant use of the terrain and utilisation of his army. Having taken Reading, and even if Essex's army had not contracted camp fever, they would not have been able to make a direct assault on Oxford by the shortest route for the reason given above. The artillery had travelled by barge to Reading and utilised local horses to bring the guns into position. The heavy guns were returned to London by the same method.

Colonel John Urry – a cavalry commander of some note and Scottish mercenary – had fought under the command of the Earl of Brainford, the King's general. Urry had kept some correspondence with Brainford, a reference perhaps? Colonel Urry was party to Essex's Edgehill humiliation and watched how he had blundered from one tactical error to the next. Lifting the siege at Reading under such generous terms and after so much suffering may have caused Urry, as a mercenary, to consider his position. Supplies for his regiment of horse were probably lacking, pay spasmodic, and, after Reading, the prospect of defeating the King on the battlefield ever more remote. Oxford had been resupplied from York in mid May, which enabled the Royalists to operate guerilla warfare across the Home Counties towards London without opposition. They drove sheep, cattle and especially horses back to Oxford to keep its army supplied at the expense of supporters of Parliament. The Army of the North was lacking horse and had been pushed back onto the defensive. Warburton reported, 'Her Majesty also states that she has left two thousand foot and "twenty companies of horse" under Charles Cavendish, to protect Nottinghamshire and Lincolnshire. Her own accompanying forces consisted of three thousand foot, thirty companies of horse and dragoons.'[41] The Queen had left York and was advancing towards Newark with a huge convoy of arms and supplies. Rob Goodwin, in contrast, writing to Colonel Sir Thomas Barrington, remarked, 'my Lord Fairfax is in great want of horse ; the Queene advanceth'.[42] For a mercenary to be on the losing side, and should he survive the final battle, could be injurious to one's health, wealth and reputation. Colonel John Urry had given excellent service

---

40 John Steane, *Medieval Bridges in Oxfordshire* (Oxford: Oxfordshire Council and Vale and Downland Museum, 1997).

41 Warburton, *Memoirs of Prince Rupert*, vol. II, p.221.

42 British Library (BrL) MS Egerton 2646, f. 293: Rob. Goodwin's letter to Sir Thomas Barrington sent from Thame, 26 June 1643. See Appendix IX, Item 11, for text.

to Parliament to the detriment of his reputation to the Earl of Brainford. Urry required an excellent reason for the King to accept his offer to turncoat. Clarendon wrote, 'Whilst the Earl of Essex remained at Thame, and his Army quartered thereabout, Hurry came to Oxford in the Equipage that became a Colonel of Horse who had received good pay … he went to Prince Rupert, acquainted him where the Parliament Horse lay, and how loose they were in their Quarters'.[43] Circumstantial evidence suggests that Colonel Urry left Thame as late as 16 June 1643. Clarendon wrote, 'and to give a testimony of his fidelity to the King, he desired to march a Volunteer with a good Party, to make an attempt upon the Enemy'.[44]

Sir Samuel Luke's New Bedfordshire Levies was sent to Thame to reinforce Essex's army. It consisted of a fully equipped dragoon regiment that was oversupplied with horse. Chinnor, some three miles from Thame and situated below the ledge of hills on the Chilterns, was their quarters. Chinnor is on the ancient Icknield Way, which has many paths ranging from the lower, other paths in between, to the upper winter route, on which attackers could be upon the village without disturbing Essex's main army. Urry may have spotted an opportunity that would ingratiate him to the King. Urry, the cavalry commander, would be aware of Essex's military vulnerability because of his desperate need for horses. It is easy to reason that depriving Essex of 300 or 400 newly acquired horses and having the enemy use them against him would have contained the army's ability to take the fight to the Royalists.

Scout Master General Sir Samuel Luke's intelligence reportedly stated that his scouts had found an unguarded bridge across the River Ray at Islip that offered a way into Oxford. At Priest End in Thame was a bridge over the River Thame where the road to Crendon crossed the river. By taking this route, they could travel across country through Ickford along the edge of Otmoor by Beckley on through Noke to Islip, where a bridge crossed the River Ray. From Islip to the eastern gate in Oxford is five miles across open country. Other than a show of bravado to satisfy the Committee of Safety that he was taking the fight to the Royalists' camp, it is difficult to understand Essex's objective. The route described by Luke into Oxford is a march of over 20 miles and is across difficult and boggy terrain. Had Parliament's contingent crossed the bridge into Islip and came in sight of Oxford City, the exhausted men would have been overwhelmed four to one. Bletchingdon, three miles east from Islip, housed 3,000 Royalist horse. Any thought that the exhausted men had of a hasty retreat would be dashed by troopers coming out of Bletchingdon on their way to Oxford. On the early morning of 17 June 1643, 2,500 troops left Thame, which included Sir Samuel Luke's regiment of dragoons from Chinnor, crossed the River Thame and headed towards the village of Crendon. The boggy route around the edge of Otmoor and then 15 miles of torturous marching brought them to Islip. Had Prince Rupert showed a little patience that morning when Parliament visited Islip and not lined the hill with his troopers and allowed Parliament's troops to cross the River Ray, he could have escorted his captives

---

43 Hyde, *The History of the Rebellion* (1702–1704), vol. II, p.202.
44 Hyde, *The History of the Rebellion* (1702–1704), vol. II, p.201.

to Oxford. Three thousand Royalist horse were stabled at Bletchingdon, and these were soon lining the ridge above the moor where Parliament's army halted. Prince Rupert surveyed the pathetic scene and watched the men set up fires. He could have chased Parliament back into the bogs around Otmoor but considered he could lose men and horses in the treacherous ground. Without a shot being fired, Parliament's army returned to Thame tired, hungry and dejected after a 30-mile march. Sir Samuel Luke's dragoons, who had set off from Chinnor at dawn, returned and settled their nags at dusk before falling exhausted into their beds.

Colonel John Urry's intelligence of the terrain and how loose Sir Samuel Luke's dragoons were from Parliament's main army, along with the ease of which Chinnor could be approached without Essex's men being aware, ensured the raid's success. That Essex had blundered yet again on sending his men on a fool's errand to Islip would have curbed any doubt that Urry might have held of his decision to turncoat. Urry reportedly told Rupert that the pay convoy was to come to Thame on 18 June 1643; pay warrants confirm the convoy came to Thame on the due day. Examination of the narrative in the *Late Beating Up*, written 10 days after the action, shows, 'Parting from this town, we missed narrowly, and but half an hour, of Twenty one thousand pound then coming to the Earl of *Essex:* but the conductors hearing of the Alarm, drove the Carts into the wood, and so we missed it.'[45] Only the highest-ranked senior staff officers would be party to information about when a pay convoy would arrive. Secrecy was everything: officers would be informed in the loosest terms or given false information about when their regiments would be paid. The Earl of Essex and Colonel John Hampden were likely to be the only persons with full knowledge of pay train's value. However well informed Essex and Hampden had been as to when to expect the pay waggon, they would not know the time of its arrival until it came into Thame. The vagaries of bringing such valuable heavy carts across hostile countryside ensured that it was impossible to predict an arrival time. The statement in the past tense accurately reports the event. The narrative has the reader assume that the Royalists knew the convoy was in the area and searched the surrounding countryside, writing, '… the conductors hearing of the Alarm, drove the Carts into the wood, and so we missed it'.[46] Had Rupert known the pay convoy was in the area, his instinct would have been to seek it out. The statement is most probably true, but Rupert's narrator made the case from his desk in Oxford.

---

45 Bodleian Library, Wood 376 (14): *His Highnesse Prince Ruperts Late Beating Up of the Rebels Quarters at Post-comb & Chinner in Oxford Shire. And his Victory in Chalgrove Field on Sunday morning, June 18th 1643. Where unto is added Sr John Urries Expedition to West-Wickham the Sunday after : June 25. 1643*, pp.4–5.

46 BoL Wood 376 (14): *Late Beating Up*, pp.4–5.

4

Time and Place

'Time and Place' is a method that enables the movements of named groups or individuals to be plotted across a landscape.[1] Any combination of groups can be drawn onto a map, each in relation to the others' time at a given place. The method takes into account whether the groups are on foot or on horseback galloping with all speed. This Time and Place example examines the movements of Royalist troops after leaving Oxford at 4:00 p.m. on Saturday, 17 June 1643, to their return on the Sunday with those of Parliament's over the same period. The routes traversed by the parties from their various starting points is reconstructed by referring to statements in contemporary documents that name or give a clue as to that groups' location at a given time. The movements of all the parties that get to Chalgrove are followed in accordance with the Time and Place method, each from their point of origin. The data is taken from contemporary documents, notably the *Late Beating Up*, which, using the Time and Place method, has been found to be an accurate account of events leading to the Battle of Chalgrove.[2] The *Late Beating Up* was compiled by the narrator, probably Bernhard de Gomme, who was alongside Prince Rupert throughout the campaign, and it was published around 10 days after the battle. The Earl of Essex's letter dated 19 June 1643 from Thame is used to cross-reference events in the *Late Beating Up*.[3] The Time and Place method has shown that Essex's *Two Letters* is riddled with propaganda.[4] Sir Edward Hyde, who became known by the title 'Earl of Clarendon' in 1661, was the King's chief advisor, and both were

---

1 Derek Lester, *Time and Places in the 'Late Beating Up' Compared with the Essex Letters in Chronological Order* (Chalgrove Battle Group, 2023, Flipbook), <https://johnhampdensregiment.org.uk/Time%20and%20place/mobile/index.html#p=1>.
2 BoL Wood 376 (14): *Late Beating Up*.
3 British Library (BrL) Thomason Tracts (TT), E 55 (19): *Two Letters from his Excellencie Robert Earl of Essex. The one unto the Speaker of the House of Commons; relating the true state of the late skirmish at Chinner, between a party of the King's and Parliament's Forces, on the Sabbath day the 19 June 1643. With the number of such persons as was taken and slain on both sides. The other to the well affected of the County of Essex.*
4 BrL: TT, E 55 (19): *Two Letters*.

in Oxford to offer a triumphal welcome to Colonel John Urry, back from 'his' victory at Chalgrove and Chinnor. Sir Edward Hyde recorded for his private journal testament taken from Essex's most senior officers, captured from Chalgrove, as they came as prisoners into Oxford.[5] Hyde's document is used to cross-reference or collaborate evidence taken from other documents.

In 1612, William Webb was commissioned by Magdalen College to draw an estate map of Golder Manor.[6] Webb's map was drawn to the most accurate of scale, with colour representing the field systems. Trees, hedges and pastures still in evidence are precisely located, as is the ancient church and Golder Manor. Highways shown on the map are today's bridleways, and the great hedge, partly in evidence today, divided the parishes. The *VCH*'s historical survey of Chalgrove and Warpsgrove included finding that *English Heritage Battlefield Report: Chalgrove 1643* had wrongly identified Warpsgrove Manor Farm Cottage, believing it to be the ancient Warpsgrove House.[7] The present Warpsgrove Manor Farm was built early to mid eighteenth century.[8] The *VCH* referenced and cited the information on Warpsgrove House from *Oxoniensia*.[9] Historic England amended its records of the English Heritage registered battlefield report of Chalgrove to include the revised location of Warpsgrove House and a reinterpretation of the battle according to that found in *Oxoniensia*.[10] Chalgrove's St Mary's Church recorded that St James' Church was located in the area of Warpsgrove House. In all probability, it is the parish church referred to as 'In tymes past a Parish Church' on the 1612 map.[11] There is barely a trace of Warpsgrove House left except for the odd pegged tile or a piece of dressed stone turned up by the plough. A hedge detail that was a sheep pen hedge was tangible and could be measured in relation to other markers, such as a field corner. Ordnance Survey's 1881 map concurs precisely with the location of the hedge detail and field corner, which confirms that William Webb's map is not a work of art.[12] Warpsgrove House's possible site was shown as being in a featureless ploughed field, which precluded using the technique of simply measuring and comparing to find its location. Webb's fascination for accuracy may have included drawing the thumbnail sketch of the house in its precise location. Golder

---

5   Bodleian Library (BoL) MS. Clar. 112, f. 366: Sir Edward Hyde's Private Journal, 1641–1646.
6   Oxfordshire History Centre (OHC) Magd. Coll. MP/1/77: William Webb map 1612 – Golder Manor Estate.
7   Simon Townley (ed.), *A History of the County of Oxford: Volume XVIII: Benson, Ewelme, and the Chilterns (Ewelme Hundred)* (Woodbridge: Boydell and Brewer, 2016); English Heritage, *English Heritage Battlefield Report: Chalgrove 1643: Chalgrove Field (18 June 1643)* (Swindon: English Heritage, 1995).
8   Townley (ed.), *History of the County of Oxford*, p.425.
9   Lester, 'Military and Political Importance', p.30.
10 'Battle of Chalgrove 1643', *Historic England*, <https://historicengland.org.uk/listing/the-list/list-entry/1000006>, accessed 18 Feb. 2023; Lester, 'Military and Political Importance', p.36.
11 OHC: Magd. Coll. MP/1/77: William Webb map 1612 – Golder Manor Estate.
12 Oxfordshire History Centre (OHC) Ordnance Survey, Epoch1, sheet XLVI.4 (1881), 1:5,000, North East of Chalgrove.

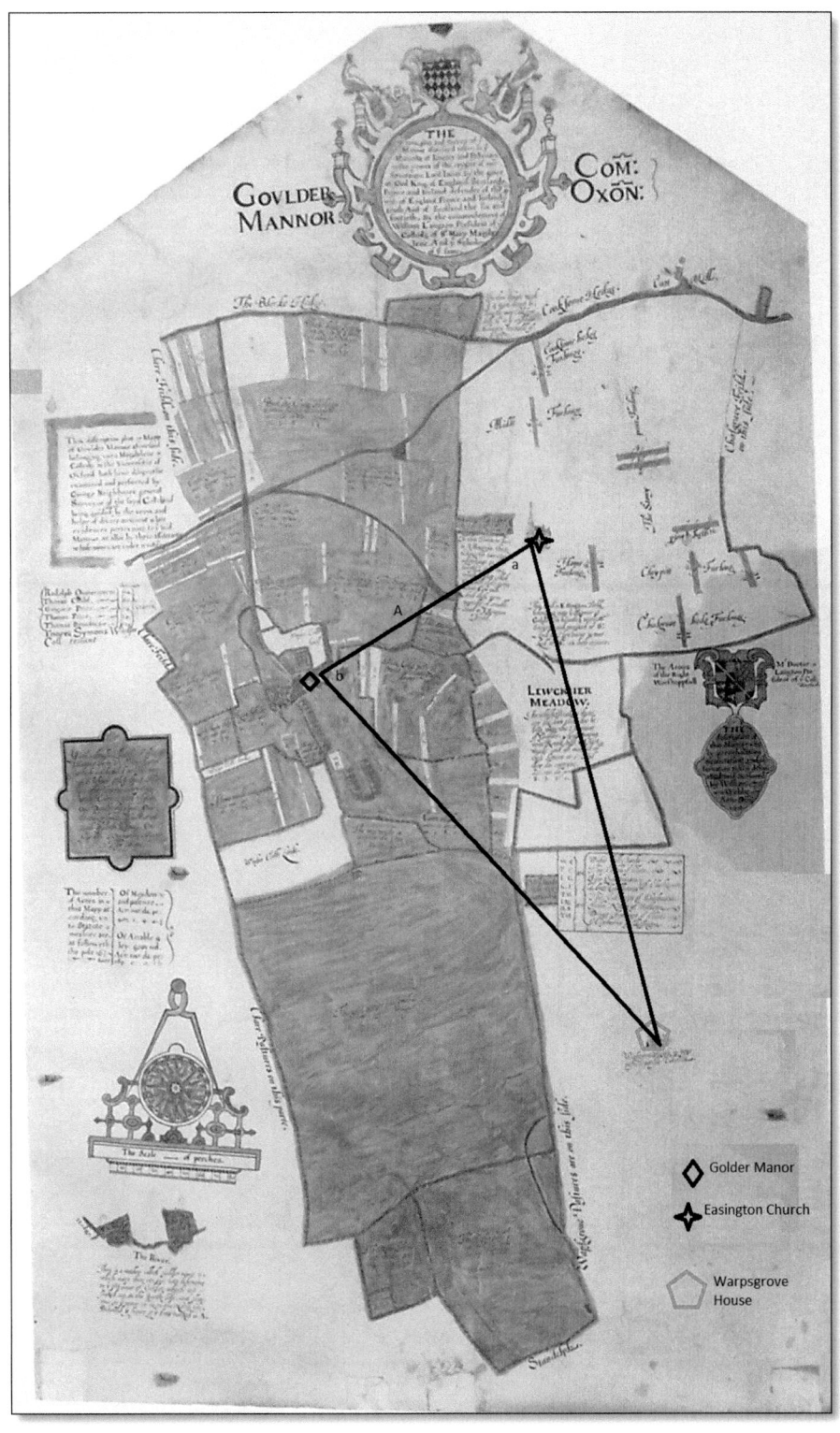

Magdalen College Estate Map, William Webb, 1612, Golder Manor. (By the kind permission of the president and fellows of Magdalen College, Oxford)

Manor to Easington church are fixed locations that still exist; therefore, by drawing lines between these two points and the thumbnail sketch of Warpsgrove House, a triangle is formed. Trigonometrical calculation allows for this triangle to be reproduced onto other maps regardless of their scale and orientation. The scale of the map was so accurately drawn that it was possible to transfer the information to an Ordnance Survey map – therefore revealing the most likely location of Warpsgrove House. The *VCH* and Abingdon Archaeological Geophysics conducted a geophysical survey of the area defined by the calculation and found evidence of a structure. Lidar images of the given area revealed foundations of a building. The evidence is sufficient that Historic England has now extended the listed area relating to the Battle of Chalgrove to include the site of the newly rediscovered site of Warpsgrove House.

At 4:00 p.m. on Saturday, 17 June 1643, Prince Rupert crossed Magdalen Bridge, Oxford, at the head of 2,000 troops flanked by Colonel John Urry and Bernhard de Gomme.[13] Soldiers on the march walk at a little over two miles an hour, and, although the cavalry is capable of much higher speeds, they usually stay with the foot to offer protection. It follows that, knowing an army's direction of travel, its time of arrival at a particular destination can be closely estimated. While the Royalists were leaving Oxford the Earl of Essex, with his army loosely quartered, was in Thame waiting for his troops to return from their expedition to Islip.[14] Sir Samuel Luke's New Bedfordshire Levies had ridden, on the morning of 17 June, 20 miles from Chinnor to Islip. Upon facing the Royalists at Islip and without a shot being fired the levies turned for home and, by 4:00 p.m., were somewhere around Wheatley with many more miles to go to reach their quarters at Chinnor. As Rupert made his way to Tetsworth in the early hours Luke's levies were returning from Islip.[15] After 40 miles in the saddle and then looking after the horses the levies fell into bed.

Leaving Oxford at 4:00 p.m., the Royalists would have covered the seven miles to Chiselhampton Bridge at a slow march in three hours. The Prince, by 1:00 a.m., was at Tetsworth, some six miles or three-hours' march from Chiselhampton Bridge. This determines that the Royalist troops rested at Chiselhampton for three hours before setting off into no man's land at nightfall. The Prince's entourage may, at the invite of the Stonors, have been entertained in Camoy's Court, which is close to Chiselhampton Bridge. The Royalists, it can be assumed, after crossing Chiselhampton Bridge, took the shortest route across country to Great Haseley. By taking this route, Stadhampton and Little Milton are bypassed.

Latchford Lane at Great Haseley leads across the fields bypassing Tetsworth, which are 400 to 500 yards away from the village. 'With this little Army, without any *Ordnance*, after some *Halts* on purpose by the way; by one a clock next morning, was the Prince advanced as high as over against

---

13   BoL Wood 376 (14): *Late Beating Up*, p.1.
14   BoL Wood 376 (14): *Late Beating Up*, p.1.
15   BoL Wood 376 (14): *Late Beating Up*, p.3.

Tetsworth, and upon the right hand of it.'[16] Warning shots were fired into the darkness from the church walls that look over the out-of-range Latchford Lane. Parliament's men had suffered from frequent surprise raids upon the outposts and were relieved when their shots were not answered. A troop of Colonel Morley's of Sussex dragoons occupied Postcombe, and, forewarned by Urry, the hamlet was approached with caution. At three o'clock in the morning, having taken two hours to travel two miles from Tetsworth, the dragoons entered Postcombe. Morley's dragoons were in a state of readiness, and, as the Royalists' dragoons dismounted, the rebels mounted their horses and fled. Bernhard de Gomme, the probable narrator, wrote, 'Some Pistols, with other Horsemen's Arms and Horses were here taken: together with 9 Prisoners, and one Cornet of Colonel *Morleys of Sussex*, as we were informed. This town was beyond *Tame*, and upon the south of it.'[17] The Earl of Essex wrote of this incursion, 'About two of the clock on Sunday morning the Enemy with about twelve hundred Horse and a great body of Dragoons fell into a Towne called *Porcham*, where one Troop of Horse (being Colonel *Morleys*) was Quartered, of which they took the greatest part, and from thence went not far to another Village called *Chinner*'.[18] One mile from Postcombe is the ancient track Icknield Way, which leads to the village of Chinnor two miles along the track. Gomme described the time and place of the advance to Chinnor, 'Hence after half an hour, his *Highness* advanced somewhat towards the *left*, along under the ledge of hills, not far from *Stokenchurch*, and the Villages in the bottom. Before 5 in the morning; were we got to *Chinner,* some 4 miles beyond *Tame:* being the very farthest of the Rebels Quarters towards *London*.'[19]

De Gomme described the raid on Chinnor:

> The Town was presently entered by Sergeant-Major *Legg* and his Partee, and by & by surrounded by the rest of the *Princes* Forces. Within it lay some 200 Dragooners of Sir *Samuel Luke's Bedfordshire* Regiment: under their Sergeant-Major *Edwards*. These, though but new levied men, yet had already actually appeared in Rebellion: as being part of that strong *Partee,* which the day before had marched out against *Islip*. These all weary and new come into the Quarters, were taken sleepers in the Barns and Houses. Diverse were killed as they bustled up: and others, that upon the Alarm, had already gotten themselves to their Arms.[20]

It was reported that 50 were killed, and six score (120 men) were taken prisoner. The dragoon's horses were saddled up and used as pack animals to carry away the booty. Farriers who attended horse regiments had carts to carry the smithying equipment and, being offered good money to work for the King, would have been ready to march to Oxford. Chalgrove is seven

---

16 BoL Wood 376 (14): *Late Beating Up*, p.3.
17 BoL Wood 376 (14): *Late Beating Up*, p.3.
18 BrL: TT, E 55 (19): *Two Letters*.
19 BoL Wood 376 (14): *Late Beating Up*, pp.3–4.
20 BoL Wood 376 (14): *Late Beating Up*, p.4.

miles from Chinnor, and the narrator wrote, 'This Action having taken up about some hour and halfs time, His *Highness* commanded away to Horse, bending His march homewards all along under the ledge of hills to the South and South-westward.'[21] The action began at around five o'clock in the morning, and Rupert left Chinnor at six-thirty. Seven miles at two miles an hour is three-and-a-half hours and, added to six-thirty, would imply the battle at Chalgrove began at around ten o'clock. Twice Gomme stated that the battle began at nine o'clock. This anomaly can be explained. The duration of the fighting at Chinnor was very short. The soldiers immediately began to saddle up the horses and load them with booty, probably aided by those dragoons just captured. The vanguard formed on the Icknield Way, ready to bring the soldiers into column and ready to march. Before six o'clock in the morning, the vanguard moved off, with the foot soldiers leading horses with their booty. The soldiers – loaded with bounty, with a skip in their step and at two-and-a-half miles an hour – would be at Chalgrove before nine o'clock. Prince Rupert and the cavalry on their fine steeds could gallop away from Chinnor and soon be up behind the foot.

Map 1 shows schematically the movements and interactions of how these groups, listed by letters in the diagram, came together to be at Chalgrove for nine o'clock in the morning to engage in battle. Data from *Time and Places*, a document published by the Chalgrove Battle Group, has taken information from contemporary documents, analysed the contents' findings and integrated them into this chapter.[22] In the early hours of 18 June 1643, the long-awaited pay convoy came to Thame. Numerous pay warrants are on record to confirm that Essex's troops were paid.[23] The payment ritual decreed that regimental officers were dressed ready for battle to present themselves to the Lord General and confirm their allegiance. When the alarm came from Chinnor, the elite of Essex's army were gathered around the headquarters, dressed ready for battle. Colonel John Hampden, second-in-command, had the authority to order that his regiment's pay remain on the cart and be delivered to Watlington, where his regiment was quartered. Having sent the cart with the regiment's pay on ahead, John Hampden – along with Colonel Sir Samuel Luke and Colonel John Dalbier – left Thame for Watlington before the alarm came from Chinnor, probably around 6:00 a.m.

A footnote in Nugent's *Some Memorials* refers to 'a very ingenious little *History of Watlington*'.[24] John Badcock, a resident of Pyrton, kept a journal that included a *History of Watlington*.[25] Within the pages of the *History of Watlington*, John Badcock wrote:

> †– p.29 It is said that the headquarters of one of the contending armies (probably Hampdens from the then political sentiments of the inhabitants) was at this Town,

---

21 BoL Wood 376 (14): *Late Beating Up*, p.5.
22 Lester, *Time and Places*.
23 The National Archives (TNA) SP 28/7, f. 395; SP 28/7, f. 440; and SP 28/143, unfol.
24 Nugent, *Some Memorials* (1832), vol. II, p.431.
25 Oxfordshire History Centre (OHC) PAR 279/9/M5/1: *History of Watlington 1816*.

at an Inn kept by Robert Parslow, which is supposed to be the house inhabited by Mr. Thomas Slater, Painter & Glazier and that a Military chest of great value left there previous to the Battle was never called for afterwards, by which means Parslow became enriched (applying to the contents to his own use) and was enabled thereby, to bequeath a very liberal amount.

The *History of Watlington* is in two parts. John Badcock's sons, Joseph and Richard, wrote in reply to Lord Nugent's affront against their father:

> … applying the contents to his own use †– p.29 … In a modern publication the author has represented this as a species of dishonesty, & the legacy to the poor was to satisfy the benefactor's conscience, but it is believed by many that from the attention of the Landlord to his guests he was desired to accept this chest (which might have been private property) by the owners if they fell in the field. It is difficult to say at this distant period how it became Parslow's, but as there is no authority whatever for believing Mr Brewer's account of it, it is surely right to lean to the most favourable opinion.

Robert Parslow may have been aware that John Hampden had been wounded in battle from a combatant who had fled the battlefield. Parslow, the landlord of the Hare and Hounds and field headquarters of Hampden's regiment, witnessed Hampden's regiment decamping Watlington on the morning of the battle to a man. When the pay wagon's conductors arrived at the Hare and Hounds, they would have been unaware that Colonel John Hampden had been mortally wounded. Parslow took charge of the 'Military chest', probably under the strict order to deliver it personally into the hands of Colonel John Hampden and no other. The chest remained with Robert Parslow until his death in 1683. St Leonard's Church, Watlington, has a plaque on the wall stating that Robert Parslow gave £200 to the poor of Watlington – a testament to Parslow's honesty. The Earl of Essex concurred that Hampden was, as is discerned, in the area of South Weston with the words in his letter, 'Colonel *Hampden* being abroad with *Sir Samuel Luke* and only one man and seeing Major *Gunters* Forces they did go along with them, Colonel *Dulbier* the Quarter-Master General did likewise come to them: with these they drew near the Enemy, and finding them marching away, kept still upon the rear for almost five miles'.[26] Colonel Sir Samuel Luke and Colonel John Dalbier were with Hampden when they met with Sergeant Major John Gunter's troops while on their way to Watlington.

The party were close to South Weston when the skirmish began but came up to Gunter after the fighting had ended. Prince Rupert raided Chinnor at around 5:00 a.m. (**A**): 'Before 5 in the morning; were we got to *Chinner* … The Town was presently entered'.[27] Essex reported in his letter to the Speaker on 19 June 1643, '… they beat up those of the new Bedfordshire Dragons and took some of them Prisoners, and three of their Colours, and some

---

26 BrL: TT, E 55 (19): *Two Letters*.
27 BoL Wood 376 (14): *Late Beating Up*, p.4.

- A ┆┆ Royalist Vanguard with Foot and booty leave Chinnor at 6.00am.
- B ┆┆ Prince Rupert's cavalry leaves Chinnor at 6.30am for Aston Rowant.
- C ┆┆ Royalist sight line from the Icknield Way over 'the village hard upon the left hand of us', Aston Rowant, to Beacon Hill.
- D ‖‖ The alarum left Chinnor at 6.30am for Sir Philip Stapleton in Thame at 7.00am.
- E ‖‖ Sanders' & Buller's dragoons sent by Stapleton to Chinnor, arriving at 7.30am.
- F ‖‖ Detachment sent back to Stapleton to report. They reported back to Thame before 8.00am.
- G ‖‖ Sanders & Buller chase after the Royalists down Icknield Way via Aston Rowant.
- H ┆┆ Major Gunter, Capt. Crosse and Capt. Sheffield at Aston Rowant.
- J ┆┆ Sanders' & Buller's troops join Gunter's men and harass the Royalists.
- K ┆┆ These 300 men skirmish with Rupert's 1,000 cavalry at South Weston.
- L ┆┆ Dundasse's dragoons leave Thame at 7.30am to arrive at South Weston after the skirmish.
- M ‖ Detachment of Dundasse's dragoons returns to Stapleton in Thames reporting after 9.15am.
- N ┆┆ Hampden & Luke set off from Thame at 6.00am arriving at Stokefield at 8.15am.
- P ┆┆ Gunter's men with Sanders & Buller meet Dundasse and then greet Hampden at Stokefield.
- R ‖‖ Scratch force of 700-800 principal officers leave Thame at around 8.00am to arrive at Clare Crossroads at 8.30am to join with the skirmishers.
- S ┆┆ Royalists march on via Clare Crossroads to Easington and Chalgrove.
- T ┆┆ Highway to Weston from Clare as shown on 1721 map.

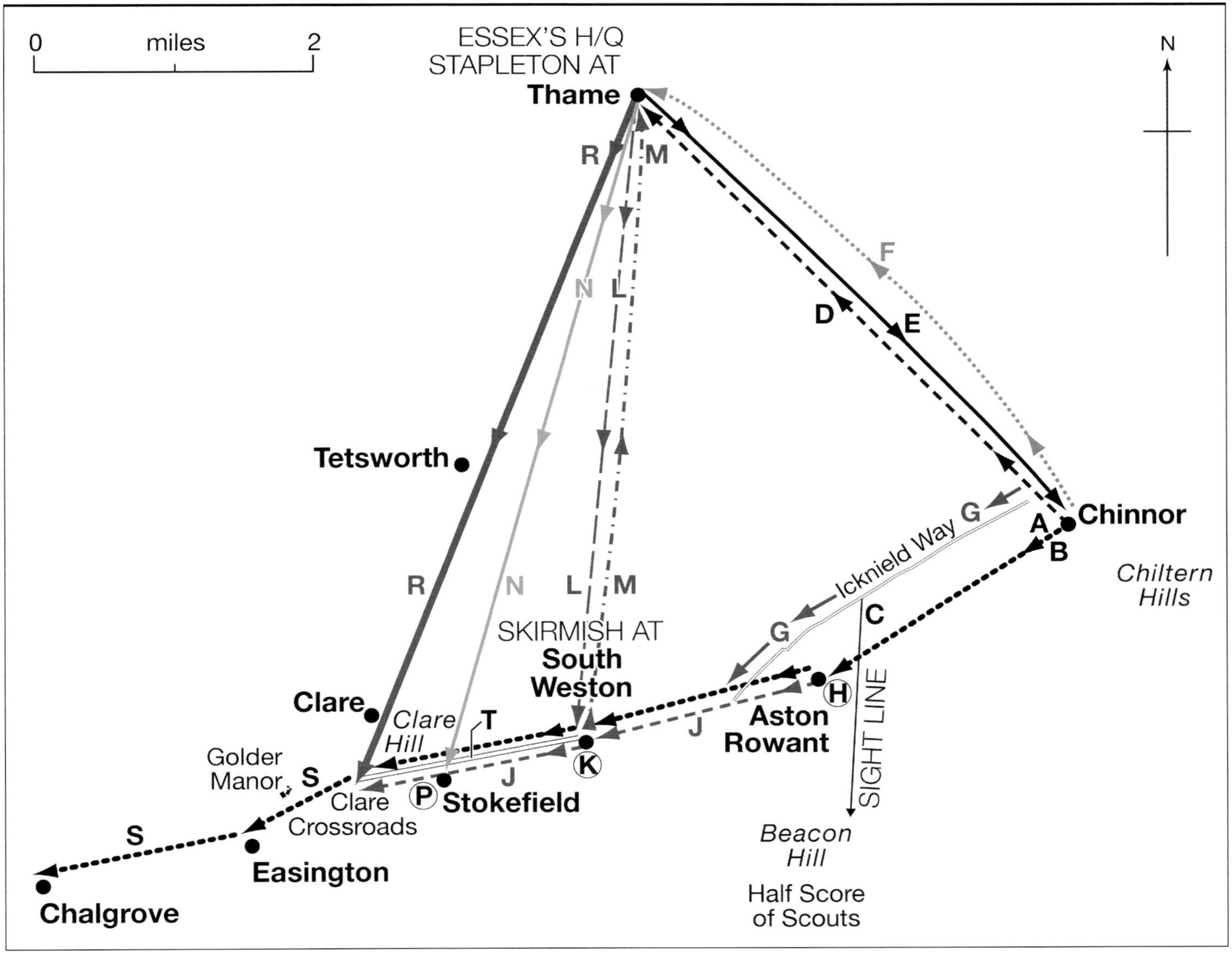

Map 1 – Royalist and Parliamentarian movements of troops prior to the battle.
(Commissioned by the author and copyright shared with *Oxoniensia* and the writer)

Officers behaving themselves very well defending the Houses wherein they were; they set fire on the Town'.[28] Gomme related:

> Our men report that they killed some 50 or more in all of them: eight of which they say were slain in one Barn. Which number alone amounts to more than some of the Rebels will confess, who say they buried but 5 in all *Chinner*. Prisoners we brought away about Sixscore: so that very few of all that were Quartered there, escaped. Almost all their Horses and Armes were taken, with three of Sir *Samuel Luke's* Dragoon Cornets. Their *Field* or Ground was *black*, with 1, 2, 3, 4, or 5 *Bibles* bost and bufft, depainted in them.[29]

The foot with the prisoners left Chinnor before 6:00 a.m. (**B**) Gomme recounted:

> This Action having taken up about some hour and halfs time, His *Highness* commanded away to Horse, bending His march homewards all along under the ledge of hills to the South and South-westward. But yet on purpose with so slow a march, that the Rebels (if they pleased) might have leisure to confront Him. And so it happened: news being brought us betwixt 7 and 8 a clock, that a body of the Rebels were discovered in the village hard upon the left hand of us.[30]

(**H**) Essex related that 'the Alarm came where Major *Gunter* lay with three Troops (*viz.*) his own, Captain *Sheffields* and, Captain *Crosses* whom he presently drew out and marched towards the Enemy'.[31] (**J**) Sanders and Buller's commanded men joined with Gunter's troops in the vicinity of Aston Rowant. (**C**) 'Presently whereupon some half score of their Scouts were discovered upon the sides of the *Becon-hill*, beyond the Village'.[32]

The sight line from the Icknield Way to '*Becon-hill*' reveals that Rupert was looking directly over the village of Aston Rowant to discover the scouts. (**D**) Once the Royalists had departed from Chinnor, an 'escapee' ran the three miles to Thame to raise the alarm. (**E**) Essex stated, 'Captain *Sanders* Troop, and Captain *Buller*, [each] with [50] commanded men, which were sent to Chinner by *Sir Philip Stapleton*, who had the watch here at *Thame*'.[33] This statement establishes that, at around 7:00 a.m., Stapleton was in Thame. (**G**) Sanders and Buller sent a detachment back to Stapleton and reported sometime before 8:00 a.m. that Chinnor was in flames and that the Royalists had taken 'Almost all their Horses and Armes'.[34] (**F**) Essex wrote that, 'when he [Stapleton] discovered the fire there, to know the occasion of it', he sent out dragoons to gather more information. (**L**) Essex also related, 'he likewise

---

28 BrL: TT, E 55 (19): *Two Letters*.
29 BoL Wood 376 (14): *Late Beating Up*, p.4.
30 BoL Wood 376 (14): *Late Beating Up*, p.5.
31 BrL: TT, E 55 (19): *Two Letters*.
32 BoL Wood 376 (14): *Late Beating Up*, p.5.
33 BrL: TT, E 55 (19): *Two Letters*.
34 BoL Wood 376 (14): *Late Beating Up*, p.4.

sent one Troop of Dragoons under the command of Captain *Dundass*, who came up to them. There were likewise some few of Captain *Melves* Dragoons that came to them.'[35] These dragoons met up with Gunter's troops after the skirmish at South Weston. (**G**) Sanders and Buller's 100 commanded men chased off down the Icknield Way in pursuit of the Royalists and found 200 men of Gunter, Crosse and Sheffield's troops who had watched the Royalists pass by Aston Rowant. The Royalists' foot with the prisoners, by 8:00 a.m., were within two miles of Chalgrove. Stapleton was still in Thame at this time directing operations. The Prince, Gomme, and his Lifeguard were close behind the foot, protecting their rear. (**T**) The highway to Weston, shown on the Map of Clare 1716, was on the Earl of Macclesfield's estate and shows the route the armies took to reach Chalgrove.[36] (**K**) The Prince, with his Lifeguard and Gomme by his side, was close behind the Royalists' foot and well ahead of Gunter's troops, who were harassing Percy's and the Prince's own regiments when the skirmish that is confused with the Battle of Chalgrove happened around South Weston, about three miles from Chalgrove. This is discerned from a comment made by Gomme (**K**):

> After a little farther march, the *Princes* own Regiment, and General *Percyes* being in the rear, and at that time over-marched by the *Princes* Troop of *Life-guard*, the Rebels Horse fell upon their rear; skirmishing lightly with them for a while. It would seem by my Lord of *Essex* Letter, that these Rebels were Major *Gunter*, with his own Troop, Captain *Sheffield*'s & Captain *Crosse*'s Troops, with Colonel Dulbeir, their Quarter-Master-General. These being once or twice faced by General *Percy*, and Lieutenan*t* Colonel *O'Neale*, they so far retreated, that ours had time to recover up to the *Prince*, and *Van* of the Army.[37]

Essex described the skirmish as:

> … we having not above 300 Horse; our men charged them very gallantly, and slew divers of them; but while they were in fight, the Enemy being so very strong, kept a Body of Horse for his reserve, and with that Body wheeled about and charged our men in the rear, so that being encompassed and overborne with multitude, they broke and fled, though it was not very far.[38]

Essex and Stapleton were in Thame, six miles away from where the skirmish took place, which Essex referred to as 'we having not above 300 Horse; our men charged them very gallantly'.[39] It is farcical to believe that Essex and Stapleton were at South Weston and Thame at the same time. Following on from 'though it was not very far', Essex described what took

---

35 BrL: TT, E 55 (19): *Two Letters*.
36 Bodleian Library (BoL) Map (R) C17:49 60: John Badcock's map of Pyrton, 1835.
37 BoL Wood 376 (14): *Late Beating Up*, p.5.
38 BrL: TT, E 55 (19): *Two Letters*.
39 BrL: TT, E 55 (19): *Two Letters*.

place after the Battle of Chalgrove, but his words are a deliberate attempt to deceive the reader into believing the skirmish at South Weston was the battle:

> For when I heard that our men marched in the rear of the Enemy, I sent to Sir *Phillip Stapleton* who presently Marched toward them with his Regiment; & though he came somewhat short of the Skirmish, yet seeing our men Retreat in disorder, he stopped them, caused them to draw into a Body with him, where they stood about an hour: Whereupon the Enemy marched away.[40]

(**M**) Dundasse's dragoons may have heard the gunfire from the skirmish and came to Gunter. Dundasse relayed the message to Gunter that Essex's officers were riding with all speed towards Chalgrove. Gunter gave Dundasse's detachment a message to give to Essex and Stapleton in Thame that was received there at around 9:30 a.m. This is the message that Essex referred to and made sense of: 'For when I heard that our men marched in the rear of the Enemy, I sent to Sir *Phillip Stapleton*'.[41] Stapleton left Thame after 9:30 a.m. and galloped with his regiment with all speed, '& though he came somewhat short of the Skirmish [Battle of Chalgrove] … he stopped them, caused them to draw into a Body with him [sometime after 10:00 a.m.]'[42] This information gives the duration of the Battle of Chalgrove as being over an hour. Sir Edward Hyde wrote of the battle:

> Hereupon they quickly engaged in a sharp encounter, the best, fiercest, and longest maintained that hath been by the horse during the war; for the party of Parliament consisted not of bare regiments and troops which usually marched together, but of prime gentlemen and officers of all their regiments, horse and foot, who being met at the head quarter, upon the alarum, and conceiving it easy to get between prince Rupert and Oxford, and not having their own charges ready to move, joined themselves as volunteers to those who were ready.[43]

(**N**) Colonel John Hampden left Thame with Luke and Dalbier before the alarm came from Chinnor.

(**P**) The route from Thame to Watlington would take Hampden's party through Stokefield, close to South Weston, at around 8:30 a.m. – during which they met Gunter's 300 skirmishers. This logically infers that Hampden and company left Thame around two hours earlier and before the alarm came from Chinnor. *The Parliament Scout* reported, 'Colonell Hambden [sic] who came by accident into this Skirmish, and charged in Captaine Crofts [Crosse's] Troope was shot in the shoulder, but is now dead.'[44] (**R**) Parliament's officers,

---

40 BrL: TT, E 55 (19): *Two Letters*.
41 BrL: TT, E 55 (19): *Two Letters*.
42 BrL: TT, E 55 (19): *Two Letters*.
43 BoL: MS. Clar. 112, f. 366: Sir Edward Hyde's Private Journal, 1641–1646.
44 British Library (BrL) Thomason Tracts (TT), E 96 (10): The Parliament Scout, Communicating His Intelligence to the Kingdome, From Tuesday the 20. June, to Tuesday the 27. of June 1643, no. 1.

mentioned by Hyde above, joined with Gunter's men at Clare Crossroads at around 8:30 a.m. These 1,150 troops were under Sergeant Major John Gunter's command, for he came first into the battle and who hurriedly planned to outflank the Royalists as they turned westward towards Oxford. The Royalists continued on the highway down Golder Hill through Easington until:

> His *Highness* was now making *halt* in *Chalgrove* cornfield … Just at this time (being now about 9 a clock) we discerned several great Bodies of the Rebels Horse and Dragooners, coming down *Golder-hill* towards us; from *Esington* and *Tame*: who (together with those that had before skirmished with our Rear) drew down to the bottom of a great Close, or Pasture: ordering themselves there among trees beyond a great hedge, which parted that Close from our Field.[45]

A great hedge is a double row of stock-proof hedges a few feet apart, often with a modest ditch running between them. It is a formidable barrier and impossible to leap by horse as suggested of Prince Rupert in some chronicles. The location of the great hedge, the marker for the parish boundary and in evidence today, determined the armies' manoeuvres to the battlefield.

---

45   BoL Wood 376 (14): *Late Beating Up*, pp.5–6.

5

The Battle of Chalgrove

The near exact location of where Prince Rupert made halt in a Chalgrove cornfield can be discerned by relating the topography of a modern Ordnance Survey map to that shown in the Magdalen College Estate Map of Golder Manor. Until very recent times, most of the hedges and trees shown on the 1612 map were found in the landscape and identically on modern Ordnance Survey maps. It is on this terrain that Sergeant Major John Gunter found himself in command of Parliament's scratch force, leading and giving orders to officers more senior than himself. Colonel John Hampden, second-in-command of Essex's army, put himself in Captain Richard Crosse's troop to fight as trooper. The valiant aspiration of Essex's officers, who volunteered as one to bring honour back to Essex and stop the Royalists escaping with the prisoners and booty taken from Chinnor, was brought into sharp relief. Officers of the highest rank, who were used to giving orders, had to form into companies and fight as troopers. They had to learn how to respond to 'their' captain's orders and maintain a fighting unit: training a trooper took time, and they were about to engage with the elite of the Royalist cavalry.

The Prince's own regiment, his 150-strong Lifeguard, the Prince of Wales' regiment and General Percy's regiment were elite regiments – Rupert's Lifeguard, in particular, hand-picked for their loyalty to the Prince and their horsemanship. At Edgehill, Prince Rupert's tactics forced Essex into battle on the Royalists' terms. In the manoeuvring on the battlefield, Prince Rupert, the master tactician, was able to force the Parliamentarians into making rash decisions. Prince Rupert watched from the advantage of the higher ground as the Parliamentarians 'drew down to the bottom of a great Close, or Pasture: ordering themselves there among trees beyond a great hedge, which parted that Close from our Field'.[1] Parliament had blundered, by its haste, into a position that gave Rupert the advantage of the terrain. To 'zugzwang' an opponent, as in a game of chess, is when the adversary is forced to move a piece to a disadvantageous position. In this case, Gunter was compelled to put his 'pieces' of the army into a difficult or dangerous situation. The alternative was to admit defeat. By Rupert's actions – manoeuvring his troops from the Chalgrove

---

1 BoL Wood 376 (14): *Late Beating Up*, pp.5–6.

cornfield and taking advantage of Parliament's compromised position – he was able to influence Gunter's manoeuvring of his troops.

The ancient track in the folds of Golder Hill was extant until 1933. It was the cart route from Chalgrove to Easington and onwards, and it is today's bridleway. The Royalists' line of march from Clare Crossroads led them down the folds of Golder Hill, through Easington, across the fields to one of the few gaps in the parish boundary's great hedge and into the Chalgrove cornfield. The Royalists' three regiments of horse, from the vanguard to the troop bringing up the rear, stretched for around half a mile. As the rear of General Percy's regiment cleared the great hedge, Prince Rupert – along with Gomme – was looking from their viewpoint towards Golder Hill (**F**). Gomme recorded from this vantage point in the Chalgrove cornfield:

> Just at this time (being now about 9 a clock) we discerned several great Bodies of the Rebels Horse and Dragooners, coming down *Golder-hill* towards us; from *Esington* and *Tame*: who (together with those that had before skirmished with our Rear) drew down to the bottom of a great Close, or Pasture: ordering themselves there among trees beyond a great hedge, which parted that Close from our Field.[2]

Essex's letter expunged mention of the battle or that his officers were fighting as troopers. Essex failed to mention that his officers had suffered a humiliating defeat and that they had fought to Chalgrove. Gomme was at pains to remind Essex of his injudiciousness and wrote, 'My Lord of *Essex's* Relation, here mentions Captain *Sanders* Troop, and Captain *Buller* with 50 commanded men; Captain *Dundasses* Troop of Dragooners, with some few of Colonel *Melves*. But surely these were not all their Forces.'[3] The Parliamentarians came from Easington and Thame, Gomme stated. Easington is near due east from where the Prince stood in the Chalgrove cornfield, and Thame is six miles away towards the north-west. This statement suggests that the Parliamentarians were racing in ragged order across a wide arc of Golder Hill in a bid to outflank the Royalists.

Parliament's troops were brought to an abrupt halt by the great hedge that forms the parish boundary. A great hedge usually has a double line of stock-proof hedges with a ditch running in between and is intended to be a physical barrier. The Parliamentarians looked beyond the hedge, and 75 yards up the hill was the Prince. Rupert ordered his troopers to turn from column into line, which brought them into battle formation. The Royalists' foot and dragoons with the prisoners and booty were over one mile to the west, heading towards Chiselhampton Bridge and safety. The dragoons had been ordered to create a rolling ambush. This involved the dragoons hiding in hedgerows that lined the lane in ambush as the foot and prisoners made their way to safety. Once the foot was a way ahead, the dragoons would retreat then set another ambush. The longer Gunter prevaricated the closer the foot with the prisoners came to the safety of Chiselhampton Bridge. Gunter was aware that to attack the foot

---

2   BoL Wood 376 (14): *Late Beating Up*, pp.5–6.
3   BoL Wood 376 (14): *Late Beating Up*, p.6.

A – Parliament attempts to outflank retiring Royalists.
B – Gunter's force follows Royalists along the 'ancient track' down Golder Hill.
C – Highway from Clare joins the 'ancient track'.
D – Royalist vanguard at Easington at 8:30 a.m.
E – Royalists enter Chalgrove Parish on the 'ancient track'.
F – Royalists stand to face Parliamentarians on the north side of the great hedge.
G – Gunter's force joins main Parliamentarian body in Lewknor Meadow.
H – Combined Parliamentarian force organises itself.
J – Royalist vanguard – foot, dragoons and prisoners – cross Warpsgrove Lane at 8:45 a.m.
K – Royalist horse continue retirement across Solinger Field into Upper Marsh Lane.
L – Parliamentarians gallop down the north side of the great hedge to Warpsgrove Lane.
M – Parliamentarians deploy through the great hedge onto the battlefield.
N – Position of Parliamentarian reserves.
P – Royalist horse deploy behind a low hedge on west side of the 'ancient track', at that point called Upper Marsh Lane.
R – Prince Rupert jumps the low hedge, followed by his men, and throws back Parliamentarians.

Note: The crossed swords on a black disc indicate where the battle was believed to have taken place as marked on the 1881 Ordnance Survey map. The crossed swords on a pale disc mark where the battle actually took place.

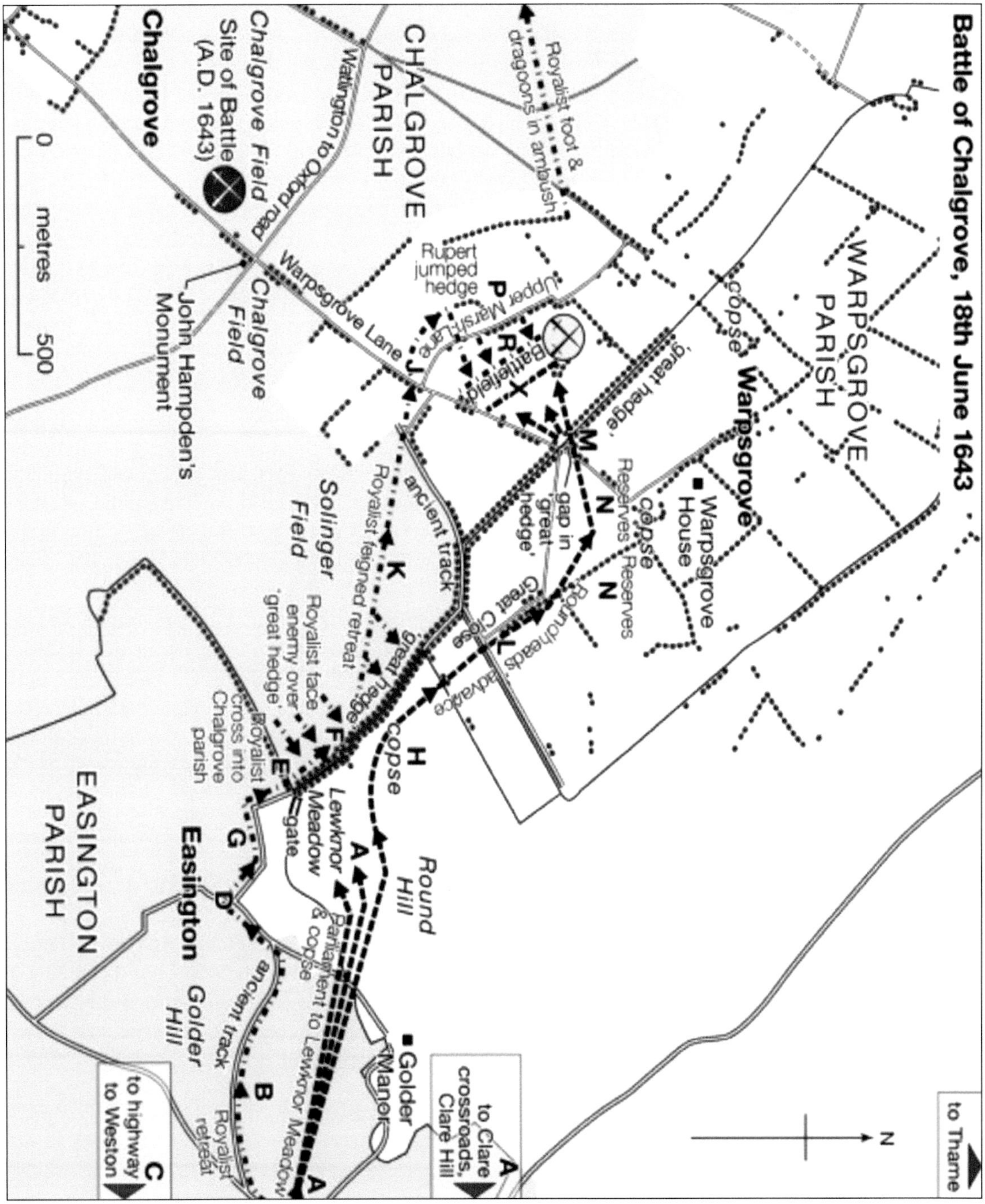

THE BATTLE OF CHALGROVE

Map 2 – The approach to, and deployment on, the battlefield of Chalgrove.
(Commissioned by the author and copyright shared with *Oxoniensia* and the writer)

and dragoons would be a suicidal mission. Having over a 1,000 troopers close behind as your men rode into an ambush was the prospect that faced Gunter. Another option was to admit defeat and allow Prince Rupert to march away, but Gunter had his reputation to consider. The recriminations would be unbearable, and Gunter's military career would be over. Gunter's only option, and probably spurred on by his superiors, was to confront Prince Rupert on the battlefield.

The great hedge stretched unbroken for 1,000 yards to where the lane to Warpsgrove House passed through the great hedge. (**L**) Rupert could hear the orders being barked out as they were 'ordering themselves there among trees beyond a great hedge, which parted that Close from our Field'.[4] The Prince gave an order to his cavalry to turn from line into column and march to the corner of the cornfield farthest away from the gap in the great hedge by Warpsgrove House. In the few minutes available, Gunter formed the men into 13 cornets of horse and a company of dragoons commanded by Captain Middleton. Captains Sanders and Buller's commanded men were formed into a 'Forlorn Hope of Horse' led by Colonel Dalbier. Gomme wrote, 'The better to entice them on, the *Prince* with Horse made show of a Retreat: whereupon the Rebels advanced cheerfully: doubling their march for eagerness, and coming up close to us.'[5] Gunter led his men on the 1,000-yard gallop to the gap in the great hedge and Warpsgrove Lane, which are extant (**M**). The gap in the great hedge is adjacent to Warpsgrove House, upon which Gomme remarked, 'Besides which, they had left a *Reserve* of 3 Cornets in the Close aforesaid among the trees by *Wapsgrove* [sic] *House*, and two Troops more higher up the hill, they were in sight of one another, by 9 a clock in the morning.'[6]

Around 300 men was the strength of the Prince's own regiment, and his Lifeguard was 150 hand-picked men. Two troops from the Prince of Wales' regiment, about 140 men, led by Lieutenant Colonel O'Neale joined with the Prince. These 600 men made a front equal to the Parliamentarians' eight cornets of around 560 men. Sergeant Major John Gunter came through the gap in the great hedge on Warpsgrove Lane, followed by eight cornets of horse. The dragoons led by Captain Middleton stormed down the battlefield to the hedge line to where Prince Rupert's Lifeguards were located and began firing their carbines at close range. Some saddles of the Lifeguard were emptied. The riders in the Forlorn Hope of Horse, as the name suggests, were not expected to return. Gomme reported, 'Some of ours affirm, how they over-heard *Dulbiere* (who brought up some of the Rebels first Horse) upon sight of the *Princes* order and dividing of his *Wings* , to call out to his People *to retreat, least they were hemmed in by us*.'[7] The commanded men acting as dragoons were so close to General Percy's regiment that they overheard Colonel Dalbier's order for his troops to retreat.

The purpose of deploying a Forlorn Hope of Horse is to disrupt the enemy's cavalry's battle order before they charge. Once a troop or regiment

---

4   BoL Wood 376 (14): *Late Beating Up*, pp.5–6.
5   BoL Wood 376 (14): *Late Beating Up*, p.6.
6   BoL Wood 376 (14): *Late Beating Up*, pp.6–7.
7   BoL Wood 376 (14): *Late Beating Up*, p.8.

of horse has charged out of order, it precludes the brigade from charging the enemy. Colonel Dalbier had the opportunity to charge into the flank of General Percy's regiment either before the battle began or after as they waited in reserve. Colonel Dalbier and his illustrious troopers, it seems, faltered in carrying out their duty as a forlorn hope. Losing a couple of officers and a number of troopers in a 'forlorn' charge against the enemy was acceptable, the leader of the charge being mentioned as a gallant gentleman and officer and his widow being compensated for her loss. The 100 commanded men of the Forlorn Hope of Horse were officers, some of whom may have been close to the royalty, lords of the realm or gentry of the highest order. Commanding the regiment in a gallant charge against the enemy and to die with honour on the battlefield was an accolade to be treasured. The ignominy for a lord or gentleman of rank fighting as a dragoon was a humiliation beyond the call of duty. It was not the fear of dying that caused the commanded men to baulk at charging against General Percy's troops but the dishonour it would bring to their family's name and regiment. At the moment the commanded men were to charge as a forlorn hope, the thought that they would be remembered for being a dragoon when they fell would have been too much for them to bear. Colonel Dalbier's order to retreat may have been made to save his commanded men's honour and his own. The commanded men obeyed their commanding officer's order, and Dalbier had saved face by giving an order they would obey without question. Captain Middleton's dragoons were taking a toll on Rupert's Lifeguard, and Colonel Dalbier's Forlorn Hope of Horse was a threat to the Royalists' order, which Rupert was aware could bring his troops into confusion.

Major John Gunter deployed eight cornets of troops in battle order about 100 yards beyond the great hedge, inviting the Royalists to come onto the battlefield:

> … for that (saith he) the Rebels being so near us, may bring our Rear into confusion, before we can recover to our ambush. Yea (saith he) their insolency is not to be endured. This said, His *Highness* facing all about, set spurs to His Horse, and first of all (in the very face of the Dragooners) leapt the hedge that parted us from the Rebels. The *Captain*, and rest of His Troop of *Lifeguards* (everyman as they could) jumbled over after him: and as about 15 were gotten over, the *Prince* presently drew them up into a Front, till the rest could recover up to him.[8]

Prince Rupert set spurs to his horse and, in grand and dramatic style, crashed through the hedge onto the battlefield. 'At this the Rebels Dragooners that lined the hedge, fled', and the Forlorn Hope of Horse retreated. Some of his Lifeguard followed the Prince through the hedge while the remainder and his regiment followed 'Lieutenant-Colonel *O'Neale* having passed with the *Princes* Regiment beyond the end of the hedge on the left hand'.[9] 'Captain *Martins*, and Captain Thomas *Gardiner's* Troops, in Prince *Ruperts* Regiment' spearheaded the charge into Gunter's men. Gunter's troops' 'first Volley of Carbines and Pistols [was] at a distance, as ours were advancing: yea they

---

8   BoL Wood 376 (14): *Late Beating Up*, p.7.
9   BoL Wood 376 (14): *Late Beating Up*, p.7.

had time for their second Pistols, ere ours could charge them. The hottest of their charge fell upon Captain *Martins*, and Captain *Gardiner's* Troops … indeed the whole Regiment endured the chief shock of it'.[10] Parliament's horse made a stand to receive Prince Rupert's charge.

Firing a pistol at incoming troops at a distance was a futile gesture, as its range was very short. Breastplates were proofed for pistol shots, and the wearing of buff coats further protected a rider from a hail of bullets. Pistols fired at close range were more effective, but it was a daunting prospect to have a wounded horse stung with pain smashing into the ranks. In the turmoil, the Royalists who charged with swords raised came in among Parliament's ranks then used their pistols at the closest range. Backplates were not proofed for shot – you would not cowardly present your back to enemy was the thinking. The Royalists used their pistols to great effect. Being among the enemy's ranks, the unsuspecting target received a double-loaded pistol shot into their back from the closest range, maybe with the barrel touching the victim. Colonel John Hampden was wounded, possibly targeted, in such a manner.

Being an early casualty, and in the confusion and disorder, Hampden was able to retire from the battlefield to the reserves by Warpsgrove House. A troop from Percy's regiment chased up to the gap in the great hedge by Warpsgrove House and challenged Parliament's reserve to attack. This manoeuvre was to deny Parliament's reserve the opportunity to come to their fellow officers' rescue. General Percy's regiment entered the fray and engulfed Parliament's left flank with overwhelming numbers. Time and again, the Royalist troopers wheeled around, reloaded their pistols and charged in amongst Parliament's men, carefully choosing the best targets before firing their pistols at close range. Parliament's men stood their ground but, having little time to reload their pistols, were reduced to slashing at fleeting shadows as they galloped passed. The near impossibility of reloading a pistol on horseback while in the thick of battle was emphasised by the necessity to first sheathe one's sword. The left flank had witnessed the badly wounded Colonel John Hampden leaving the battlefield and Sergeant Major John Gunter killed before their eyes. The onslaught was relentless.

Prince Rupert, taking his chance, swept in on the left flank and put them in rout. The term 'rout' can mean 'every man for himself', the troop or individuals not being under command of their officers. Troops, once routed, usually flee for their lives, but this was not an option. The battle raged – blood and gore spilled as bodies of the fallen were trampled under the hooves of the horses of those fighting. Parliament's right flank had faltered, perceiving that, by bringing on his reserves, Sergeant Major Daniel's men could cause great execution. The Prince of Wales' regiment had lost a cornet in the fight at Hopton Heath, and Sergeant Major Daniel saw his chance to recover the regiment's honour by Law of Arms in taking a colour from the rebels. Captain James Sheffield, rallying his troop and cornet in hand, was shot and wounded by Major Daniel. In the melee to save their colour, Major Daniel was unsaddled from his horse, but the

---

10   BoL Wood 376 (14): *Late Beating Up*, pp.7–8.

cornet was won, and the right to bear arms was the regiment's battle honour.[11] 'As on the other wing did Major *Daniel* with the *Prince of Wales* his Regiment: so that now were the Rebels wholly routed.'[12]

The Royalists outnumbered the Parliamentarians on the battlefield near two to one and had time to peel off and reload their pistols 'so that now were the Rebels wholly routed' but still unable to flee the battlefield. Parliament's men ceased to put up resistance, and they were all Prince Rupert's prisoners. They could not flee as usually happened when an army was routed and overwhelmed. The gap in the great hedge by Warpsgrove House was too narrow to accommodate 500 or 600 men on horseback racing through in panic. The great hedge to the north closed all possibility of galloping out and away from the enemy. Directly westward, the land was deep marsh with a small lake that was fed by a spring. Avoiding the bog and marshy ground to the westward would have taken them into the dragoons' ambush. The Royalist reserves waiting where the Royalists first formed up in Upper Marsh Lane would have picked off those trying to flee to the southward. The eastward on Parliament's left offered the best hope, and, in the early part of the battle, some Parliamentarians had escaped this way. Gomme highlighted again that Essex's account of the battle was false, commenting, 'for that the *Prince* with his *Lifeguards*, with Sword and Pistol charging them home upon the *Flank*, (not wheeling about upon their Rear, as the *London Relation* tells it) put them in rout at the first encounter'.[13]

But there was a problem: the Royalists' horses had been saddled up and ridden for over 20 hours. Galloping back and forth in a hectic battle drained them of any reserves of energy. The riders were also weary. Chasing around in bright sunshine in heavy woollen and leather clothing left them sapped of energy. Rupert's problem was more profound: how could he end the battle and march victorious for home? The foot and dragoons with the prisoners would, in the hour's duration of the battle, be across Chiselhampton Bridge and safe from attack. It was unheard of for officers to fight as a company of troopers, and this lack of understanding left them leaderless and bemused. Parliament's officers trapped on the battlefield understandably had no training for this situation. They were wholly routed, in that individuals within companies had stopped taking orders – everyman for himself. Parliament's command structure had completely broken down. They were utterly and wholly routed, and their reserve was unable to come to their aid. Parliament's 350 reserves were on fresh horses fully armed and, like a bottle of champagne that had been shaken and left out in the sun, were about to blow the cork. For Rupert to walk away with 400 or 500 prisoners would leave Percy's troop with an impossible task and facing certain death. If Percy's troop had abruptly turned and galloped away, it would be as though the cork of an agitated champagne bottle had suddenly been released. The great release of anger could cause devastation to a Royalist force already exhausted from battle. The Royalists, having raided Chinnor and skirmished heavily at South Weston, after the hour-long battle

---

11   BoL Wood 376 (14): *Late Beating Up*, pp.9–10.
12   BoL Wood 376 (14): *Late Beating Up*, p.8.
13   BoL Wood 376 (14): *Late Beating Up*, p.8.

at Chalgrove, were desperately low or out of gunpowder. Rupert's prisoners would be released from their word of honour to be true prisoners if they were recaptured by Parliament's reserves. Rupert's troops, although victorious, were vulnerable to an attack that they would have had difficulty in repelling.

By studying the archive of material on the battle, Rupert's brilliant solution to the dilemma is revealed. Sir Edward Hyde, the King's chief advisor, gleaned from Colonel John Urry and the prisoners coming into Oxford that, 'with the new prisoners he had taken, retired orderly to the pass where his foot and former purchase expected him'.[14] This statement calls attention to Parliament's reserve being unable to break through Percy's troop's cordon at the great hedge. The Royalists retreated in an orderly manner with the newly acquired prisoners to Chiselhampton Bridge, Hyde confirmed. Hyde reported that Rupert returned with 'near 200 prisoners, seven cornets of horse and four ensigns of foot, to Oxford'.[15] This short sentence speaks volumes about the battle. Essex was short on details in his 'letter' but did write in his own words of the New Bedfordshire Levies being overwhelmed and that three colours were taken. Gomme recorded in the *Late Beating Up*, 'Prisoners we brought away about Sixscore', and, by deduction and subtraction, it states that 80 prisoners were taken from Chalgrove.[16] Only cavalry were involved in the battle, yet four ensigns of foot were taken at Chalgrove, which were paraded through Oxford. Hyde described in his manuscript, 'for the party of Parliament consisted not of bare regiments and troops which usually marched together, but of prime gentlemen and officers of all their regiments, horse and foot', which reveals that the 80 prisoners from Chalgrove were officers of quality selected from those corralled by Rupert when Parliament's men were wholly routed.[17]

Gomme disclosed how the Prince resolved the dilemma in writing:

> The Rebels now flying to their *Reserve* of three *Colours* in the Close by *Wapsgrove* house, were pursued by ours in execution all the way thither: who now (as they could) there *rallying*, gave occasion to the defeat of those three *Troops* also. So that all now being in confusion, were pursued by ours a full mile and quarter (as the neighbours say) from the place of the first encounter. These all fled back again over *Golder hill* to *Esington*: and so far Sir *Phillip Stapleton* with his Regiment was not yet come.[18]

The last sentence highlights that Stapleton was still in Thame at the time of the skirmish at South Weston. At around 9:30 a.m., Dundasse's dragoons relayed the information to Essex that Gunter and the officers he had sent were following the Royalists. Gomme's remark 'and so far Sir *Phillip Stapleton* with his Regiment was not yet come' exposed Essex's statement in his letter to ridicule.[19] Essex had alluded that the following statement was before the battle, '… Sir *Phillip*

---

14 BoL: MS. Clar. 112, f. 366: Sir Edward Hyde's Private Journal, 1641–1646.
15 BoL: MS. Clar. 112, f. 366: Sir Edward Hyde's Private Journal, 1641–1646.
16 BoL Wood 376 (14): *Late Beating Up*, p.4.
17 BoL: MS. Clar. 112, f. 366: Sir Edward Hyde's Private Journal, 1641–1646.
18 BoL Wood 376 (14): *Late Beating Up*, p.8.
19 BoL Wood 376 (14): *Late Beating Up*, p.8.

Stapleton who presently Marched toward them with his Regiment; & though he came somewhat short of the Skirmish, yet seeing our men Retreat in disorder, he stopped them, caused them to draw into a Body with him, where they stood about an hour: Whereupon the Enemy marched away'.[20] Essex's account in his letter is shown to be what it was: propaganda to serve the citizens of London to allay their fears of rumours that the King was to march on the city.

Where Warpsgrove Lane passed through the great hedge, it formed a bottleneck. The narrowness of the gap precluded more than three riders in disciplined order from galloping through the great hedge at a time. As described earlier, 400 or 500 men on horseback fleeing in panic would result in a crush. Having such a large body of riders racing through such a narrow gap in good order could only be achieved with agreement of those Parliamentarians involved. Why should these officers agree to fly to their reserves in good order? These officers were the prisoners of Prince Rupert, and he could trade their word to do as asked for their liberty. Disarmed of their pistols and swords, Parliament's men would not pose a threat even if they banded together with the reserves. The Royalists selected 80 prisoners of quality for their exchange value or for those who could be persuaded to give their loyalty to the King. The lives of these 80 prisoners could also be at forfeit should Parliament's men turn with the reserves and mount an attack. Those who had pursued Parliament's troops over Golder Hill returned to the scene of their victory.

Prince Rupert was master of the battlefield. All was quiet except for the groaning on what minutes earlier had been the site of a raging battle with gunfire, neighing horses and men screaming. The troops were sent out to scour the fields and search for their injured or fallen comrades, as well as those of the enemy. Those Royalists who had fallen or had been wounded were brought into a rudimentary dressing station for their wounds to be dressed. At Mr Steven's house in Easington, 10 sorely wounded men were found having their wounds dressed.[21] Carts were commandeered to carry the dead and wounded back to Oxford. Useful articles found littering the battlefield or upon the enemy's dead were piled into carts, and loose horses were rounded up to add to the bounty of the two encounters.

His duties to the wounded and fallen Royalist troops fulfilled, and the battlefield scoured for items of value:

> … the victorious *Prince* retired his Troops over *Chiselhampton* bridge leisurely. There having ordered Mr. *Percy* with his Horse Regiment, and Colonel *Washington* with his Dragooners for that night to quarter near the *pass*, and to send out strong *patrols* or *rounds* for scouting all along the River Charwell [Thame]: His Highness by two a clock came safely back into *Oxford*. He had sent the news of all before by Colonel Urrey whom the King presently Knighted. The report of these *two* Victories, were so much the welcomer to His Majesty, for that he had heard the Prince have been engaged.[22]

---

20 BrL: TT, E 55 (19): *Two Letters*.
21 BoL Wood 376 (14): *Late Beating Up*, p.14.
22 BoL Wood 376 (14): *Late Beating Up*, pp.13–14.

JOHN HAMPDEN AND THE BATTLE OF CHALGROVE

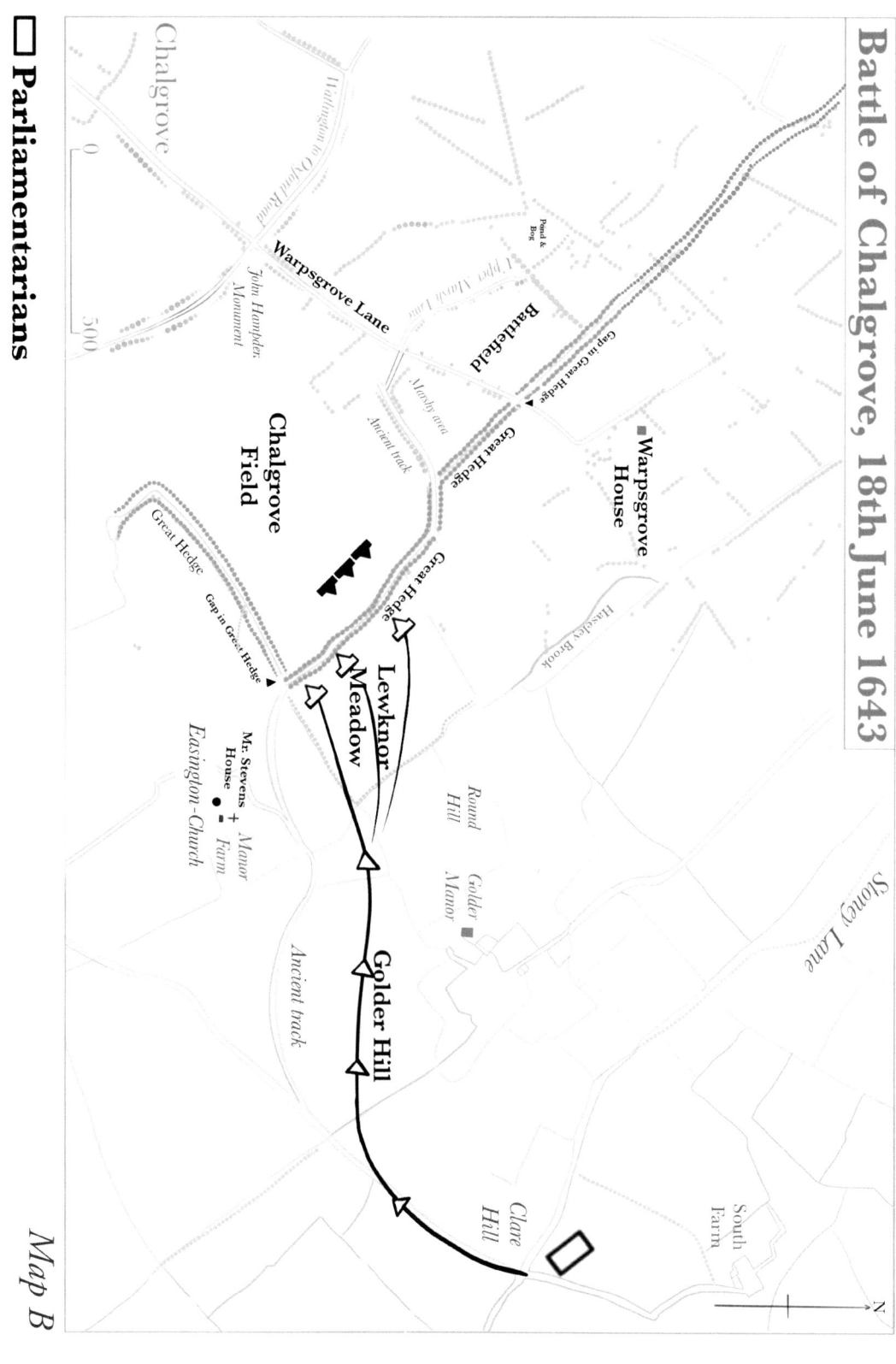

Map B

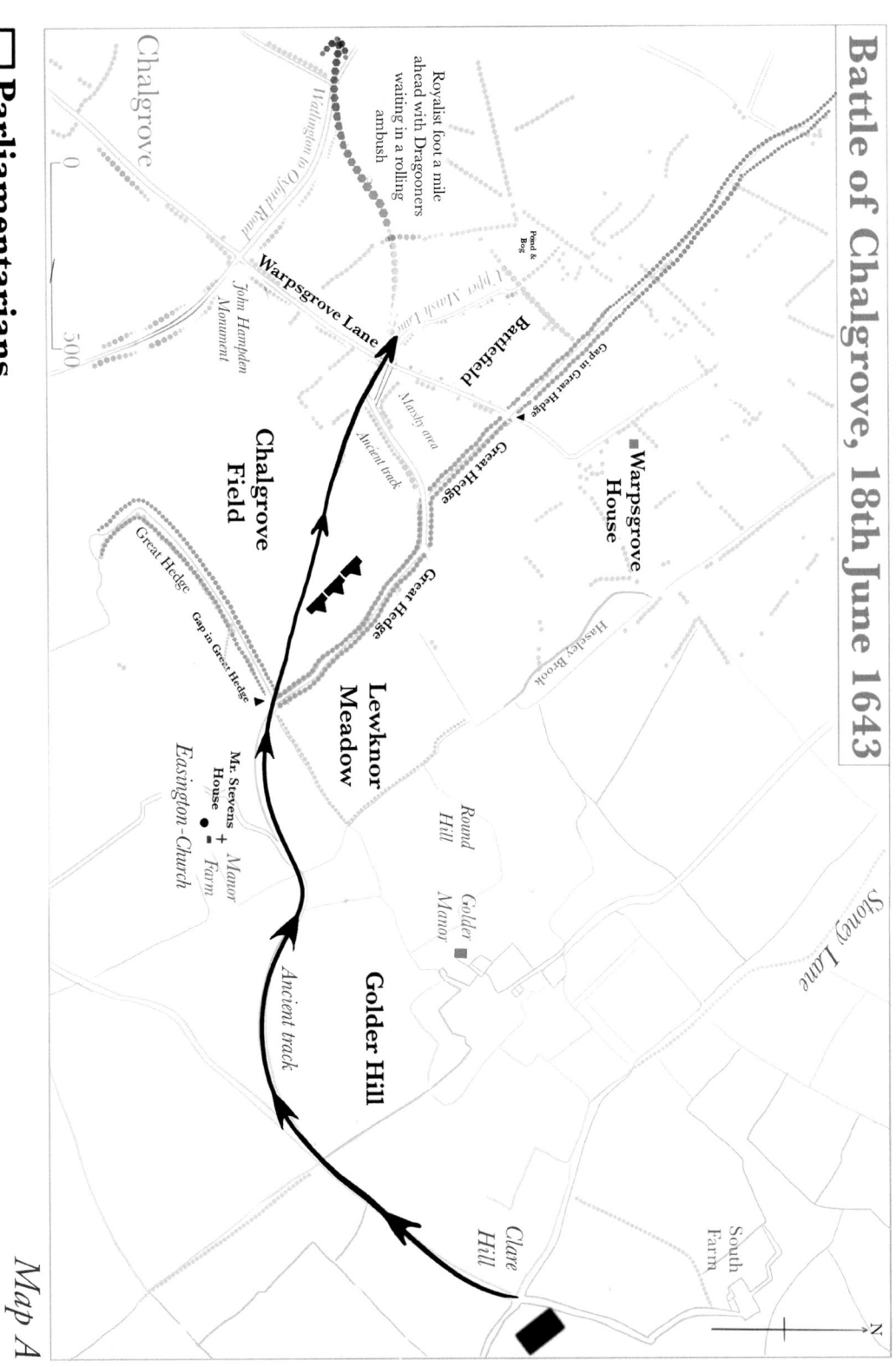

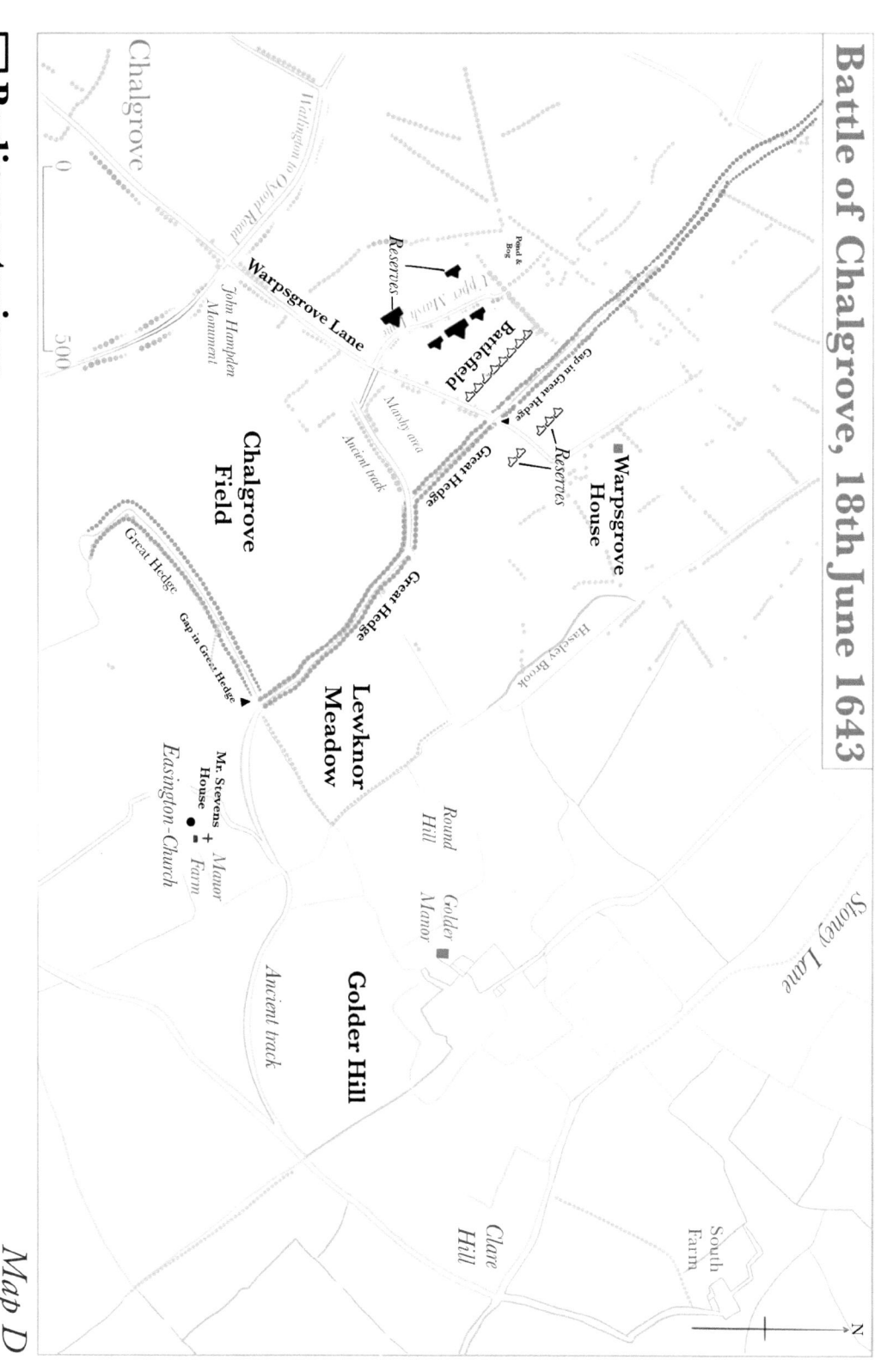

THE BATTLE OF CHALGROVE

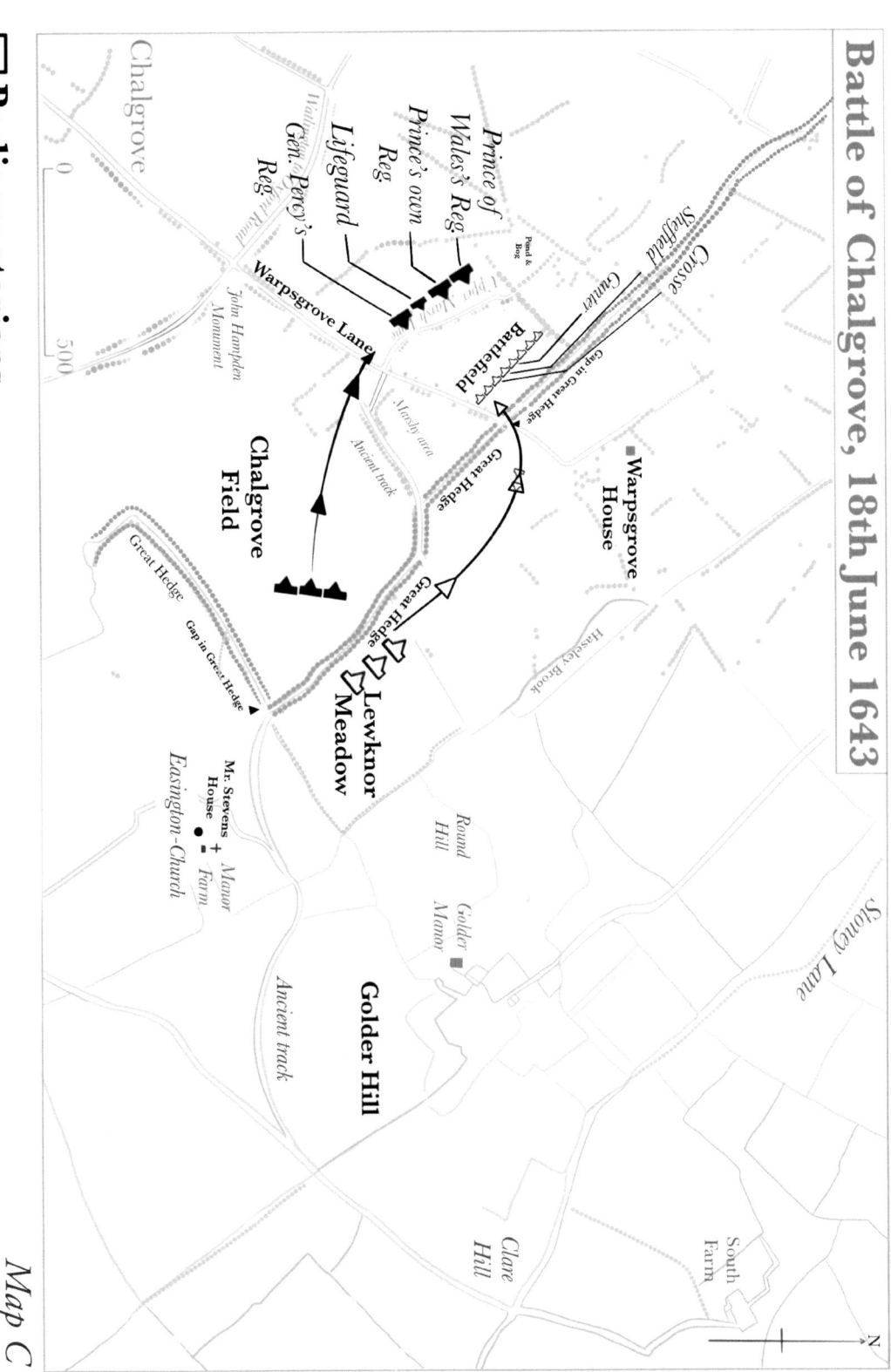

Map C

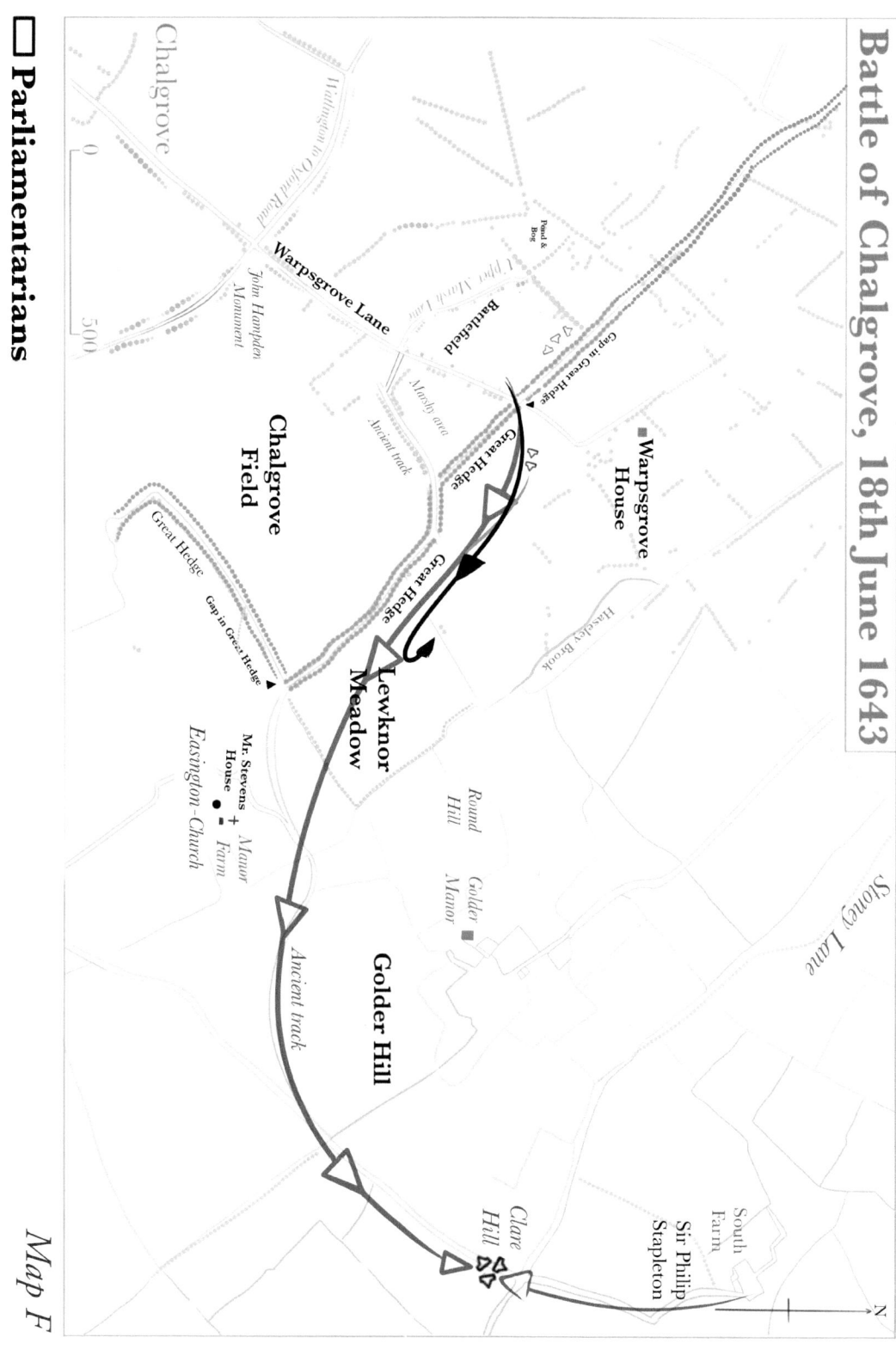

THE BATTLE OF CHALGROVE

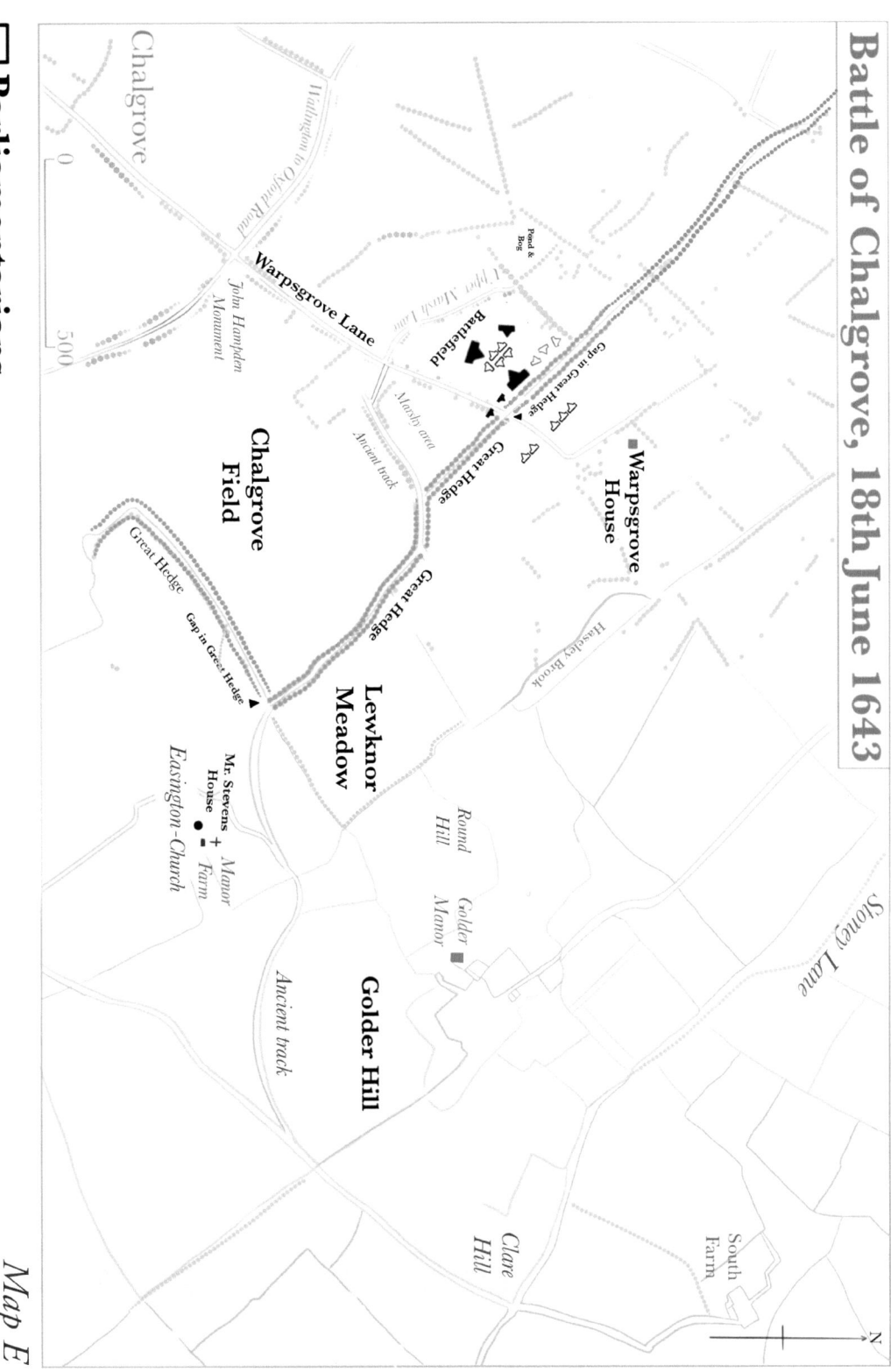

6

Aftermath

The guards who had been left to defend Chiselhampton Bridge the previous night when Prince Rupert had led 2,000 troops out into no man's land to raid Chinnor were called to attention. Horses were seen coming up from Stadhampton towards Chiselhampton. The guards raised the defences on the bridge, and musketeers lined the banks of the Thame in readiness to fight off those that might try to come across the river. The River Thame flows lethargically under Chiselhampton Bridge, and the fields all around are marshy: it would be a foolhardy rider that made an attack across the river against these defences. Sergeant Major Legge, who led the vanguard, approached and with due ceremony, asked the guards' permission to cross the bridge. A guard of honour may have welcomed the vanguard across the bridge to cheers all around. Behind the vanguard came the foot, leading 120 prisoners and hundreds of horses laden with booty. The dragoons brought up the rear. The cavalry were still fighting at Chalgrove – their fate as yet unknown. Sir Samuel Luke's dragoons lost three of their colours during the raid on Chinnor. Colonel Morley of Sussex's troops had a cornet taken at Postcombe as the Royalists made their way to Chinnor. The seniority of companies within a regiment was denoted by 'devices'. These took the form of crescents, stars or bibles (as on the colours of Sir Samuel Luke's dragoons) emblazoned across them: 'Their *Field* or Ground was *black*, with 1, 2, 3, 4, or 5 *Bibles* bost and bufft, depainted in them.'[1] One such device on a standard denotes the first captain's colour, and two the second captain's and so on. The colour was the embodiment of the regiment and held the memory of battle honours won. It was a Sunday ritual for the padre to deliver a hellfire sermon that put the fear of God into the troops, with slogans such as 'fear none but the Lord'. Alongside the padre during the hellfire sermon was the regiment's ensign proudly flying the colour. On command, the ensign trooped the colour between the ranks of soldiers, and the standard was held forward at head height so that the soldiers could see the colour at close quarters. The ensign had the message of Trooping the Colour 'drummed' into the soldiers' heads: 'Know your colour, BOOM, know your colour well, BOOM'. The

---

1   BoL Wood 376 (14): *Late Beating Up*, p.4.

drummer underlined each phrase as the ensign marched between the ranks. By the time the ensign had called out the phrases below several times, the message would be drummed into the soldiers:

> Know your Colour, know your Colour well for in times of battle when all seems lost reform on the Colour. Defend the Colour with your life if they should fall it is a dishonour to have the name of the regiment dragged through the mud. Keep up your Standard. Fall upon the enemy in multitude should they take the Colour. Keep up your Standard. When the Ensign is weary or injured in battle 'Raise your Standard' flagging to the enemy that the Regiment is beaten will bring the wrath of God. Keep up your Standard.[2]

The padre closed the Trooping of the Colour with the Lord's Prayer.

On the battlefield, as the troops closed upon the enemy across an open field, staring down the barrels of the enemy's guns, the words of the ensign to 'know their colour' rang in their ears. As shot from field pieces and muskets ripped through the ranks, they prayed silently that they would 'fear none but the Lord'. Should a musketeer's morale falter and he in terror throw down his gun, the lieutenant would scream at him to stand his ground. The lieutenant carried a halberd that had a long spike and below a curved-axe-style blade, ideal for hooking an ankle and severing a foot. If the musketeer broke rank, the lieutenant would spear the 'coward' through the thigh or hook the offender with the blade. Above the noise, the sergeant would scream, 'March on, fear none but the Lord, follow the Colour'.

The scene at Chiselhampton Bridge was one of jubilation, the soldiers jeering at their prisoners and toasting their good health with ale taken from the alehouse in Chinnor. The prisoners had been roused from their beds before they were able to 'break fast' on being woken so rudely. The hungry prisoners, who had been made to walk from Chinnor carrying a heavy load of spoil, had not eaten since the previous evening. The smell of food cooking and watching with envy as their tormentors scoffed with great exhibition in front of them could cause uproar among the ravenous prisoners. Those who became too loud or insulting to their captors could be forced to chew on a large chunk of gristle and then have it forced down their throat until they choked.

At Mr Steven's house in Easington, after the battle, 10 sorely wounded men were found having their wounds dressed.[3] The steward of Captain Henry Stevens, who was the Royalists' waggon master general, was allowed to charge the rebels for the use of a cart to carry the injured back to their quarters in Thame.[4] Close by, lying amongst the corn seriously injured and at first left for dead, was Captain James Sheffield, the son of the Earl of Mulgrave.

---

2   Trooping the Colour in the seventeenth century was an ad hoc affair, but these words have been gleaned from various contemporary sources by English Civil War Society members and have been used in re-enactments.
3   BoL Wood 376 (14): *Late Beating Up*, p.12.
4   Margaret Toynbee (ed.), *The Papers of Captain Henry Stevens, Waggon-Master-General to King Charles I* (Oxford: Oxfordshire Record Society, 1961).

As cornet, he had led his troop into battle, but now all was lost. The cornet he had been flourishing was taken by Sergeant Major Thomas Daniel as a trophy to restore honour to his regiment. Captain Berkeley, a Scotsman, (or possibly Captain James Barclay) was lying alongside him also wounded. The pair are said to have promised 'upon the word and *Parole* of a Soldier, to become true Prisoners' – that is, to take themselves to Oxford when they were able and become prisoners.[5] Sheffield and Barclay were accused of breaking their parole, for as recorded by Gomme:

> … both these [Sheffield and Barclay] by the *Princes* courtesy, were left near the place to be dressed; each promising upon the word and *Parole* of a Soldier, to become true Prisoners, which whether they forgot or no, I know not. Sure it is, that on *Monday* night, they excused themselves by their soreness and disability, to come away hither in Sir *Lewis Dives* [a Royalist officer] his Coach, on purpose sent for them which notwithstanding they were next morning fetched away by their own party.[6]

The Royalists had pursued the rebels over Golder Hill after the battle – which in the confusion of the chase caused Mr Henry Howard, son of the Earl of Berkshire, and Captain Thomas Gardiner of Prince Rupert's regiment, who spearheaded the first charge, to become prisoners. The Earl of Berkshire, upon learning of his son's capture, wrote to Prince Rupert on 21 June 1643 suggesting, 'Captain James Sheffield and the Scotchman Berkeley who abused your favour contrary to their word be exchanged for my son'.[7] The Earl of Essex replied to Prince Rupert's letter on 22 June 1643 in denial that Mr Sheffield agreed to be 'a true prisoner', but, on the proviso that he release Sergeant Major Thomas (captured at Chinnor), he would send Captain Gardiner and Mr Howard to him.[8]

The guard on Chiselhampton Bridge, upon seeing hundreds of horse coming towards them again, raised the defences. It was probably Sergeant Major Thomas Daniel of the Prince of Wales' regiment who led this great party of men over the bridge. Daniel's troop had lost a colour at Hopton Heath, but, by capturing Sheffield's cornet, he had restored his troop's right to fly a standard. Gomme stated, 'His troop, henceforth again to bear a Cornet which (having heretofore in fight at *Hopton* Heath lost their own) it seems by Law of Arms they might not bear, till some of theirs again in fight had won a Colour from the Rebels.'[9] A commanding officer's battle standard bore the family's coat of arms or a motto and, when flourished on the battlefield, stated (in the case of Earl of Essex) that he personally was on

---

5   BoL Wood 376 (14): *Late Beating Up*, p.12.
6   BoL Wood 376 (14): *Late Beating Up*, p.12.
7   Warburton, *Memoirs of Prince Rupert*, vol. II, p.211, Letter dated 21 June 1643 from the Earl of Berkshire, Ewelme Lodge, Ewelme, Oxon., to Prince Rupert.
8   Warburton, *Memoirs of Prince Rupert*, vol. II, p.212, Letter dated 22 June1643 from the Earl of Essex to Prince Rupert.
9   BoL Wood 376 (14): *Late Beating Up*, p.10.

the battlefield. His motto, '*Cave Adsum*', roughly translated means, 'beware, I am here'. Mercurius Aulicus of 'The five and twentieth Weeke' advertised Essex's humiliation with 'Colours taken in the fight, some were of the Earle of Essex his own Colours, and had painted in great Capital letters, CAVE ADSUM, to let us see with what a fury his Excellency intended to have fallen upon us; yet Cave Adsum was an admirable Motto for one who never shewed his face in the battaile.'[10] Behind Daniel came two more of Essex's standards, possibly flown upside down or dragged through the dust and dirt as a contemptuous statement to the wild cheers of the soldiers. A standard is only allowed to touch the ground to honour the King or as mark of respect at a special burial. Verbal abuse against the Earl of Essex would have filled the air, with taunts of his lack of prowess on the battlefield and elsewhere jeered through the crowd. The insinuation was that the Earl of Essex was a coward who never led his troops into battle. The tale of the defeat of Essex's regiment would grow upon every telling among the soldiers around the campfire. The Earl of Essex's reputation among his fellow officers was so severely tarnished that, four weeks after the humiliation of Chalgrove, he offered to resign his commission, but the offer was refused.

Among the troops crossing the bridge were a number of Parliamentarian officers who had been taken prisoner. They were to quote Hyde's private journal, 'the new prisoners he [Prince Rupert] had taken, retired orderly to the pass where his foot and former purchase expected him'.[11] The Royalist soldiers stood in wonder as 80 senior officers from Essex's army and who had fought at Chalgrove rode across Chiselhampton Bridge on their fine steeds. Prince Rupert ordered that Colonel Urry lead the foot and dragoons with the prisoners and booty back to Oxford for a triumphal parade: 'He [Rupert] had sent the news of all before by Colonel Urrey whom the King presently Knighted.'[12] '… the messenger for his good service, returned, with near 200 prisoners, seven cornets of horse and four ensigns of foot, to Oxford'.[13] Each of the 500 musketeers, barring those who had other duties, had to attend to a horse, one of the many taken from Chinnor. Hyde wrote, 'his own [Rupert's troops] being harassed and tired with near twenty miles' march and laden with spoil and prisoners, scarce a soldier without a led horse'.[14] The musketeers, many of whom were farm labourers, were well acquainted on how to handle horses. The horses, again laden with spoil, were soon made ready for the seven-mile march from Chiselhampton back into Oxford: 'His Highness by two a clock came safely back into *Oxford*'.[15] An 'express' was sent that afternoon by the King to his Queen at Newark Castle with the message that Essex's army was no longer a threat. Upon receiving the message, the

---

10 British Library (BrL) Thomason Tracts (TT), E 245 (36): *Mercurius Aulicus Communicating the Intelligence and affaires of the Court, to the rest of the Kingdom*, The five and twentieth week.
11 BoL: MS. Clar. 112, f. 366: Sir Edward Hyde's Private Journal, 1641–1646.
12 BoL Wood 376 (14): *Late Beating Up*, pp.13–14.
13 BoL: MS. Clar. 112, f. 366: Sir Edward Hyde's Private Journal, 1641–1646.
14 BoL: MS. Clar. 112, f. 366: Sir Edward Hyde's Private Journal, 1641–1646.
15 BoL Wood 376 (14): *Late Beating Up*, p.13.

Queen began making ready for the arms convoy to leave Newark, which set out for Oxford on 27 June 1643. Essex's defeat at Chalgrove quelled the Queen's fear that Essex would steal the convoy before it reached the King.

Colonel John Hampden had been shot in the shoulder with a brace of pistol bullets early in the battle and managed to get through the gap in the great hedge before it was closed. From leaving the battlefield to John Hampden's death in the early evening of Saturday, 24 June 1643, little is known. A 'Will Hales', in a letter dated 22 June 1643, related, '… the worst news. I know is that Colonel Hampden is in great danger'.[16] He wrote to Colonel Sir Thomas Barrington that 'The Lord General I hear intends to march today from Thame'.[17] Essex wrote addressing his letter, 'To my honourable brother Sir Thomas Barrington Knight. I desire you to raise sixty horses … and send them unto me for the mounting of my own Regiment'.[18] The letter was received on 28 June 1643 by Barrington and underlines Essex's desperation for horses. Essex was desperate for horses, it seems, for he was unable to retreat because of the lack of means to transport equipment. Essex's regiment's loss of horse and the officers taken with them at the Battle of Chalgrove was a principal cause of his inability to command the army.

Sir Philip Stapleton, who had drawn the men into a body after they fled from the Chalgrove battlefield, sent a runner to Essex to prepare him for the worst. Whether Hampden's fate was known by those who had been fighting with him on the battlefield is unclear. It is possible that two of the five troops that had been held in reserve by Warpsgrove House escorted the wounded John Hampden back to Thame Park, Essex's headquarters, which is located in an isolated position out of town. Circumstantial evidence shows that a trooper from the Chalgrove battle found his way to Watlington, Colonel John Hampden's field headquarters. The trooper, it is speculated, told the officers of Hampden's regiment that their colonel was wounded. On this news, the regiment decamped from Watlington and headed for Thame. These points will be expanded upon in a later chapter. It was reported that 'an angry mob of Green-coats broke down the organ, defaced Popish images in St Mary's church, Thame and pulled the cross down to the ground'.[19] It was soon common knowledge that Hampden had been wounded, but his whereabouts were unknown to the general populace. Great Hampden, John Hampden's estate, was 10 miles away from Thame, and he could easily have been taken there. The popular notion that John Hampden was taken to Ezekiel Browne's house, reportedly above Greyhound Walk in Thame High Street, where he died after suffering six days of agony, is a fallacy. The story of John Hampden's last days was published in *The Gentleman's Magazine*, the full transcript of

---

16   British Library (BrL) MS Egerton 2646, f. 285: Letter by Will Hales to Sir Thomas Barrington, 22 June 1643, sent from Thame. See Appendix IX, Item 12, for text.
17   BrL: MS Egerton 2646, f. 285: Letter by Will Hales to Sir Thomas Barrington, 22 June 1643, sent from Thame.
18   British Library (BrL) MS Egerton 2646, f. 289: Letter from the Earl of Essex to Sir Thomas Barrington, 24 June 1643.
19   Barrès-Baker, *Siege of Reading, April 1643*, p.184.

which is found in Appendix II. John Hampden's grand funeral, supposedly at Great Hampden, was a figment of Lord Nugent's imagination. In 1847, Nugent published a booklet commonly referred to as '*A Worthy Discourse*', which told of a funeral that Lord Nugent believed John Hampden deserved.[20] Rob Goodwin, Arthur Goodwin's brother and close friend of Hampden, in a letter wrote, 'my Lord General is yet at Tame; but we had this day an intimation given us by Mr Pym that he would goe [sic] forward upon some designe [sic] tomorrow [Sunday, 25 June 1643]'.[21] Rob Goodwin would have been close enough to the headquarters to receive this type of news, and this indicates that Hampden was at Thame Park. Rob Goodwin continued, 'You shall understand that this present Monday morning, being the 26 of June, we received the sad tidings of Colonel Hamdens [sic] death; he died on Saturday night last'.[22] Rob Goodwin reported that John Hampden died on Saturday, 24 June 1643, but he received the sad tidings on Monday, 26 June 1643. The parish register states that John Hampden was buried on 25 June 1643 in St Mary Magdalene Church, yet Rob Goodwin failed to mention this monumental event. This failure to mention a funeral or burial of John Hampden and that no tombstone marks his grave add to the certainty that he was spirited away from Thame Park and buried in secret. Essex's diseased, ragged army was starving and unable to defend itself. Essex, with his last hope gone, prepared his army for retreat to London. John Hampden was not expected to live, but, even in death and after burial, his body had to be protected.

Following John Hampden's death, it is speculated that his son Richard Hampden, with others, collected the body from Thame Park and took it to Great Hampden. In the early hours of the 25 June 1643, Colonel John Hampden was lowered into a pre-dug grave. Upon covering the coffin with earth and replacing the tiles, Richard Hampden closed and locked the door to 'his' church. West Wickham is three miles from Great Hampden, and, while Hampden was being buried, Colonel Sir John Urry beat up West Wickham: 'His Majesty … was pleased to command him [Urry] out upon a new partee the Sunday after, for the beating up the Quarters of some new-levyed Kentish and Sussex men, then lodged at West-Wickham. Intelligence was given in, that enemies were some 500 foot, & one Troop of horse: a considerable number, indeed , and well worth the beating'.[23] As with the Sunday before at Chinnor, the Royalists took all the horses and everything they could carry. Rob Goodwin wrote, 'the last night the Cavaliers plundered Wickham and tooke a troope of my Lo: Generals horse; and this City [Thame] tooke an

---

20 Lord George Nugent, *Tract Entitled True and Faithful Relation of a Worthy Discourse, Between ye late Colonel Hampden and Colonel Oliver Cromwell held June ye Eleventh, in ye Yeare of Grace 1643* (London: Chapman and Hall, 1847).

21 BrL: MS Egerton 2646, f. 293: Rob. Goodwin's letter to Sir Thomas Barrington sent from Thame, 26 June 1643.

22 BrL: MS Egerton 2646, f. 293: Rob. Goodwin's letter to Sir Thomas Barrington sent from Thame, 26 June 1643.

23 BoL Wood 376 (14): *Late Beating Up*, p.15.

alarum upon it and were up in armes all night'.[24] After 24 June 1643, John Hampden was never seen or heard of again. There was no memorial stone raised to mark his grave, and his place in the church remained unknown. The secret of Hampden's death and burial site was well guarded, for Sir Edward Hyde recorded in his private journal, 'Mr Hambden [sic]; Who, being shot into the Shoulder with a brace of Bullets, which brake the Bone, within three Weeks after died with extraordinary pain; to as great a consternation of all that Party, as if their whole Army had been defeated; or cut off.'[25]

Parliament strengthened its defences in the expectation that the Royalists would attack London, which was saved, as was Essex's army, because the King had concentrated his forces to bring his Queen and the arms convoy from Newark to Oxford. On 27 June 1643, the Earl of Newcastle – along with reportedly 10,000 men – left Newark and headed north. Newcastle's opponents in the north were Parliamentarian Commander Ferdinando (Lord Fairfax) and his son Sir Thomas Fairfax. The Fairfax duo had raised an army from Parliament's supporters in the cloth-manufacturing towns of the West Riding of Yorkshire, and Sir Thomas soon gained a reputation as a determined officer in a series of small actions in defence of barricaded towns and for attacks on Royalist quarters. Newcastle marched and crushed their army at Adwalton Moor on 30 June 1643. Fairfax retreated to Bradford and on to Halifax before being chased into Leeds. He briefly defended Leeds, probably as a rearguard action to cover his father's retreat, but the town was untenable, and he broke out with his cavalry. Caught up in a running fight, Sir Thomas only had two officers and three troopers left with him when he finally rejoined with his father. Sir Thomas' wife, Anne, who had left Leeds with him, riding behind one of his officers, was captured in the pursuit. The Fairfax duo abandoned Leeds and retreated to Hull. Ever the gentleman, Newcastle treated Lady Anne Fairfax with all civility and respect and provided a cavalry escort and his own coach to return her to her husband in Hull. On 27 June 1643, the convoy of arms left Newark bound for Oxford. News of Essex's defeat and retreat out of Oxfordshire was sent into the West Country. Thousands of Cornish men took up arms and marched north. On 30 June 1643, at Adwalton Moor, Parliament's Army of the North was destroyed. On or around 2 July 1643, Queen Henrietta left Newark with her Lifeguard to follow in the convoy's tracks. Colonel Sir Phillip Stapleton's and Colonel Arthur Goodwin's horse were involved in a heavy skirmish on 2 July 1643 as Essex's troops were retreating towards Bierton, Buckinghamshire.[26] Essex reported the event as 'the King had sent more Forces to Buckingham …' and, in a deluded account, wrote that the Royalists retreated when he had sent his foot towards the town.[27] On 4 July 1643, having left Thame a couple of days earlier, Essex's beleaguered army made camp at Bierton. On the same

---

24 BrL: MS Egerton 2646, f. 293: Rob. Goodwin's letter to Sir Thomas Barrington sent from Thame, 26 June 1643.
25 BoL: MS. Clar. 112, f. 366: Sir Edward Hyde's Private Journal, 1641–1646.
26 Warburton, *Memoirs of Prince Rupert*, vol. II, p.223.
27 BrL: TT, E 64 (3): The Earle of Essex His Letter to Master Speaker, 9 July 1643.

day, the Royalists' vanguard took Burton-on-Trent, allowing the convoy to proceed unhindered on its way to Oxford. On 6 July 1643, Queen Henrietta was at Ashby-de-la-Zouch, seven miles before Burton-on-Trent. Edward Nicholas, the King's secretary, relayed the Queen's message that had been sent from Ashby to Prince Rupert. The letter recounted that Fairfax's Army of the North was utterly broken and that the Parliamentarian strongholds of Leeds, Halifax and Bradford had been taken for the King.[28]

On 7 July 1643, the King ordered that Prince Rupert head north for the 'secure conveying of the Queen'.[29] Despite heavy losses on 5 July 1643, Launceston was taken by the Cornish men, and they continued their march north. Sir William Waller tactically retreated to Devizes after Launceston but was followed by Sir Ralph Hopton's troops and Royalist reinforcements released from protecting Oxford as Essex was no longer a threat. By 9 July 1643, Essex's army had retreated to Great Brickhill. In a letter to the Speaker dated 9 July 1643, Essex wrote, 'The enemie being so strong in Horse, and this Armie being neither recrewted with Horses, Armes, nor Saddles, it is impossible to keep the Countries from being plundered, nor to fight with them … If it were thought fit to send his Majestie to have Peace'.[30] On 12 July 1643, Essex resigned his commission, but this was refused by the Committee of Safety. On 13 July 1643, the Royalists took Devizes at the Battle of Roundway Down. Sir William Waller's army was all but destroyed, with a great loss of horse, and he blamed Essex for his defeat for 'reposing complacently' at Thame. Another consequence of the Battle of Chalgrove was the irreparable dissension between those who supported Waller's camp and those in the Committee of Safety who backed Essex. On 15 July 1643, the Queen arrived in Oxford with the convoy of arms to a jubilant welcome. On Tuesday, 18 July 1643, Prince Rupert led an army towards Bristol, and, on 26 July 1643, after a hard-fought battle, Nathaniel Fiennes surrendered the town and port of Bristol. On 20 July 1643, having made Colonel Thomas Tyrill commanding officer of Colonel John Hampden's Regiment of Foot, Essex abandoned Oxfordshire and Buckinghamshire to the mercy of the Royalists. Thanks to the Battle of Chalgrove, the King had control of the north, west and south of England – only Cromwell's army in East Anglia remained that could come to London's aid if threatened by the Royalists. Essex departed Great Brickhill the last week of July and made camp at St Albans. Essex's letter, 'To the Speaker', from Uxbridge on 6 August 1643 states:

> Sir, – I should not so often trouble you in your great affairs, but that I could not discharge the duty I owe, holding so great a charge as I do, but to acquaint you, that unless present order be taken for the supplying the army with money, their necessities are so great, it will be impossible for me to keep them together. For

---

28 Warburton, *Memoirs of Prince Rupert*, vol. II, p.225, Letter dated 8 July 1643 from Edward Nicholas, the King's Secretary to Prince Rupert.

29 Warburton, *Memoirs of Prince Rupert*, vol. II, p.223, Letter dated 7 July 1643 from the King to Prince Rupert.

30 BrL: TT, E 64 (3): The Earle of Essex His Letter to Master Speaker, 9 July 1643.

besides their former arrears, they are now three weeks without pay; many sick men recover, but finding no money they have small comfort. I am now marching to a fresh quarter, where, if they may have pay, recruits and clothing, most of them being almost naked, and our soldiers not drawn away with new levies, I doubt not but in a short time to have a considerable army.

Sir, I am your assured friend, ESSEX.[31]

The King decided to try and take Gloucester, but the time expended allowed the Earl of Essex to refresh his army and take the fight to the King. From Gloucester to the Second Battle of Newbury, the revitalised Parliamentarians found new courage. Did the King make a tactical error by not marching on London? Would it have been a different story had the King consolidated his forces and marched on London? Cromwell's Eastern Association had remained strong all through 1643. Essex's and the Committee of Safety's incompetency at prosecuting the war, along with John Hampden's demise, handed Oliver Cromwell the power to speak for the army in Parliament. The ignominy that Essex had to bear, much through his own incompetency but aided by the Committee of Safety and particularly by John Pym, left his position as captain general vulnerable. John Hampden, a loyal supporter of the Earl of Essex, was dead and gone. This was shortly followed by the demise of Arthur Goodwin in August 1643. Sir William Waller in the west was pressing to take over Essex's position, emphasising his and the Committee of Safety's ineptitude. John Pym, Essex's closet ally in Parliament, died in December 1643, which led to the Committee of Safety's inability to prosecute the war. Cromwell's persuasive argument and unassailable position led to the Committee of Safety's disbandment in February 1644 in favour of the Committee of Both Kingdoms. Colonel Oliver Cromwell was able to argue his case in Parliament from a position strength to remodel the army. The rest of Cromwell's Civil War exploits are history – perhaps another indication of the importance of the Battle of Chalgrove.

---

31 Bodleian Library (BoL) MS. Tanner 62/1B, fols. 233, 240.

7

Political Aftermath

Hampden's death in the cause for which he fought was to have a significant influence on political and ideological debates in succeeding centuries, not only in Britain but also in the North American colonies. It is evident in the political struggle between Crown and colonies in the seventeenth and eighteenth centuries, and likewise in the historical interpretation of the Civil War and Commonwealth that emerged in the early eighteenth century, that Hampden's name and reputation became an exemplar. In the process, Hampden's memory not only served different purposes but also promoted distortion of the reality of his life and death. Before the English Civil War, English pounds had been the dominant currency in the colonies, with pieces of eight finding favour. Funding the Civil War restricted the supply of British currency to the colonies. Oliver Cromwell's overthrow of the monarchy rendered the colonies' Royal Charter null and void, which constrained the means of trading. John Hull, the treasurer for the Massachusetts Bay Colony, became the mint master and, in 1652, produced cash for the colonies. After the Restoration of the Monarchy in 1660, King Charles II endeavoured to reassert Royal authority and stop the colonists from minting coinage. The Royal Navy was a formidable force that Charles used to his advantage. The Royal Charter was reinstated, and trading relations – which had always been difficult – resumed. In 1684, the Royal Charter was revoked, which was followed in 1685 with the death of Charles II. James II was crowned King of England, and, early in his reign, he instilled the Dominion of New England, an administrative union, over the colonies. James II was deposed in 1688 mainly because of his religious intolerance – an issue that clashed with the puritanical colonists. When news of the 'Glorious Revolution' under William and Mary reached Boston, it sparked what became known as the 'Boston Revolt'. The Massachusetts Bay Colony revoked the Dominion of New England and reverted to its rule under the Royal Charter until 1691, when a new charter was issued for the Province of Massachusetts Bay.

John Hampden (1653–1696), grandson of John Hampden (1595–1643) of Ship Money fame, is said to have coined the phrase 'Glorious Revolution' – an event that brought in the reign of King William III and Queen Mary II (1689–1702). Hampden was imprisoned for his alleged involvement in the Rye House Plot of 1683 but was spared of the death sentence. In 1685, after the failure of the Monmouth Rebellion, John Hampden was again brought to trial and condemned to death, but the sentence was not carried out. John was elected MP for Wendover in the Convention Parliament of 1689 – an action that may have caused him to exclaim, 'Glorious Revolution', for the threat of imprisonment had been lifted and he was accepted into Court.

The War of Grand Alliance ran concurrent with King William's War (1689–1697). The War of the Spanish Succession (1702–1714) overlapped with what was called 'Queen Anne's War' in the Americas. The European Wars tangled with the North American Wars, which ran into the War of the Austrian Succession (1742–1748). The latter (known as 'King George's War' in North America) followed, and, after four years, the French and Indian War, which had never really ended, developed into the Seven Years' War, which began in 1756. By 1763, Britain was in control of what is now Canada and most of North America. Details of the above wars are the subject of many publications that can be consulted for a better understanding of these events. The battles over land and sea projected the politics of the warring factions, with alliances being made and broken. The Court was an arena in which powerful Whigs and Tories could assert opinion. Reputations, the loss of liberty, personal fortunes and even one's head were won and lost in eighteenth-century feudal politics.

Reverend James Blair obtained a Royal Charter to commission the College of William and Mary in Williamsburg, Virginia, in 1693. To honour King William and Queen Mary, Williamsburg became the colonial capital of Virginia in 1699. Throughout the 1680s, Princess Anne came under intense political pressure, for she was heir to the English throne. In 1694, the third royal governor of the Province of Maryland, Francis Nicholson (1655–1728), overthrew the Catholic second governor, Thomas Lawrence (1645–1714). He re-sited the royal colony's capital from St Mary's City to Anne Arundel's Town, which Nicholson later renamed 'Annapolis' after Princess Anne of Denmark and Norway, sister of Queen Mary. In 1694, upon the death of her sister Mary, Anne became heir apparent and succeeded to the English throne in 1702.

Edmund Ludlow (1617–1692) was a regicide and judge at Charles I's trial. After the Restoration, and with his life in jeopardy, he escaped England to Vervey, Switzerland. While in exile, Ludlow wrote *A Voice from the Watch Tower*, which was heavily rewritten after his death to produce the *Memoirs of Edmund Ludlow*, 1698–1699. This publication and many others written in a similar vein were viewed as a threat to the monarchy, whose succession was becoming less certain. Lawrence Hyde (1642–1711), 1st Earl of Rochester and the second son of Edward, Earl of Clarendon, was a minister in Queen Anne's Court along with Robert Harley (1661–1724), 1st Earl of Oxford, and Robert Walpole (1676–1745). Lawrence Hyde was close to Queen Anne, as she was his niece. Lawrence Hyde's father was known to have written about the English Civil War. It is remarkable to state that Edward Hyde's handwritten documents were not published in his lifetime. *The History of the Rebellion and Civil Wars in England* was compiled by Lawrence Hyde, and the first edition was published in 1702 – 28 years after the Earl of Clarendon's death on 9 December 1674. Lawrence's *The History of the Rebellion* has on the title page, 'Written by the Right Honourable Edward Earl of Clarendon'.[1] The 1702–1704 *The History of the Rebellion and Civil Wars in England* is an adaption of his father's work that was published to counter the like of Ludlow and to favour the Tory's interpretation of events. Lawrence's *The History of the Rebellion* abounds with poetic licence and gross inaccuracies of fact. One particular sentence has resonated throughout the pages of biographers:

> … that he was confident Mr Hambden was hurt, for he saw him ride off the Field before the Action was done, which he never used to do, with his head hanging down, and resting his hands upon the neck of his Horse; by which he concluded he was hurt.[2]

The absurdity of this passage reads as if John Hampden was a veteran commander with a great military reputation, whereas, in reality, he had only been involved in a handful of skirmishes by the time of the Battle of Chalgrove. Had Colonel John Hampden, or any officer, deserted a battlefield 'before the Action was done', he would have been branded a coward and stripped of rank and reputation. John Hampden's stand against King Charles over Ship Money and subsequent debates in the Short and Long Parliaments had to be accurately recounted, as the facts were in the official record. Lawrence Hyde's description of the Battle of Chalgrove is sparse and has gross errors of misinterpretation. Robert Walpole, Robert Harley and Lawrence Hyde were all involved with the publication of the 1702–1704 edition of *The History of the Rebellion*. In 1711, Robert Harley (1661–1724) became Queen Anne's chief minister or first prime minister – a claim given to Robert Walpole. Robert Harley had Robert Walpole removed from office as secretary of war, provoking bitter exchanges between them. In 1712, Walpole was impeached, most probably on the orders of Harley, was expelled from Parliament and spent six months in the Tower of London. After his release, Walpole published anonymous pamphlets attacking the Harley ministry. Harley created the South Sea Company in 1711 – which, until 1720, was a very successful enterprise.[3] Harley retired to his country estate upon the accession of George I and, a few months later, was impeached and accused of high treason, high crimes and other misdemeanours. These alleged crimes could carry the death penalty, but he was incarcerated in the Tower of London for two years.[4] Upon his release from the Tower, he was informed by George I that he was no longer welcome at Court.

Richard Hampden (1674–1728), the great-grandson of John Hampden, married Sarah Foley (1661–1724). While Treasurer of the Navy, Richard used naval funds to make a personal profit. It is possible that Richard was

---

1   Hyde, *The History of the Rebellion* (1702–1704), vols I–III.
2   Hyde, *The History of the Rebellion* (1702–1704), vol. II, book VII, p.204.
3   Brian W. Hill, *Robert Harley: Speaker, Secretary of State and Premier Minister* (New Haven, CT: Yale University Press, 1988).
4   British History Online (BHO) *Journal of the House of Lords*, vol. 20, 25 May 1717, 'Earl of Oxford and E. Mortimer impeached'.

dealing in slaves and sending them to Jamaica, where Hampden may have had plantations. Robert Walpole, who was close to the South Sea Company directorship, knew of its impending collapse, sold his holding and made a 1,000 percent profit. Paul Foley (1645–1699) campaigned with his nephew Robert Harley and was elected to be Speaker of the House of Commons in Queen Anne's first Parliament. Thomas Foley (1670–1737), Paul's eldest son, held office in Parliament almost continuously from 1691 to his death in 1737. Seventy-eight years after Hampden's death, the de facto first Prime Minister Sir Robert Walpole tried to slur the reputation of the Hampdens, Pyes, Harleys and Foleys, who were interrelated families, for his own political purposes. Laurence Echard (1670–1730) wrote *The History of England* in three volumes.[5] The work was presented to King George I by Sir Robert Walpole in 1719. An Appendix of Errata was published in 1720, in which is found:

> Volume II Page 415, dele the last Period of the Paragraph, and add these Words.] As his Death was a great surprise, so the manner of it was very uncommon, and generally unknown, as I am assur'd by a great man, who says his death's Wound proceeded from the Breaking of one of his Pistols, which happened to be more than doubly charg'd. This was one of a choice Case presented to him by his Son-in-law Sir Robert Pye, to carry on the War and at the first sight of him in his illness he cry'd out to him 'Ah Robin, your unhappy Present has been my ruin!'[6]

Echard wrote 'as I am assur'd by a great man' to add veracity to the story.[7] The only person who could have given that assurance was Robert Walpole. The Civil War was a memory, which begs the question: why did Walpole invent the story of Hampden's pistol exploding at Chalgrove? The answer may be for political and personal revenge for being incarcerated in the Tower of London by Robert Harley.

During the political turmoil of William and Mary's reign and Queen Anne's succession, Robert Harley, Paul Foley, Richard Hampden and Richard Pye were at various times political allies with Robert Walpole, but each had fallen out with him over political infighting. Sir Robert Walpole's intention of tarring his political enemies with the same brush is brought into sharp focus by Echard being assured by a great man the veracity of Hampden's pistol exploding at the Battle of Chalgrove. Norman Lawrence, Pink Floyd's road manager and direct descendant of Sir Robert Pye, overheard the writer's comment that a paper the equivalent to an autopsy of the exhumation that had taken place on 21 July 1828 at St Mary Magdalene Church, Great

---

5   Laurence Echard, *The History of England. From the First Entrance of Julius Cæsar and the Romans, To the Conclusion of the Reign of King James the Second, and the Establishment of King William and Queen Mary upon the Throne, in the Year 1688* (London: Jacob Tonson, 1707–1720), vols I–III and an Appendix of Errata.
6   Echard, *The History of England*, Appendix of Errata, p.572.
7   Echard, *The History of England*, Appendix of Errata, p.572.

Hampden, had been found.⁸ Norman's extensive, unpublished compilation of his family's genealogy, *Of Royal Descent The Pye Family*, contained Echard's account of the exploding pistol, which was said to have been given to him by Robert Pye Jr and had burst at the Battle of Chalgrove.⁹ In 1701, Sir Robert Pye (b. 1620) died. He was married to Anne Hampden (19 October 1625–1701/2), a daughter of John Hampden the Patriot (1595–1643), and she died in the same year as her husband and was buried together with him in the Pleydell Aisle of All Saints Church, Faringdon.¹⁰ The inscription on the tomb reads, according to an unattributed book, *The Pye Family of Faringdon – Historette 1613–1813*:

> On the north side of Faringdon Church called the Pleydell aisle is a white marble slab on the floor thus inscribed with 'Here lies Sir Robert Pye Kt Lord of this Manor and here also lies Dame Anne his wife daughter to the famous Mr Hampden. He was with him in Chalgrove field. They lived together for sixty years and both died 1702.'¹¹

Sir Robert and Anne Pye's tombstone is found half hidden under an altar in the Pleydell Aisle and has the legend:

> Here lies SIR ROBERT PYE, KNT., Lord of this manor. He was esteemed a fine gentleman by all who knew him. Here also lies DAME ANNE, his wife, daughter of the famous Mr Hampden. They lived together sixty years with great reputation and both died A.D. 1701. His grandson Henry Pye Esq. laid this stone over them A.D. 1730.

Sir Robert Walpole dominated Parliament, his term in office being termed the 'Robinocracy'. In 1725, an opposition group formed – a faction titled 'Patriot Whigs' later to become known as the 'Patriot Party'.¹² Sir Robert Pye was proud to state on his tombstone, 'He was with him in Chalgrove Field'. Henry Pye (1709–1766), upon coming of age in 1730, covered his grandfather's gravestone with another that omitted the phrase 'He was with him [Hampden] in Chalgrove Field'. This is an indication that, throughout the period, Walpole was actively using the bursting pistol story to his

---

8   Buckinghamshire Archives (BA) AR 62/92 (Box File) A6: Letter from Dr James Grace to Earl of Buckinghamshire, Union Club, Cockspur Street, London, 22 July 1828.
9   Norman Lawrence, *Of Royal Descent The Pye Family – Of Most Honourable and Ancient Extraction* (Private Collection, Unpublished).
10 Buckinghamshire Archives (BA) PR 90/1/1: Great Hampden Register of Baptisms and Burials, 1557–1812, Microfilm. Extract: 'Anne Hampden daughter of Mr John Hampden Esquier and Elisabeth his wife was baptized the 19 day of October Anno D'nj p^{rdict} 1625.'
11 Norman Lawrence, 'Notes on The Pye Family as written by Norman Lawrence (a descendant of the Pyes) in his unpublished *History of the Pye Family*, held by his son. Included is *The Pye Family of Faringdon – Historiette 1613–1813*, not attributed [Note by Norman Lawrence – Possibly by Samuel James Arnold, son-in-law to H. J. Pye (1745–1813)]', (Unpublished).
12 H. T. Dickinson, *Walpole and the Whig Supremacy* (Aylesbury: Hazell, Watson and Viney, 1973).

advantage. Victorian historians decreed that Chalgrove was a skirmish – a term adopted by those entrusted to look after English Civil War history.

Goodwin's regiment was formed by 8 August 1642 but only had four troops at that stage – probably his own, Major Sigismund Alexander's, Captain Thomas Tyrell's (or Tyroll) and Captain Thomas Sanders' as these troops are identified in early October 1642.[13] Records show that Robert Pye was serving in Arthur Goodwin's regiment by 21 June 1643.[14] Up to 800 of Essex's officers, including the young Robert Pye, were sent to intercept the Royalists heading back to Oxford.[15] Contemporary reports of the exploding pistol during the Battle of Chalgrove cannot be found. Edward Hyde reported on the day of the battle and in the presence of the King in Oxford, 'colonel Hambden, who was shot into the shoulder with a brace of pistol bullets'.[16]

John Hampden's name, reputation and political importance to the ideals from the time of King John (1166–1216) and the signing of the Magna Carta were bought into sharp focus by Walpole's attempt to slur his name. Lord Cobham's elevation of Hampden into a patriot's hall of fame blunted Walpole's attack on his name and reputation. Sir Robert Walpole's scheming to take revenge on his political enemies by inventing stories about John Hampden was to have repercussions for King George III. Walpole could not have foreseen that his ill-gotten words may have elevated John Hampden's name to champion of the American of War of Independence. Richard Temple (1675–1749), 1st Viscount Cobham, succeeded his father in 1697. He was elected in 1730 as a Whig MP for Buckinghamshire – a post held by John Hampden in 1640–1643. Cobham's opposition to Walpole was measured until 1733 when the Excise Bill was presented to Parliament. In 1733, Lord Cobham erected on his vast estate at Stowe the 'Temple of British Worthies'. It features 12 Whig heroes and patriots being divided into men (and one woman) of action and those of contemplation. Hampden is among the former and is there together with Alfred the Great, the Black Prince, Elizabeth I, Raleigh, Drake and William III. The emphasis on 'virtue' and 'liberty' would explain Hampden's selection, his reputation as a hero of liberty being well established by the eighteenth century. The inscription on the medallion under the bust of Hampden has, 'John Hampden, Who, with Great Spirit and consummate Abilities, began a noble Opposition to an arbitrary Court, in Defence of the Liberty of his Country; supported them in Parliament; and died for them in the Field'.

Archbishop William Laud, Oxford University's chancellor from 1630–1641, obtained the privilege from the Crown in 1636 to print and distribute the King James Bible, the authorised version of the scripture. These authorised bibles were shipped to the colonies. The first edition of *The History of the Rebellion and Civil Wars in England* (1702–1704) that had been compiled by Lawrence Hyde was re-edited and periodically edited again, and these

---

13 The National Archives (TNA) SP 28/2B, ff. 321–24.
14 The National Archives (TNA) SP 28/7, f. 438.
15 Lester, 'Military and Political Importance', p.35.
16 BoL: MS. Clar. 112, f. 366: Sir Edward Hyde's Private Journal, 1641–1646.

were sent to the colonies with the bibles. In 1752, Thomas Villiers (1709–1786) married Lady Charlotte Capell, the heir to Clarendon's manuscripts. In 1759, Villiers published *The Life of Edward Earl of Clarendon – Lord High Chancellor of England, and Chancellor of the University of Oxford: In which is Included a Continuation of His History of the Grand Rebellion – Written by Himself. MDCCLIX*. Villiers' publication was a work of fiction based on previous propaganda said to have been written by Clarendon.

The Seven Years' War (1756–1763) involved the British fighting mainly the French for control of North America and its colonies. Britain was victorious and gained control of Canada from France (it was previously called 'New France, Quebec'). In America, this war is called the 'French and Indian War' and, in Pennsylvania, was fought on the borders in the Pittsburgh area. Thomas Villiers' association with Oxford University allowed him to export his publication with the authorised bibles to the colonies. Villiers' publication *The Life*, as it commonly became known, came to the colonies in the 1760s, a time of political upheaval. Parliament sought to recoup the cost of the Seven Years' War, requiring the American colonists to pay for their own defence. Villiers' interpretation in *The Life* of English Civil War events was 'used' by the Boston press to create a dialogue between aliases posing as seventeenth-century politicians. It is difficult to explain the circumstance or the reason why, but, on 14 June 1776, Thomas Villiers became the Earl of Clarendon. With the proceeds from Clarendon's manuscripts, Villiers rebuilt The Grove, West Watford, into a palace fit for a king's visit. King George II died on 25 October 1760, and, according to law, 'Writs of Assistance' (a law passed by Parliament that allowed British tax officials to enter a property) expired six months following his death. Lord Nugent's grandfather George Grenville (1712–1770) became prime minister by the resignation of Lord Bute in April 1763. George Grenville introduced the Stamp Act of 1765, and this act imposed a direct tax on the British colonies in America. There were no American seats in the House of Commons, and this raised the question of 'no taxation without representation' that John Hampden had established after the Ship Money trial of 1637.

Boston lawyer James Otis Jr (1725–1783) defended those who had refused entry to the British tax collectors. John Adams (1735–1826), who would become the second president of the United States, was moved by James Otis' speech that opposed the British tax collectors' right to impose laws passed by an arbitrary court.[17] John Adams later declared, 'Then and there the child Independence was born', which referred to Otis' court action.[18] Adams continued to state that Otis had 'the satisfaction of seeing his constitutional doctrine of no taxation without representation embodied by that body' at

---

17   Lorenzo Sabine, *The American Loyalists: Or, Biographical Sketches of Adherents to the British Crown in the War of the Revolution; Alphabetically Arranged; with a Preliminary Historical Essay* (Boston: Thurston, Torry and Co., 1847), pp.328–29.

18   Eric Burns, *Infamous Scribblers: The Founding Fathers and the Rowdy Beginnings of American Journalism* (New York: Public Affairs, 2006), pp.141–42, 201.

the 1765 Stamp Act Congress.[19] The Stamp Act was passed by Parliament as a way to tax the American colonies to pay for the enormous cost of the Seven Years' War. It can be argued that the Stamp Act of 1765 was a principal cause of the American War of Independence. James Otis, the leader of the Stamp Act Congress (7–25 October 1765), was reported by his contemporaries to have 'plucked up his courage and under the pseudonym "John Hampden" published in the Boston press a sweeping denial of Parliament's right to tax the colonies'.[20] James Otis was able to express the colonists' political endeavour through the Boston press from 1765 to 1783 using the name of 'John Hampden' as an alias. John Hampden, John Pym and other seventeenth-century Parliamentarian notables voiced an opinion and objective through their aliases throughout the American War of Independence. The saga was captured by the diligence of Harbottle Dorr, who made a collection of these newspapers.[21] In 1765, George III sacked his prime minister, George Grenville. The Stamp Act, like all taxes, was very unpopular in America and, after months of protest, was repealed in March 1766. However, Parliament still wanted to exert its sovereignty over its colonies, so Parliament passed the American Colonies Act, commonly known as the Declaratory Act, making Parliament's position clear that the British Parliament '"had hath, and of right ought to have, full power and authority to make laws and statutes of sufficient force and validity to bind the colonies and people of America … in all cases whatsoever"'.[22] This in turn was followed by the Mutiny Act, which indirectly required provincial assemblies such as Pennsylvania to provide quarters for British troops in the colonies. This act caused a lot of bad blood and turned otherwise loyal Americans away from England and towards a fight for independence.

From 1765, the Boston press carried philosophical debate between 'John Hampden', the alias of James Otis, and John Adams, who signed under the pseudonym of Humphrey Ploughjogger. Philosophical debates between names of distinction from the early English Civil War Ship Money trial period were published as if these gentlemen of the seventeenth century were alive in Boston.[23] These debates carried controversial proposals that could have led to the writers being arrested. Otis guided the thoughts and actions of the colonists through the Boston press to act as one against Parliament's arbitrary courts in John Hampden's name. Hampden's stand against King Charles I's arbitrary courts of 1637 that resulted in Parliament later declaring that only it had the right to raise taxes was an analogy too close to the colonies' reality to ignore. Hampden-Sydney College in Virginia was founded in 1775, and the name was chosen to symbolise the devotion to the

---

19 Richard B. Morris, '"Then and There the Child Independence was Born"', *American Heritage: The Magazine of History*, 13:2 (1962), pp.36–39. See Appendix VII.
20 Morris, '"Then and There"', pp.36–39. See Appendix VII.
21 Massachusetts Historical Society (MHS) *The Annotated Newspapers of Harbottle Dorr, Jr.*
22 'Declaratory Act', *Wikipedia*, <https://en.wikipedia.org/wiki/Declaratory_Act>, accessed 18 Feb. 2023.
23 MHS: *The Annotated Newspapers of Harbottle Dorr, Jr.*

principles of representative government and full civil and religious freedom that Otis, in the name of John Hampden (1595–1643) and Algernon Sydney (1622–1683), instilled in the colonists' minds. Hampden and Sydney, in their lifetimes, had outspokenly supported and had given their lives to the ideals that Otis was passing to the colonists. Throughout the War of Independence, John Hampden, by Otis' direction, was leading the minds of the troops and giving guidance to the colonists. When the war ended, John Hampden's name was venerated. Following the war, land was granted in exchange for services rendered, which became known as the 'Great Migration'. In western Massachusetts, when the county names were being selected, they continued to identify with the English patriot whose cause Otis championed. Hampden County, Springfield, Massachusetts, in the heart of the 13 states set the tone. Hampden townships are found in Alabama, Maine, Baltimore, Massachusetts, North Dakota, Ohio, West Virginia and Wisconsin. In Canada, Hampden townships are found in Newfoundland, Labrador and Quebec. Australia has Hampden townships in Queensland; South Australia; the County of Hampden, Victoria and Shire of Hampden, Melbourne, Victoria. New Zealand has Hampden townships in North Otago, and Murchison was home to a Hampden township until 1882.

Following the end of the American War of Independence, the venerated name of John Hampden returned home to spearhead the Whigs' cause for social reform. The *St. James Chronicle* is believed to have commissioned Horace Walpole to write the 'exploding pistol' story for its opening publication in March 1761. Horace's father, Sir Robert Walpole, was the author of the exploding pistol story and was versed in the account.[24] The story remained and circulated in polite society. In 1784, Mark Noble FSA (Fellow of the Society of Antiquaries) (1754–1827) published *Memoirs of the Protectorate-House of Cromwell 1784*. Volume II has *Memoirs of the Hampdens*, and it recounts the burst pistol story as stated by Echard's *The History of England*.[25] Guy Fawkes' (1570–1606) country estate was Farnley Hall, Otley, North Yorkshire, which latterly became the residence of Walter Ramsden Fawkes (1769–1825). Walter was approved by Lord William Grenville (1759–1834), 1st Baron Grenville, to stand as the MP for Yorkshire in the 1806 general election. At this election, William Grenville became prime minister. In 1810, at the age of 21, Lord Nugent (1789–1850) was elected as a Whig MP for Buckingham, a Grenville-held rotten borough.

Lady Mary Nugent married George Nugent-Temple-Grenville, 1st Marquess of Buckingham of Stowe, and, in 1789, gave birth to George, who became Lord Nugent upon the death of his mother. George Nugent-Grenville (1789–1850), 2nd Baron Nugent of Carlanstown, was brought up in the Whig

---

24 See Appendix IV.
25 Mark Noble, *Memoirs of Several Persons and Families, Who, by Females Are Allied To, or Descended From, the Protectorate-House of Cromwell, Chiefly Collected From Original Papers and Records: To Which Is Added, a Catalogue of Such Persons Who Were Raised to Honors or Great Employments by the Cromwells; With the Lives of Many of Them* (Birmingham: Pearson and Rollason, 1784), vol. II, p.98.

George Grenville, Lord Nugent (1789–1850). (Private collection. By the kind permission of Mr and Mrs G. R. Anson)

tradition. He was educated at Brasenose College and, in 1810, received an honourary degree, Doctor of Civil Law. Nugent was familiar from an early age with John Hampden's history and Walpole's attempt to slur his name, as much of the story was played out at his childhood home in Stowe.[26] George Nugent-Grenville stood as a Whig MP (1810–1812) in the rotten borough of Buckingham that was controlled by the Grenvilles. Nugent used John Hampden's name and reputation as an exemplar of his own honesty and integrity, and, in the 1812 general election, Nugent was returned to Aylesbury and continued to represent the town until 1832. Lord Nugent became Lord of the Treasury, followed by Lord High Commissioner of the Ionian Islands. After standing for Aylesbury in 1837, 1839 and 1843 and failing to get elected, Nugent secured re-election for John Hampden's old constituency in 1847 and died in late 1850.

On 20 April 1812, at the Thatched House Tavern in St James', London, Walter Ramsden Fawkes was in the chair at the inauguration of the Hampden Club for reform. Fawkes had previously enrolled as a committee member of the Union for Parliamentary Reform. The second resolution of the Hampden Club was 'no taxation without representation' – 'taxation and representation are inseparably united; God hath joined them'.[27] Major John Cartwright (1740–1824) was the driving force of the Hampden Club, and it was through his good offices that many more Hampden Clubs were formed, especially in the industrial towns of the north. Cartwright was an ardent supporter of the American colonists and had published a plea on the colonists' behalf titled *American Independence: The Glory and Interest of Great Britain* in 1774. Cartwright supported universal suffrage and John Hampden's demand of 'no taxation without representation' – a phrase in 1775 on the tongue of John Hampden's alias, James Otis, in Boston, Massachusetts. Thomas Jefferson, in an exchange of letters, praised Major John Cartwright for his support during the American War of Independence and for his continuing work to gain universal suffrage.[28]

---

26 Derek Lester and Gill Blackshaw, *The Controversy of John Hampden's Death* (Oxford: Parchment Press, 2000).

27 John Cartwright, *The Life and Correspondence of Major Cartwright* (London: Henry Colburn, 1826), vol. II, pp.24–26. See Appendix III.

28 Cartwright, *Life and Correspondence*, vols I–II.

8

Exhumation

In 1816, the 4th Earl of Buckinghamshire died, succeeding his titles to George Vere Hobart at a time when the country was in uproar. Street riots were common, and the political foment caused by the actions of the Hampden Clubs, especially in the industrial heartlands, was most fierce. A crowd said to be of the order of 60,000 came to hear speeches by leading reformers in August 1819 at St Peter's Field, Manchester, demanding in as many words 'no taxation without representation' and universal suffrage. The authorities feared that Henry Hunt, a radical orator, would whip the crowd into a frenzy and have them march on the government. Cheshire Magistrates' chairman summoned the 15th Hussars to disperse the crowd and arrest the speakers. The Peterloo Massacre that followed, so called by a newspaper in ironic reference to the Battle of Waterloo, saw 18 people killed and hundreds injured.[1] Much of the blame, however, was accorded to the Manchester and Salford Yeomanry Cavalry rather than the 15th Hussars.

Lord Nugent won his second term as MP for Aylesbury in the frenzy of a Whig revolution. Hampden's name, Hampden Clubs, riots in the streets in many cities and the Peterloo Massacre had been reborn into Lord Nugent's soul. Nugent had become an extreme radical Whig reformer and called upon John Hampden's name and reputation to promote his political cause. In 1824, the 5th Earl inherited the Buckinghamshire estates of the Hampden family and took the name of Hampden – his ancestor, Sir John Hobart, 3rd baronet, having married Mary Hampden in about 1655.[2] Unpublished family papers held by the Brookses has:

> The 3rd and last Viscount Hampden died in 1824. The Viscounts had inherited Hampden under the Will of John Hampden died 1754. That same Will devised the estates, on the extinction of that branch and the Viscounty, [sic] to the descendants of Sir Henry Hobart who became Earls of Buckinghamshire. Thus in

---

1   Cartwright, *Life and Correspondence*, vols I–II.
2   'George Hobart-Hampden, 5th Earl of Buckinghamshire', *Wikipedia*, <https://en.wikipedia.org/wiki/George_Hobart-Hampden,_5th_Earl_of_Buckinghamshire>, accessed 18 Feb. 2023.

1824 the 5th Earl inherited Hampden Estates and the gift of the living (GEC The Complete Peerage, Vol II p.440 (Buckinghamshire).[3]

The 5th Earl of Buckinghamshire was certainly aware of the Whigs' claim to John Hampden's name and reputation when he came to Great Hampden in 1824. Civil unrest filled the streets, and John Hampden's reputation as the gallant warrior losing his life in battle was once again called into question. Nugent's words engraved on the monument at Chalgrove read, 'while fighting in defence of the free Monarchy and ancient liberties of England'. The Earl's inheritance of the Hampden Estates in 1824 made him a political target, with the added barb implied that he carried his ancestors' shame for John Hampden's death. The question of whether Hampden's pistol had exploded in his hand or that he had been shot in the shoulder was troubling the Earl even in the sanctity of his Union Club.

Nugent's research had come to the attention of the Earl of Buckinghamshire, and he was curious to know if Nugent had asked for permission to visit Great Hampden. Dr Grace, the Earl's steward, in a written reply to the Earl sometime in late March 1828 informed him that he had not received any such request but that he would write to Nugent and offer him every assistance in his investigations.[4] Edward Clough's narrative was economical in the description of John Hampden's funeral, his narrative stating, 'The whole Armie at his buriall followed, singing the 90th Psalme; and at their returne the 43rd; with ensignes furled and muffled drums their heads uncovered' – leaving it to the reader to make an assumption as to where the funeral and burial occurred.[5] Neither the Earl, Nugent nor anyone knew where John Hampden was buried – that is, until an entry in the parish register was found.

Early in April 1828, Nugent was exploring the archives held at Great Hampden. Of the few items that he found of importance, only an account of a portrait of John Hampden written by the Dean of Killaloe, the old pedigree of the Hampden family, and a memorandum of the Earl of Buckinghamshire's family of Sir Miles Hobart in the reign of Charles I interested him. He also learnt while he was there that the pavement in the church was to be taken up and re-laid sometime in the summer. This information is recounted in a letter dated 5 April 1828 to the Earl from Dr Grace.[6] In this same communication, Grace begged the Earl, on Lord Nugent's behalf, for permission to find John Hampden's grave when the floor was taken up, with the words that Nugent '… depends on finding the grave of the Patriot and would very much like to look into the vault if he fails in finding any inscription when the floor is removed'.[7]

---

3   See Appendix X.
4   Buckinghamshire Archives (BA) D/MH 39/88: Letter fragment from Dr James Grace to the Earl of Buckinghamshire, March 1828. See Appendix IX, Item 1, for text.
5   British Newspaper Archive (BNA) 'Letter from Mr Urban, Stoneleigh, March 26', *The Gentleman's Magazine and Historical Chronicle*, vol. 85, part 1, 1815, pp.395–96. See Appendix II for text.
6   Buckinghamshire Archives (BA) D/MH 39/84: Letter from Dr James Grace to the Earl of Buckinghamshire, 5 April 1828. See Appendix IX, Item 2, for text.
7   BA: D/MH 39/84: Letter from Dr James Grace to the Earl of Buckinghamshire, 5 April 1828.

EXHUMATION

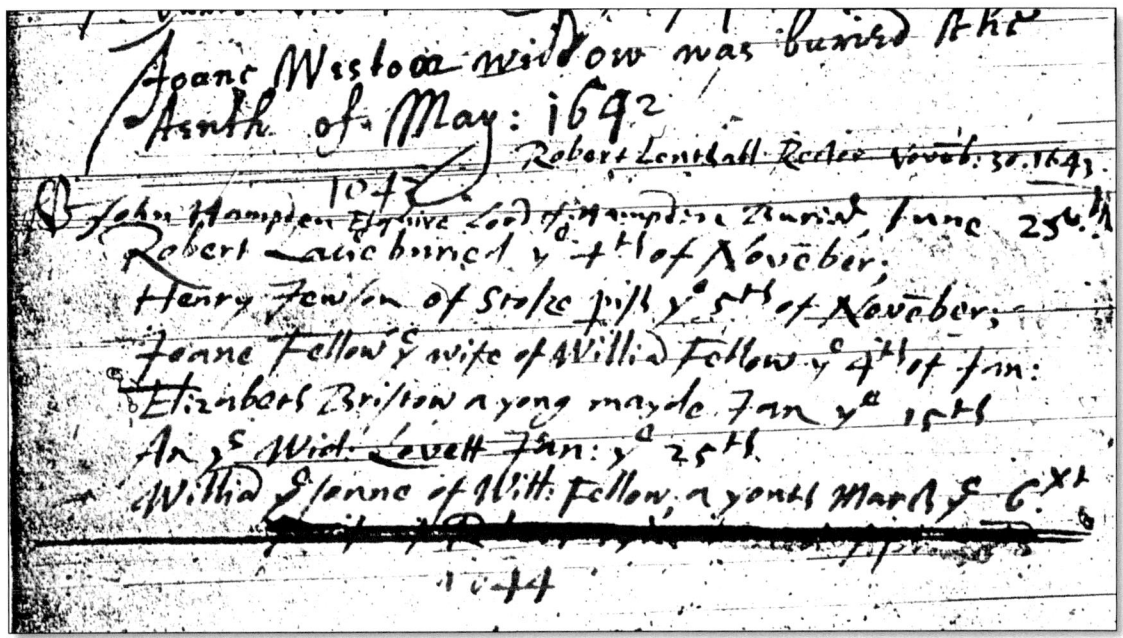

How proverbial. That the Earl gave his consent for the exhumation to take place gives an understanding of how desperate he was to settle the exploding pistol issue. Nugent did not find nor look for John Hampden's grave in Great Hampden Church during this visit in April, for he would have learnt that the Hampden family did not possess a vault – a most unusual omission for such an eminent family.

In early June 1828, during a special parochial visitation, held in the parish church and in the presence of the Earl of Buckinghamshire with the bishop and archdeacon, the circumstance of the exhumation of John Hampden was discussed. Upon examination of the parish register, the following entry was found, which satisfied the bishop and archdeacon that John Hampden was buried in the church: 'NB John Hampden Esquire Lord of Hampden Buried June 25th. 1643'.

It is customary that lords of the manor are buried in the chancel of their church. Rector Robert Lenthall – who was inducted into St Mary Magdalene, Great Hampden, on 10 November 1643 – ratified on 30 November 1643 Richard Hampden's word that John Hampden was buried in the church on 25 June 1643.[8] In a fragment of a letter to the Earl, Dr Grace wrote in excited terms, '… he has discovered the entry of the burial of John Hampden in an old register proving beyond doubt the circumstance of his being buried at Hampden'.[9] The discovery of the parish register with the name 'John Hampden' entered for 25 June 1643 gave Lord Nugent licence to embellish the events of Hampden's last days on the 'authority' of a fictitious Edward

Extract from the Great Hampden Parish Register. It reads, 'NB. John Hampden Esquire Lord of Hampden Buried June 25th. 1643. Robert Lenthall Rector Novb: 30. 1643' (BA: PR 90/1/1: Great Hampden Register of Baptisms and Burials, 1557–1812, Microfilm). (Image licence – June22/CDL/157/Lester)

---

8 Clergy of the Church of England Database (CCEd) ID 8618.

9 Buckinghamshire Archives (BA) D/MH 39/87: Letter fragment from Dr James Grace to the Earl of Buckinghamshire, early June 1828. See Appendix IX, Item 3, for text.

Clough. From this moment, Lord Nugent became the authority on John Hampden's life, his action at Chalgrove, his time lying in agony in Thame and his supposed grandiose funeral at Great Hampden.

The floor of the chancel had been taken up, and the grave markers removed prior to their lordships' visit to Great Hampden. Their lordships decided that John Hampden's unmarked and unknown grave was most likely to be found buried in front of his wife's memorial, situated on the south wall. Their lordships instructed the workmen to excavate the area in front of the memorial to Elizabeth Hampden, and there they dug down to a coffin. This coffin, their lordships declared, was the grave of John Hampden, but they were mistaken. Had their lordships uncovered the nameplate on the coffin, it would have read, 'Griffith Hampden Esq died 27 October 1591 and of Anne his second wife Daughter & Heir of Anthony Cave of Chicheley, Anne deceased the last Day of Dec 1594'. Had their lordships explored the contents of the parish chest more closely, they would have found a document titled '*Hampden Magna*'. On a previous occasion in 1663, when the floor was to be retiled, Rector John Yates recorded the location and names of the occupants of the graves in the chancel.[10] The coffin was left exposed, ready for Lord Nugent and Dr Grace to examine its contents at a later time. Dr Grace heard that the rector had been busy retiling the chancel and, on a visit, found that the excavated grave had been filled in and the chancel floor retiled over it. Dr Grace sent a letter to Lord Nugent on 17 June 1828 to explain the circumstance of Rector Brooks' defiance to their lordships desire to establish the cause of John Hampden's death. Dr Grace explained to Lord Nugent that the rector had the final decision on whether to allow the exhumation:

Risborough June 17, 1828,

My Lord,

I went to Hampden the next morning after your Lordship's last visit there intending to prevent the floor being laid over the grave containing the coffin which you wished opened; on my arrival there I found that Mr. Brooks had workmen to fill up the grave and proceed with the floor, all of which I found done. I however, lost no time communicating your Lordship's wishes to Lord Buckinghamshire, telling him the scruples Mr. Brooks had with regard to his consenting to the opening of the coffin, to which I have since had a reply, and the result is that Lord Buckinghamshire wishes by all means that the coffin should be opened and examined. I have not had an opportunity of seeing Mr. Brooks, scarcely, since I had the pleasure of meeting your Lordship, so as to have any conversation with him on the subject; perhaps you would write to him as his consent is the only thing necessary. It is true that the floor must be disarranged again, but this must have been the case if we had proceeded the time as intended, for I think it would have been impossible to have examined the coffin properly

---

10 Buckinghamshire Archives (BA) AR 62/92 Box A4: *Hampden Magna: Tombs' Location in the Chancel of St Mary Magdalene, Great Hampden (1663–1675)*.

or satisfactorily without taking up the floor. As Lord B has so strongly intimated his wishes in the matter. I apprehend Mr. Brooks will no longer hesitate about it, provided he is put to no additional expense in setting to right the floor after the examination has taken place.

I remain, my Lord, your Lordship's obdt. Servant. J. GRACE.[11]

The rector had the grave refilled and the chancel retiled somewhat to the annoyance of Dr Grace and the Earl. Lord Nugent, in a letter to the rector dated 27 June 1828, politely asked and gave many promises that disturbance of the grave would be kept to a minimum if he would grant his permission.[12] The rector agreed to Lord Nugent's request that the coffin could be examined on the morning of 21 July 1828. Rector George William Brooks' appointment at Great Hampden was probably arranged between the Earl of Buckinghamshire and the rector's father, John. A word from Rector George's father that his continuing defiance would affect the family's fortune may have been the deciding factor for him to give his consent to the exhumation. On the morning of 21 July 1828, Lord Nugent led Mr Thomas Denman and Mr William James Smith to St Mary Magdalene Church, Great Hampden. They were greeted by Rector Brooks, who was accompanied by Dr James Grace, the Earl's land steward and churchwarden. The rector made his position clear that he was utterly opposed to the exhumation and pleaded in the name of God for them go in peace and leave the church. Dr Grace reminded the rector of the special parochial visitation held in the parish church in the presence of the Earl of Buckinghamshire with the bishop and archdeacon in early June 1828. In granting permission for the entourage to enter the church, Rector Brooks reminded Lord Nugent of his promises made in his letter on 27 June 1828.[13]

The moment of truth: the gravediggers were called in, and they began digging at the site of the grave exposed earlier by their lordships. At this point, the rector left the church, 'giving orders to the clerk, before leaving the church, to have the coffin immediately closed and put into the grave'.[14] Expectations rose as the lid of the coffin was uncovered, and they continued digging until the nameplate was exposed. Lord Nugent entered the grave and read the name inscribed on the plaque. In shocked disbelief, Nugent read out to the others, 'Griffith Hampden Esq died 27 October 1591'. All the inscriptions on the coffins around the memorial were exposed in turn and examined, but none bore the famous legend. Then, with desperation

---

11 British Newspaper Archive (BNA) 'Rector Brookses copy of a Letter from James Grace, Esq., Land Steward to the Earl of Buckinghamshire and Churchwarden of Great Hampden, to Lord Nugent. Risborough dated June 17, 1828', *Derby Mercury*, Wednesday, 21 January 1863.

12 British Newspaper Archive (BNA) 'Correspondence sent by Lord Nugent 27 June 1828 to Mr. G W Brooks, the Rector at Great Hampden at the time of the exhumation', *Derby Mercury*, Wednesday, 21 January 1863. See Appendix IX, Item 5, for text.

13 BNA: 'Lord Nugent 27 June 1828 to Mr. G W Brooks'.

14 BNA: 'Lord Nugent 27 June 1828 to Mr. G W Brooks'.

setting in, they came across a coffin with the nameplate so corroded that it crumbled away upon being touched. This tomb was taken to be that of the Patriot by the fact that none of the other coffins were labelled 'John Hampden'. Therefore, this unidentified casket, in their minds, said by one observer of the exhumation, recounted in a letter to *The Gentleman's Magazine*, to be above the communion rail, had to be the correct one.[15]

Dr James Grace explained the circumstance of the exhumation in a letter to the Earl of Buckinghamshire:

Earl of Buckinghamshire, Union Club, Cockspur Street, London.

Risborough 22nd July 1828

The leaden coffin has been opened, but not satisfactory proof obtained that the body contained in it, was that of the Patriot. Lord Nugent attended, accompanied by Mr. Denman & they went away under the impression that they had discovered a fracture in the collar bone, but on Mr. Norris's examination it proved to be no such thing, and he reported all the bones to be in a perfect state. The body was in a fine state of preservation enclosed with a considerable quantity of wrapping within three coffins, one of lead. The flesh and muscles not much wasted & the face plump & must have had nearly the same appearance as when buried. There was a large quantity of hair in good preservation. Mr. Norris supposes the body has been buried upwards of two hundred years & would have remained as much longer without being disturbed. There is a description on the stone over the grave to William Hampden Esq. and it is probable that this must be the same person. It is extraordinary that no trace can be discovered of the body of the Patriot which can only be accounted by his not being buried in lead and consequently gone completely to decay.

I remain my Lord

Your Lordship's faithful servant

J. Grace.[16]

On Monday, 28 July 1828, *The Times* printed a report of the exhumation, giving details of those present, a brief history of both accounts of how Hampden received his mortal wound and, of course, the grisly details of the disinterment.[17] *The Times* sold this most interesting gruesome story to numerous news outlets. Among those who published the article in the first week of August 1828 were the *London Courier and Evening Gazette* (Monday,

---

15 Buckinghamshire Archives (BA) D/MH Trans 11: *The Gentleman's Magazine* 6 June 1829, Letter signed by P.Q.
16 BA: AR 62/92 (Box File) A6: Letter from Dr James Grace to Earl of Buckinghamshire, Union Club, Cockspur Street, London, 22 July 1828.
17 See Appendix V for a transcript of the letter.

28 July), the *Dublin Evening Mail* (Friday, 1 August), *Cork Constitution*, Cork (Saturday, 2 August), *Hampshire Advertiser* (Saturday, 2 August), *Westmoreland Gazette* (Saturday, 2 August), *Chester Courant* (Tuesday, 5 August) and the *Morning Post*, London (Tuesday, 5 August).[18]

The description of the body and its mutilation referred in *The Times* letter can be seen to be embellishments of the facts, or downright lies, when viewed from the advantage of twenty-first-century medical, physical and scientific knowledge. The tenor of the letter was one to provoke horror and disgust that the Earl of Buckinghamshire would allow his ancestor to be publicly humiliated, mutilated and butchered in order to absolve his conscience of the 'accident' that caused John Hampden's death. The real question that must be asked, when it is proved that the facts in this letter are a complete fabrication, is why this distinguished body of gentlemen thought it necessary to publish such lies. Dr Grace's letter to the Earl is proof enough, for, unbeknown to him, his description of the exhumed body was scientifically correct.

Within this little group, there were two factions: one believing in the exploding pistol theory – of which Nugent's friends, William James Smith and Mr Thomas Denman, were the fiercest adherents – and the other, which included Nugent, believing that Hampden was shot in the shoulder. Mr Thomas Denman was a lawyer of some renown whose liberal policies had caused his exclusion from office of state until 1822. He was an MP in rotten boroughs from 1818 to 1832. Denman's sponsor for these seats is not recorded. In 1830, he was made attorney general and, in 1832, the year of publication of Nugent's book, Lord Chief Justice of the King's Bench. The style of the letter's narrative is that of a lawyer covering all other possibilities of the cause of death. After reporting some evidence of the right hand being mutilated, all other scenarios of how the corpse might have met its death were covered. The letter's writer postulated that it was possible that, as Hampden's pistol exploded, he might have at the same time been shot in the shoulder. This possibility was said to have been investigated, and, to facilitate the inquiry, both arms were said to have been amputated with a penknife. The blade of an eighteenth-century penknife was possibly an inch long (25mm) and under a quarter of an inch wide (less than 6mm) and made from a thin piece of quality steel. The sole purpose of the penknife (or quill knife) at this period was for sharpening the quill of a bird's feather to fashion it into a point with a narrow slit to enable it to be used as pen. The absurdity of a quill knife being used to cut through sinew as tough as leather is too ludicrous to be taken seriously. Further discussion on the integrity of John Hampden's name and reputation being used to bolster the Whigs' political argument was dealt a crushing blow.

Smith and Denman being the likely authors of the letter to *The Times* and Denman becoming attorney general in 1830 and Lord Chief Justice in 1832 made further discussion futile, except those who squabbled for attention in *The Gentlemen's Magazine*. The opening two paragraphs of the letter to *The*

---

18 Hatfield Library (HL) Letter to *The Times* published 28 July 1828, Microfilm reel. See Appendix V for text.

Times cite the reason for them being at Great Hampden and the names of some of the people who attended. What follows can only be described as a one-sided view, conditioning the reader to accept that Hampden's hand was shattered by the exploding of his pistol. Within the next few paragraphs, they had dismissed all contemporary evidence of the episode and had promoted the Pye story from a contradictory statement to a fact. Any lingering doubts as to whether they were about to open John Hampden's coffin are cast aside with an oblique reference to Edward Clough's discredited narration of the grand procession and the entry of Hampden's interment in the burial register.[19] *The Times* letter states:

> It [the coffin] was lying under the western window, near the tablet erected by him, when living, to the memory of his beloved wife, whose virtues he extols in the most affectionate language. Without positive proof, it was reasonable to suppose that he would be interred near his adored partner, and this being found at her feet, it was unanimously agreed that the lid should be cut open to ascertain the fact, which proved afterwards that we were not mistaken.[20]

The black marble tablet to Elizabeth Hampden hangs on the south wall of the chancel, and the reference to the western window could be construed as an insult, as lords of the manor are buried in the chancel.

Previous to this paragraph, the letter has:

> On the morning of the 21st July we all assembled in the church, and commenced the operation of opening the ground.

> After examining the initials and dates on several leaden coffins, we came to the one in question, the plate of which was so corroded, that it crumbled and broke into small pieces on touching it. It was therefore impossible to ascertain the name of the individual that it contained.[21]

'After examining … several leaden coffins' is contrary to the previous paragraph's statement that Hampden's coffin was found on the first attempt beneath the marble tablet dedicated to his first wife. Which leaden coffins? And how many did the writer of the letter presume were unearthed before coming to the one it is said to be beneath the memorial to Elizabeth Hampden? How susceptible to suggestion was Nugent when they came to the tomb that the nameplate had crumbled off upon being touched? With his peers egging him on, Nugent agreed to have the coffin cut open. Dr Grace said that this tomb was under a stone marked 'William Hampden', which is on the

---

19 BNA: 'Letter from Mr Urban, Stoneleigh, March 26', *The Gentleman's Magazine and Historical Chronicle*, vol. 85, part 1, 1815, pp.395–96.
20 See Appendix V.
21 See Appendix V.

north wall by the communion rail.[22] Once the ensemble, Nugent included, had convinced themselves that this coffin was the one that contained John Hampden, there was no turning back.

Mr John Yates was inducted as rector to St Mary Magdalene Church, Great Hampden, on 20 July 1663. The floor of the church was to be re-laid, and Yates was asked to record the inscriptions and position of where tombs were sited. The original documents listing the tombs were transcribed, and copies were made into a booklet. *Hampden Magna* is an unpublished booklet that has a copy of the original document on the left-hand page and a transcription of it on the facing page.[23] John Hampden was buried in secret. There was no stone edifice or slab to mark his tomb. Richard Hampden, lord of the manor, knew the spot where Hampden was buried – a secret he kept to himself. Yates did not describe the chancel's decoration, yet he wrote, 'At the Entrance into the Chancel hang a Surcoat of Arms belonging to the Hampdens with Mantle Helmet & Crest bet : 4 Penons One whereof is torn the other are as follows'.[24] The torn pennon under Hampden's surcoat of arms could be interpreted as John Hampden being torn away from his friends. His friends' arms in the pennons under are first pennon 'viz Paget', second 'Hampden impa (*led*) a Lyon rampant Arg^t' and third 'viz : *Foley*'.[25] These are some of John Hampden's friends. 'Under these Penons hangs a Shield thereon the Arms of Hampden', which is interpreted as 'the Hampden beneath will protect you after death'.[26] The above describes the grave of John Hampden being at the entrance to the chancel. Assuming the gravediggers began digging underneath Elizabeth Hampden's memorial, they would have found the first coffin near the south wall, not the western window as was stated. No grave marking is shown in *Hampden Magna* under Elizabeth's memorial. There may have been room for one more grave between the memorial and the rood screen, although, again, none is recorded.

By the time they got to William Hampden's tomb near the northern wall, they could have disturbed up to five other coffins. *The Times* letter states, 'The parish plumber descended, and commenced cutting across the coffin, then longitudinally, until the whole was sufficiently loosened to roll back, in order to lift off the wooden lid beneath, which was found in such good preservation, that it came off nearly entire. Beneath this was another lid of the same material, which was raised without materially giving way.'[27] This

---

22 BA: AR 62/92 (Box File) A6: Letter from Dr James Grace to Earl of Buckinghamshire, Union Club, Cockspur Street, London, 22 July 1828.

23 BA: AR 62/92 Box A4: *Hampden Magna: Tombs' Location in the Chancel of St Mary Magdalene, Great Hampden (1663–1675)*.

24 BA: AR 62/92 Box A4: *Hampden Magna: Tombs' Location in the Chancel of St Mary Magdalene, Great Hampden (1663–1675)*.

25 BA: AR 62/92 Box A4: *Hampden Magna: Tombs' Location in the Chancel of St Mary Magdalene, Great Hampden (1663–1675)*.

26 BA: AR 62/92 Box A4: *Hampden Magna: Tombs' Location in the Chancel of St Mary Magdalene, Great Hampden (1663–1675)*.

27 See Appendix V.

statement suggests that the coffin comprised of two wooden casks, probably constructed with beech wood, that were inside a leaden sarcophagus. Dr Grace mainly concurs with the description of the coffin, how it was opened and the condition of the corpse at first sight. With the coffin stripped of its lids and the body in its cerecloth wrapping exposed to the elements, the moment of truth had arrived. The cloths were carefully cut away from the face and body to reveal the head, arms and upper torso – which were not unwrapped as stated in the letter, as this would entail lifting the heavy, fragile body. How the features of the face can be so differently described from the same scene is quite remarkable.

Dr Grace wrote that the body had a chocolate colour, but the newspaper report stated that the face had a death-like whiteness.[28] The body had lain in sawdust in a wooden coffin for many years. Tannin, a chemical inherent in wood, migrates into the flesh of a body that is sealed in an airtight container and causes the skin to darken. Of course, Smith, the most probable author of *The Times* letter, had no inkling of this chemistry and so reported what everybody knew: that faces of dead bodies went a ghostly, ashen white. No one in the party had ever seen an exhumation of a body from an airtight coffin filled with sawdust, so it seems that they recorded what they expected to see. The rigid corpse was lying on its back, obscured by sawdust, in a coffin that lay five or six feet down in the bowels of the chancel. Lord Nugent, it is said, 'descended into the grave' and removed the cerecloths: without lifting the body, unwrapping the cerecloths would be an impossible task. Smith wrote:

> Finding that a difference of opinion existed as to the indentation in the left shoulder, where it was supposed he had been wounded, it was unanimously agreed upon to raise up the coffin altogether, and place it in the centre of the church, where a more accurate examination might take place … Being placed on a trestle, the first operation was to examine the arms, which nearly retained their original size, and presented a very muscular appearance.[29]

Lifting a lead coffin from the bowels of earth is an almost impossible task to achieve unless a block and tackle was to hand. Imagine the scene: the height of the lead coffin's side was about four feet (1.22m) to accommodate the large wooden coffins within. Trestles were common and used for tables that stood about two feet and six inches (0.75m) from the ground. The top of the coffin perched on the trestle would be six feet and six inches (less than 2m) from the ground, which brings home the absurdity of Smith's account of the exhumation. Dr Grace was at the exhumation. He also assisted Mr Norris, the local physician, the following day, when together they examined the body. That night, Tuesday, 22 July 1828, Grace wrote to the Earl of

---

28 Buckinghamshire Archives (BA) D/MH 39/86, Transcript 11: Letter from Dr James Grace to Richard Cumberland at the Exchequer, Palace Yard, London, 9 August 1828. See Appendix IX, Item 8, for text.

29 See Appendix V.

Buckinghamshire at the Union Club in London with the details of the two days' events.[30] He said:

> ... The leaden coffin has been opened, but not satisfactory proof obtained that the body contained in it, was that of the Patriot. Lord Nugent attended, accompanied by Mr. Denman & they went away under the impression that they had discovered a fracture in the collar bone, but on Mr. Norris's examination it proved to be no such thing, and he reported all the bones to be in a perfect state ...[31]

Who were Smith and Denman trying to convince, for they knew this was just plain lying? It was not a case of being mistaken. How did he think he could perpetrate such lies?

The body was left out in the chancel until the following day for all to see. The local physician, Mr Norris, had been invited to thoroughly and professionally examine it, and this he did on the Tuesday. How the writers of the narrative thought that they could get away with such audacious lies is beyond comprehension. One can only speculate why they indulged in so much invention. An exhumed body is not a pleasant sight. Although the corpse had been sealed in an airtight coffin, biological processes had continued for a while, mainly in the stomach area, until all the oxygen was depleted. Even Mr Norris did not understand these chemical reactions, neither did any scientists of the day. However, in burials from the sixteenth and seventeenth centuries, the arms of a corpse were not bent with the hands on the shoulders like now but were left straight with the hands resting on the lower abdomen.[32] Around this area, the hands and the wooden coffin were partly eaten away by bacterial action – probably sufficiently so to convince the expectant and untrained eyes of Nugent, Smith and Denman to truly believe that the hand had been shattered.

The Times printed the letter on 28 July 1828, but Dr Grace had not read it when he wrote to Mr Richard Cumberland at the Exchequer, Palace Yard, London, on 9 August 1828. He had heard about the article and had seen several accounts in other papers, about which he stated '... have all been incorrect'. He reiterated that Nugent examined the hands himself '... and went away with the fancied idea that both were fractured'. This letter also describes in detail the examination on Tuesday and does not include any mutilation of the body whatsoever – except, that is, for the hand – and this is best told in Dr Grace's own words:

> ... I saw nothing like a fracture of either hands or shoulders, nor was there any dislocation.

---

30 BA: AR 62/92 (Box File) A6: Letter from Dr James Grace to Earl of Buckinghamshire, Union Club, Cockspur Street, London, 22 July 1828.
31 BA: AR 62/92 (Box File) A6: Letter from Dr James Grace to Earl of Buckinghamshire, Union Club, Cockspur Street, London, 22 July 1828.
32 Jane Huggett, *The Shaking of the Sheets : Death 1350–1660* (Bristol: Stuart Press, 1997).

The account you saw describing the hand as being found in a separate bag (which on being examined proved to have been sawn off) was altogether incorrect, it might have been separated at the wrist by the action of moving the body from its position. There certainly was no fracture or anything of the kind and although separated at the wrist was not from a wound or by amputation – my opinion of this at the time of the disinterment was fully corroborated by Mr. Norris when he examined it afterwards the legs and lower parts of the body were not examined that part of the coffin was filled with sawdust. There was nothing appeared in the examination which could in any way prove, or so make it even supposable that the body was that of The Patriot on the contrary, if the prints and portraits we have seen of him can give one any idea of his person the features of this which could be seen perfectly were of a different character altogether. Instead of that high nose and thin visage which I have always pictured the Patriot to have had, this was a short nose and fat round face and Mr. Norris thinks it much older than the Patriot's time, and would he says if not disturbed have remained as much longer the same state. I think it not unlikely that it was Mr. William Hampden as the coffin was immediately under the stone bearing his inscription upon it. In my last letter from Lord Buckinghamshire he mentions the 20th August for coming to Hampden …[33]

The location of the coffin was confirmed by a letter to *The Gentleman's Magazine* that read:

that one of the party whose name is mentioned in the narrative as having been present on that occasion, unhesitatingly confessed that the account published was extremely incorrect; that the body described was not found in the spot mentioned, but under the floor within the communion rails; and that the hand discovered separate from the arm, had every appearance of having been detached by decay, and no appearance whatsoever of artificial amputation …[34]

By 19 August, Dr Grace had read the narrative in *The Times*, and, in a letter of the same date, in a reply to inquiries by the Earl, he wrote:

… I daresay Lord Nugent imagined that the hand was separated from the body and that it must have been so buried, but when Mr. Norris examined the arm and shoulder bones the hand although separated at the wrist was not by a fractured wound, or by amputation, in all probability it was done by the action of moving the body from its position. Mr. Norris assures me that all the bones and joints of the arm and shoulders were in a perfect state …[35]

---

33 BA: D/MH 39/86, Transcript 11: Letter from Dr James Grace to Richard Cumberland at the Exchequer, Palace Yard, London, 9 August 1828.
34 Buckinghamshire Archives (BA) D/MH Trans 11: *The Gentleman's Magazine* Sept 1828, pp.199–200, Letter by J. De Alta Ripa.
35 Buckinghamshire Archives (BA) D/MH 39/85: Letter from Dr James Grace to the Earl of Buckinghamshire, 19 August 1828. See Appendix IX, Item 9, for text.

Having blinded themselves that the body was John Hampden's because of the decayed hand, it seems that Smith and Denman had the rest of the story composed to squash any conflicting theories. After Nugent and Denman's cursory examination of the body, the entourage repaired for lunch, leaving the grave open and the coffin in the chancel. It must have been immediately apparent to Nugent and the others that no bullet had hit the shoulder. There was no question in Nugent, Smith and Denman's minds that they had disinterred John Hampden. With the evidence presented, they hoped to have convinced the readers of the narrative that they had exhumed John Hampden. It was a believable story for readers in the nineteenth century, as they did not have the scientific knowledge of today to question the facts.

Except for a few men of intellect in the world at this time, it was believed that maggots and worms spontaneously generated. Francesco Redi in 1668 proved that meat kept in a vacuum jar did not produce maggots, but he and his contemporaries did not understand why.[36] It was not until 1862 that the great Louis Pasteur proved beyond doubt that spontaneous generation was not possible. It was not known in 1828 that maggots came from eggs laid by flies. Neither did they know that the incubation period of a fly's egg is a very minimum of eight hours in hot weather nor that small, immobile maggots would begin to hatch after this period. In the cool of the church, this time would have been extended by up to a factor of two. Flies, they believed, just appeared on rotting meat, and they had no concept of how a maggot evolved into a larva and then a fly. They, including Denman, Smith and Nugent, expected the spontaneous generation of maggots on a body, but few (or, indeed, perhaps no one) until this time had exhumed a body that had been buried in an airtight coffin. We now know that, had air been present in the coffin, bacteria and the said maggots would have consumed the flesh of the body very quickly, leaving just a skeleton. The fact that the corpse was in an excellent state of preservation, no doubt a great shock to their expectations, proves that the coffin was airtight. The deterioration of the hand, though, is to be expected, as it was resting on the lower abdomen, where bacterial activity would have been most active until all the oxygen had been depleted. Being as it was completely sealed, nothing, not even bacteria, was alive when the coffin was first opened. With such dedication to detail of the evidence they presented, they hoped to convince their readers that they had exhumed John Hampden without further argument.

The letter was written to impress an uninformed general readership by offering them what they themselves would have expected a disinterred body to resemble. The Earl's letters remained private, while those to *The Gentlemen's Magazine* kept the readers ignorantly informed. Following the exhumation correspondence through *The Gentleman's Magazine* was relentless and overwhelming. Correspondents and pundits not present at the exhumation evolved their opinion from the article in *The Times*. Accusation

---

36   J. R. de la Torre Bueno, 'Francesco Redi and the Spontaneous Generation of Life (Note on a New 17th Century Accession to the Library)', *The Brooklyn Museum Quarterly*, 12:1 (1925), https://www.jstor.org/stable/26459525, pp.24–26.

and counteraccusation over the minutiae of the exhumation were examined, and judgements formed from this article. The Earl of Buckinghamshire came under particular censure. Allegations that his forebears were responsible for John Hampden's death and that he was covering up the story gained credence. Dr Grace and Mr Norris, the most reliable witnesses to the exhumation, had written to the Earl the day after the exhumation with what amounted to be an autopsy on the corpse, but this was private correspondence and not available to the readers of *The Gentleman's Magazine*. The story of Hampden's pistol exploding prevailed and entered historical folklore.

Rector George Brooks was forced to reply to a letter sent to *The Times* by Mr William J. Smith on 3 January 1863. It was Smith who had sent the bogus letter to *The Times* on 28 July 1828. Brooks sent a letter to the *Derby Mercury* on 21 January 1863 that included private correspondence to and from Dr James Grace and Lord Nugent.[37] Any lingering doubts of a pistol exploding being the cause of John Hampden's death and of grand funerals were finally squashed. Historians of the nineteenth century, after Nugent resurrected his account of the Battle of Chalgrove, went along with Edward Clough's narrative. John Hampden was not disinterred, but the myths surrounding the story were 'exhumed', and the story lived on.

---

37 British Newspaper Archive (BNA) BL_000052_18630121_042_0008.pdf. *Derby Mercury*, Derbyshire, England, Wednesday, 21 January 1863. See Appendix IX, Item 7, for text.

9

History and Propaganda

The Clarendon Press published *The History of the Rebellion and Civil Wars in England* in 1826. Reference is made in the footnotes to three manuscripts. These are MS C, MS B and MS – which may account for the statement on the title page, 'with all the suppressed passages'. A footnote on page 80 of volume IV of the 1826 edition has, 'The History is thus continued in MS.C:]'. Dunn Macray's 1888 edition has, 'while the MS. of the Hist. continues as follows:-*viz*', with exactly the same footnote as referred on page 80 of the 1826 edition.[1] In mid June 1643, Sir Edward Hyde wrote for his private journal, a diary he began in 1641, the exact text found in the footnotes of the 1826 and 1888 editions of *The History*.[2] It is deduced from the term 'Hist' that MS C is taken from *The History of the Rebellion* written by Hyde between 1646 and 1660 while in exile. The *JSAHR* published a case study that concluded, 'Clarendon's actual account of the Civil War, both militarily and politically, is still to be properly accessed and understood'.[3] Pages 80–106 of volume IV of the 1826 *The History* is verbatim text taken from pages 202–212 of volume II of the 1702 edition. On page 88 of the 1826 edition, reference is made to a footnote that states, 'This part of the History which is taken from MS. B. is thus contained in that Manuscript'. This footnote begins with 'Of which Mr Hambden was one'. The 1888 edition of *The History of the Rebellion* has an identically worded footnote as that found on page 88 of the 1826 edition: 'The *Hist*. is here resumed, at p.446, the *Life* continuing thus:- "– of which Mr. Hambden was one"'. A search of all three volumes of the published 1759 edition of *The Life* for keywords such as 'Hambden', which is identically found in the 1826 and 1888 editions' footnotes, failed to find the target words. The word 'Hambden' only occurs in *The Life*, volume I, pages 110 and 120, and then not in context. It follows that MS B is the manuscript of *The Life* that Sir Edward Hyde wrote while in exile in 1646–1660.

---

1   Hyde, *The History of the Rebellion* (1888), vol. III, pp.53–55, footnote 3. See Appendix I, Part Two, for text of the footnote found in Sir Edward Hyde's Private Journal.
2   BoL: MS. Clar. 112, f. 366: Sir Edward Hyde's Private Journal, 1641–1646.
3   Derek Lester, 'Clarendon and History: A Case Study of the Battle of Chalgrove, 18th June 1643', *Journal of the Society for Army Historical Research*, 99:397 (2021), p.151.

On page 83 of volume IV of the 1826 *The History*, in the page's text, is 'no enemy was expected, and so no guards were kept there', followed by a superscript 'r'. This exact wording is found in the 1702 edition, volume II, on page 202. The footnote 'r' on page 83 in the 1826 edition reads, 'no enemy was expected, and so no guards were kept there] they expected no enemy, and so kept no guards there'. The first part of this reference is as per the 1702 edition. The footnote 'r' refers to a change from the manuscript that went into the publication of the 1702 edition. The footnote states that the manuscript had, 'they expected no enemy, and so kept no guards there' – a subtle difference from 'no enemy was expected, and so no guards were kept there'. It therefore follows that the 'MS' referred in the 1826 edition are the documents that went into the compilation of the 1702 edition of *The History of the Rebellion*. This assumption is confirmed by the statements in the preface of *The Life* published in 1759.[4] On *The Life*'s title page, it states, 'An account of the Chancellor's Life from his Birth to the Restoration' and 'A Continuation of the same, and of his History of the Grand Rebellion, from the Restoration to his Banishment in 1667, "Written By Himself" and printed from his Original Manuscripts'. The preface has:

> TO this our noble Benefactress have thought fit to prefix, as a First Part, THE HISTORY OF THE EARL OF CLARENDON'S LIFE, FROM HIS BIRTH, TO THE YEAR 1660, extracted from another Manuscript of Lord Clarendon's own Hand-writing. This other Manuscript is entitled by his Lordship, THE HISTORY OF HIS OWN LIFE, and contains likewise the Substance of THE HISTORY OF THE REBELLION. However, it is not the Manuscript from whence that History was printed, but appears rather to be the rough Draught from whence that History, or however great Part of it, was afterwards compiled. For although He tells us towards the Close of this Work, that He wrote the first four Books of THE HISTORY OF THE REBELLION in the Island of Jersey, (many Years before the Date of this HISTORY OF HIS LIFE) yet He likewise informs us, that He did not proceed to compleat [sic] that History till after his Banishment. It is therefore supposed by the Family (and the Supposition seems to carry with it great Probability) that, seeing an unjust and cruel Persecution prevail against him, He was induced at that Time to extend the original Plan of his Work, by introducing the particular History of his own Life, from his earliest Days down to the Time of his Disgrace, as the most effectual Means of vindicating his Character.[5]

The Bodleian Library states on its website, '3. The manuscript of Clarendon's *History of the Rebellion* (in seven volumes) from which the first edition was

---

4   Edward Hyde, *The Life of Edward Earl of Clarendon, Lord High Chancellor of England and Chancellor of the University of Oxford. Containing, 1. An Account of the Chancellor's Life from his Birth to the Restoration in 1660. II. A Continuation of the same, and of his History of the Grand Rebellion, from the Restoration to his Banishment in 1667* (Oxford: Clarendon Printing-House, 1759), vol. I.

5   Hyde, *The Life*, vol. I, pp.III–IV.

printed in 1702–1704 at Oxford'.⁶ The point that needs to be made, however, is that the account published by Lawrence Hyde and all subsequent editions based upon it do not reflect Clarendon's original narrative. As extrapolated from above, *The History of the Rebellion* is a compendium of propaganda that gained in the telling. Subsequent publications of *The History*, of which there were many and composed by authors from all corners of the British Empire, added further spurious details. The Bodleian's website confirms and adds to the point, stating, 'In 1667 his enemies procured his impeachment, and Clarendon fled to the Continent, where he set himself to literary labour, revising and competing [*sic*] his *History of the Rebellion* (which he had begun in 1646), writing his autobiography, and composing essays and meditations on political and religious subjects, until his death at Rouen on 9 December 1674', as recounted in the 1759 *The Life*'s preface.⁷ Sir Edward Hyde began writing his *The History of the Rebellion* in 1646, using his extensive private journal and personal experience to compose the first four books. 'He was there', biographers of the English Civil War recite when quoting from the published editions of *The History of the Rebellion*. He was there for the first English Civil War and, on that subject, wrote four volumes. Edward, Earl of Clarendon, as the Bodleian cites, spent his time after he fled to the Continent completing *The History of the Rebellion*. While the second and third Civil Wars were fought, Sir Edward Hyde was evading his enemies. In the later period of the Commonwealth, Hyde became involved in the negotiations for the Restoration of King Charles II. Sir Edward Hyde was definitely not 'there' during 1646–1660, yet, 20 or more years later, he wrote three volumes to complete *The History of the Rebellion*.

After his death in Rouen, 1674, Clarendon's manuscripts were returned to England. In the intervening 28 years to the publication of the 1702–1704 *The History of the Rebellion*, attempts were made to collate Clarendon's work, including his autobiography. It transpires that *The History of the Rebellion and Civil Wars in England* published in 1702–1704 is a mishmash of documents, propaganda and invention cobbled together, and it is this compilation of documents to which the term 'MS' refers. Like the curate's egg, parts of the 1702 edition of *The History* are excellent, but those tracts that are rotten skewed the historical record. The contents of Sir Edward Hyde's private journal may never have been examined except for those pages that he chose to put into his *The History of the Rebellion* that he compiled while in exile. Various publications of *The History of the Rebellion* have been catalogued since the 1800s as Clarendon State Papers – *The History of the Rebellion*. Hyde's private journal is catalogued as Clarendon State Papers but is not recognised as a description of events of the English Civil War. The journal was found because the archivists were asked to locate the source of a page of text handed to them. The description of the Battle of Chalgrove from Hyde's private journal is contrary to that of the 1702 edition of *The History of Rebellion and Civil Wars in England*. The 1702 edition has a number of

---

6   Bodleian Library (BoL) Clarendon State Papers – Repositories 7567, Biographical and Historical.
7   BoL: Clarendon State Papers – Repositories 7567, Biographical and Historical.

fundamental errors and inaccuracies, including a statement that, on 18 June 1643 and prior to the Battle of Chalgrove, the Royalists attacked Wickham. In volume II, page 204, of the 1702 edition – and identically in the 1826 (volume IV, page 88) and 1888 (volume III, page 59) editions – is the first reference to 'One of the prisoners taken in the action said, that he was confident Mr Hambden was hurt, for he saw him ride off the Field before the Action was done, which he never used to do, with his head hanging down, and resting his hands upon the neck of his Horse; by which he concluded he was hurt'. The inane nature of this statement determines that it was written by someone who had little understanding of seventeenth-century Civil War etiquette. Officers or soldiers who deserted the battlefield in the face of the enemy faced the death penalty. It is from this statement that the fictitious Mr Edward Clough expanded upon the scene as if he were by Hampden's side from the moment he was shot.

Lady Charlotte Capell (b. 1721) was the daughter of William Capell (1697–1743) and Lady Jane Hyde. Lady Capell married, in March 1752, Thomas Villiers (1709–1786) and, through the 'Hyde' connection, inherited Clarendon's manuscripts. Whether Villiers referenced Clarendon's papers in writing his adaption of *The Life* is an open question. Clarendon's manuscripts were sold piecemeal to the highest bidder. It was historians' fortune that the Bodleian Library was able to repurchase these papers. The Clarendon Press were later given the monumental task of editing the re-acquired documents and, in 1826, published *The History of the Rebellion* – 'with all the suppressed passages'. Thomas Villiers was created 1st Baron Hyde of Hindon, county of Wiltshire, in June 1756. George Grenville became prime minister in 1763, and, in the same year, Villiers became postmaster general and was admitted to the Privy Council. He served as chancellor of the Duchy of Lancaster from 1771 and, in June 1776, was invested as 1st Earl of Clarendon of the second creation. From the proceeds of the sale of *The Life*, Villiers built The Grove, a palace fit for a King's visit, which has become an exclusive five-star hotel by the same name. When requesting Sir Edward Hyde's autobiography of his life, the reader is offered *The Life* published by Thomas Villiers in 1759. In the preface of *The Life*, Villiers stated that Sir Edward Hyde's account of his life, his autobiography, 'is very incorrect' (note the author's comments in brackets):

> THE original Manuscript of THE CONTINUATION OF LORD CHANCELLOR CLARENDON'S LIFE FROM 1660 TO 1667 INCLUSIVE is very incorrect, [Clarendon's autobiography is incorrect?] many Words being omitted, [From what document are words being omitted if taken from the original?] that must necessarily be supplied: But it is desired that no other Alterations may be made, except in the Orthography, or where literal, or grammatical Errors require it, or where little Inaccuracies may have escaped the Attention of the Author. The Work must be printed entire, as it now stands, no Part of it left out, not an Abstract, nor a Reference omitted.[8]

---

8   Hyde, *The Life*, vol. I, p.V.

In summary, the above complicated treatise reveals that MS C is *The History of the Rebellion* written by Sir Edward Hyde while in exile after 1646. Hyde had kept a private journal (diary) from 1641 to chronicle events on the day that they happened. Hyde used this journal as an aide-mémoire to write his account of *The History of the Rebellion* of the first English Civil War. MS B is, as referred to by Thomas Villiers, *The History of His Own Life* penned during Hyde's first time in exile. It will probably be found that items were taken from his private journal for *The History of His Own Life*. None of the above items has ever been published. The term 'MS' refers to the compilation of various documents that went into the publication of *The History of the Rebellion* (1702–1704). On the title page of the 1702 *The History*, it states, 'Written by Edward Earl of Clarendon' – Clarendon died on 9 December 1674 in Rouen. This attribution was an embellishment to the publication that was endorsed by Queen Anne. She conferred for the authors by royal decree perpetual copyright for *The History of the Rebellion*, a term that decreed that subsequent publications had to be attributed to Clarendon. Thomas Villiers' publication, the 1759 *The Life of Edward Earl of Clarendon*, cleverly circumnavigates the edict of perpetual copyright with an ambiguous statement on the title page, 'Written by Himself'. Edward Earl of Clarendon, lord chancellor to Charles II (1660–1667), was forced into exile. Thomas Villiers reveals that, while in exile, Clarendon completed his autobiography and added three volumes to his *The History of the Rebellion* that he began in 1646. These papers form part of the vast collection of Clarendon State Papers but are, at this moment, lost to history, the contents appropriated in other works by those with their own agenda.

Argument that the *The History of the Rebellion* was written by Edward Earl of Clarendon is dispelled by the publication of *The History of England, During the Reigns of the Royal House of Stuart* by John Oldmixon in 1730. The title page of *The History of England* is an accusation of conspiracy against famous writers who oversaw the change from the reign of the Stuarts to the Hanoverians. The preface is more damning than the words of title page that in polite terms accuses the writers of lying is reproduced under:

> Wherein the errors of the late histories are discovered and corrected; with proper reflections, and several original letters from King Charles II, King James II and Oliver Cromwell. As also the Lord Saville's famous forged letter of invitation, which brought the Scots into England in the year 1640, and gave occasion to the beginning of the Civil Wars.
>
> This letter being never before published, led the Earl of Clarendon, Bishop Burney, Mr Echard, Dr Welwood and other writers, into egregious mistakes upon this head.
>
> To all when is prefixed some account of the liberties taken with Clarendon's History before it came to press, such liberties as make it doubtful, what part of it is Clarendon's, and what not.

Edward Hyde (later Earl of Clarendon) wrote *The History of the Rebellion* following his exile in 1646, and these papers became a small part of Clarendon's estate when he died, in December 1674. The liberties to which

THE HISTORY OF ENGLAND,

During the REIGNS of the

Royal House of STUART.

WHEREIN

The ERRORS of LATE HISTORIES are Discover'd and Corrected;

With PROPER REFLECTIONS,

And several ORIGINAL LETTERS from King CHARLES II. King JAMES II. OLIVER CROMWELL, &c.

As also the Lord SAVILLE'S Famous *Forg'd Letter* of Invitation, which brought the *Scots* into *England* in the Year 1640;

And gave Occasion to the Beginning of the CIVIL WARS.

This LETTER being never before publish'd, led the Earl of CLARENDON, Bishop BURNET, Mr. ECHARD, Dr. WELWOOD, and other Writers, into Egregious MISTAKES upon this Head.

To all which is Prefix'd,

Some Account of the *Liberties* taken with CLARENDON'S HISTORY before it came to the Press, such *Liberties* as make it Doubtful,

What Part of it is CLARENDON'S, and what Not.

The whole Collected from the most AUTHENTICK MEMOIRS, *Manuscript* and *Printed*.

By the Author of the CRITICAL HISTORY of ENGLAND.

LONDON:

Printed for JOHN PEMBERTON, in *Fleetstreet*; RICHARD FORD, RICHARD HETT, and JOHN GRAY, in the *Poultry*; and THOMAS COX, under the *Royal-Exchange*.

M.DCC.XXX.

HISTORY AND PROPAGANDA

Oldmixon refers are the exploitation of Clarendon's name, reputation and authority as an eyewitness to the Civil War while at King Charles I's side. Oldmixon's 'liberties as make it doubtful, what part of it is Clarendon's, and what not' are the inclusion of nonsensical fiction and propaganda. An entry from the preface cannot be left without an example of its content:

Facing page: John Oldmixon's 1730 publication.

> I have, in more than one 'Place of this History, mentioned the great reason there is to suspect that the *History of the Rebellion*, as it was published at Oxford, was not entirely the work of Lord Clarendon, who did indeed write a History of those Times, and I doubt not a very good one; wherein as I have been, I believe, well informed, the Characters of the Kings, whose Reigns are here written, were very different from what they appear in the Oxford History, and its Copy, Mr. Echard's. I speak this by hearsay; but Hearsay from a Person superior to all suspicion, and too illustrious to be named without leave.
>
> I also refer it to the Decision of another very honourable Person, whether there is not, to his knowledge, such a History in Manuscript still extant; and to a Reverend Doctor now living, whether he did see the Oxford Copy, by which the Book was printed, altered, and interpolated, while it was at Press. To which I must add, that there is now in custody of a Gentleman of Distinction, both of Merit and Quality, a *History of the Rebellion* of the first Folio Edition, scored in many places by Mr. Edmund Smith of Christ-Church, Oxon.

Laurence Echard invented the story of John Hampden's pistol exploding in his hand at the battle of Chalgrove, the same story that Sir Horace Walpole reinvented in 1761 and which caused the attempted exhumation of John Hampden's body in July 1828. The other writers mentioned were equally partizan with inventions of their own. *The History of England, During the Reigns of the Royal House of Stuart* was an early exposure of *The History of the Rebellion* as fiction and propaganda. Historians who still hold Clarendon's 1702–1704 publication as a fundamental source for the history of the Civil War and the supreme authority, and there are many in high places, have need to take into account Oldmixon's early publication.

The Gentleman's Magazine in May 1815 published a letter from a Mr Stoneleigh, signed by 'A'. The letter offered the words of a supposed seventeenth-century document, *A true and faithful Narrative of the Death of Master Hampden, who was mortally wounded at Chalgrove Fight, Ann. Dom 1643 and on the 18th day of June*.[9] This document was said to be the words of an eyewitness, namely Edward Clough, who was supposedly present by John Hampden's deathbed to hear his last prayer and dying breath. The said document, *A true and faithful Narrative*, does not carry the name, for instance, of the Committee of Safety to give the pamphlet the authority to be published. The said Edward Clough reported of Hampden's last breath, "'… Oh Lord, be merciful to…" Here his speech failed, and he fell back on the bed, and to the greate griefe of all good men, gave up the ghoste, after having with more than

---

9   BNA: 'Letter from Mr Urban, Stoneleigh, March 26', *The Gentleman's Magazine and Historical Chronicle*, vol. 85, part 1, 1815, pp.395–96. See Appendix II for text.

humane fortitude indured most cruel anguish for the space of 15 dayes'.[10] The pretense that *A true and faithful Narrative* is an eyewitness account is shown to be fiction. Hampden died six days after his wounding on 24 June 1643, not 3 July 1643. Between 1702 and 1704, Lawrence Hyde published *The History of the Rebellion and Civil Wars in England* in three volumes. Volume II recounts incorrectly the story of how the Royalists attacked Wickham on 18 June 1643.[11] The anonymous Edward Clough reiterated this error. Lord Nugent was enthralled by Mr Stoneleigh, the said writer of the letter, but there was something of the night about this gentleman. Clough reported, 'he received two carabine shott in his arme, which brake the bone; yet, being thus wounded, he would not presentlie leave the fielde, seeming regardless of paine and greate letting of bloode manfullie saying, "he would not onlie loose his arme, but lay downe his life in that good cause he was ingaged in"'.[12] Volume II of *The History of the Rebellion* adds, 'with his head hanging down, and resting his hands upon the neck of his Horse; by which he concluded he was hurt'.[13]

In volume II of *Some Memorials*, Nugent's poetic licence brought these stories together.[14] Hampden looked towards Pyrton, where 'he had in youth married the first wife of his love, and thither he would have gone to die', Nugent wrote. Upon leaving the Chalgrove battlefield, Clough told of Hampden's difficult journey to Mr Ezekiel Browne's house but left it for Nugent to tell that this abode was in Thame. Edward Clough was by Hampden's bedside, so he claimed, remaining vigil over him through his '15' days of agony to hear the priest give the last rites and his last prayer and dying breath.[15] The redoubtable Mr Clough supposedly escorted the coffin, with Hampden's regiment singing the 90th Psalm to the church and the 43rd on the regiment's return. The document fails to mention to which church the coffin was taken or to where the regiment returned. This story was told in *The Gentleman's Magazine* for May 1815.[16] John Hampden's heroic actions as described in *The History* and Clough's interpretation of events are the mainstay of information that Nugent used for *Some Memorials*. Lord Nugent, the extreme radical Whig politician, extolled Hampden's virtues from the pulpit of his Aylesbury constituency, which was easily overheard by the Earl of Buckinghamshire in Great Hampden. It is unclear when Nugent began to research material for his book, *Some Memorials*, that would be published in 1832. By virtue of Nugent's association with Stowe House, he was acquainted

---

10 BNA: 'Letter from Mr Urban, Stoneleigh, March 26', *The Gentleman's Magazine and Historical Chronicle*, vol. 85, part 1, 1815, pp.395–96.

11 Hyde, *The History of the Rebellion* (1702–1704), vol. II, book VII, pp.202–04.

12 BNA: 'Letter from Mr Urban, Stoneleigh, March 26', *The Gentleman's Magazine and Historical Chronicle*, vol. 85, part 1, 1815, pp.395–96.

13 Hyde, *The History of the Rebellion* (1702–1704), vol. II, book VII, p.204.

14 Nugent, *Some Memorials* (1832), vol. II, p.435.

15 BNA: 'Letter from Mr Urban, Stoneleigh, March 26', *The Gentleman's Magazine and Historical Chronicle*, vol. 85, part 1, 1815, pp.395–96.

16 See Appendix II.

with Sir Robert Walpole's (1686–1745) attempt to discredit John Hampden's name and reputation with the exploding pistol story. The principal reason for the attempted exhumation of John Hampden was to disprove this account of his death. Henry John Pye (1802–1884) came of age in 1823, and it may have been then that Nugent learnt that the story of the exploding pistol had resurfaced and gave cause to examine the paper. Nugent stated in the first person that Henry John Pye gave him to study the commonplace book of his father, Henry James Pye (1745–1813). A commonplace book was a household's diary that chronicled the family's important events. Within the pages, Nugent found reference to Hampden's death, 'In the St. James Chronicle for the year 1761', appertaining to the exploding pistol theory: 'That, at Chalgrove Field, his pistol burst, and shattered his hand'. Sir Horace Walpole (1717–1797) was at the height of his literary power in 1761. Nugent would be reading this account of the exploding pistol 70 years after its publication in the *St. James Chronicle*. The story in the commonplace book appears to be correct, in that the exploding pistol account is false. Nugent mentioning the story that is found in the *St. James Chronicle* for the year of 1761, its first year of publication, is too much of a coincidence to be false. It is possible that the *St. James Chronicle* commissioned Sir Horace Walpole for a grand headline for the first edition of its newspaper in 1761.[17]

In volume II of *Some Memorials*, Nugent described how 'He [John Hampden] was struck in the shoulder with two carabine balls'.[18] The footnote lists the contemporary sources from which the information was taken and continues with 'There is a groundless story'. This groundless story was one of political intrigue devised by Sir Robert Walpole and told by Laurence Echard (1670–1730) in *The History of England*.[19] The issue of the exploding pistol was never resolved, for it was told to cause damage to Walpole's political enemies. The argument was bilateral: either John Hampden's hand was shattered by the exploding pistol, or he was shot in the shoulder with two carabine balls. It could not be both. It is reasonable to argue that, if it can be shown, as Nugent endeavoured to do by listing the contemporary sources, that Hampden was shot in the shoulder, then the exploding pistol account is false. Nugent presumed, as was reasonable, that his account of two carabine balls being shot into Hampden's shoulder had been proved beyond reasonable doubt and negated the exploding pistol theory. It is reasonable to believe that Nugent was aware of the origin of the 'groundless story', being as he was so close to the events that occurred around Stowe House. Nugent was probably referring to Echard's account in *The History of England* as the 'story told, upon the authority of a nameless paper, by Horace Walpole, and by Echard'.[20] Credulity is being stretched to suggest that the 13-year-old Horace Walpole met Laurence Echard, who died in 1730, and composed a 'groundless story'. Horace Walpole's father, Sir Robert Walpole, was the authority whom Echard

---

17 See Appendix IV.
18 Nugent, *Some Memorials* (1832), vol. II, pp.433–34.
19 Echard, *The History of England*, vols I–III and Appendix of Errata.
20 See Appendix IV.

referred to, being the person in the phrase 'I am assur'd by a great man' who provided and falsely authenticated the exploding pistol story.[21]

Lord Nugent's research came to the notice of the 5th Earl of Buckinghamshire, who had inherited Hampden Estates in 1824. The Earl's detractors found ways to question him, and the story grew so much that the Earl invited Lord Nugent to Hampden House.[22] Dr James Grace, the Earl's steward, found the entry of John Hampden's burial, dated 25 June 1643, in Great Hampden's parish church register.[23] Agreement was reached that, to settle the argument of whether John Hampden's pistol exploded or he was shot in the back, the body had to be exhumed. The exhumation at Great Hampden that followed was a fiasco, and, whatever the motive, an anonymous letter was sent to *The Times*. The letter, an absolute fabrication, was a sensation and was published throughout the British Empire.[24] Four years later, in 1832, Lord Nugent published *Some Memorials of John Hampden, His Party and His Times*. Within its pages, there is no mention of the exhumation. Whether Nugent realised that Edward Clough's narrative was the figment of someone's imagination is unclear.

Clough's narrative states that Hampden died 15 days after the battle, which the entry in the parish register shows is incorrect. Clough's vivid description of Hampden's regiment marching 'with ensignes furled and muffled drums their heads uncovered' fails to mention Great Hampden Church.[25] Nugent's description is equally uninspiring; he only alluded to Great Hampden as the burial place with the words 'They followed him to his grave in the parish church close adjoining his mansion'.[26] Nugent not only quoted from Clough's narrative, which he cited for the description of Hampden's wounding and journey to Master Ezekiel Browne's house, but also cited *A true and faithful Narrative of the Death of Master Hampden* as being the source.[27] Nugent added, 'In great pain, and almost fainting, he reached Thame', citing *Parliament Scout*.[28] By this citation, Nugent joined Clough's narrative to his own research.

On the morning when Chinnor was raided, Hampden's regiment was in its quarters at Watlington. Essex, in a letter to the Speaker dated 19 June 1643, wrote that 'the Alarm came where Major *Gunter* lay with three Troops

---

21 Echard, *The History of England*, Appendix of Errata, p.572.

22 BA: D/MH 39/88: Letter fragment from Dr James Grace to the Earl of Buckinghamshire, March 1828.

23 BA: D/MH 39/87: Letter fragment from Dr James Grace to the Earl of Buckinghamshire, early June 1828.

24 See Appendix V.

25 BNA: 'Letter from Mr Urban, Stoneleigh, March 26', *The Gentleman's Magazine and Historical Chronicle*, vol. 85, part 1, 1815, pp.395–96.

26 Nugent, *Some Memorials* (1832), vol. II, p.440, cites Clough's narrative as the source.

27 Nugent, *Some Memorials* (1832), vol. II, p.436.

28 BrL: TT, E 96 (10): The Parliament Scout, Communicating His Intelligence to the Kingdome, From Tuesday the 20. June, to Tuesday the 27. of June 1643, no. 1.

[at Aston Rowant]'.[29] Essex stated, 'Colonel *Hampden* being abroad with *Sir Samuel Luke* and only one man and seeing Major *Gunters* Forces they did go along with them'.[30] John Hampden was, prior to the skirmish at South Weston, in the area close by.[31] Lord Nugent stated that 'he [Hampden] had, the evening before [the battle], repaired, and had lain that night in Watlington. On the first alarm of Rupert's irruption, he sent off a trooper to the Lord General in Thame'.[32] At the Battle of Chalgrove, John Hampden was without his officers and men. Nugent said, 'Some of his friends would have dissuaded him from adventuring his person with the cavalry'. Nugent would have us believe that, leaving his officers and men in Watlington, 'He [Hampden] instantly mounted, with a troop of Captain Sheffield's horse …' and rode to Chalgrove.[33] Nugent described, in his own words, the skirmish prior to the battle as 'by several charges to harass and impede the retreat, until Lord Essex should have had time to make his dispositions at the river'. Reading from the *Late Beating Up* and Essex's *Two Letters*, Nugent plucked key phrases from each document and melded them into an account of the encounter at Chalgrove.

Nugent's interpretation of the Battle of Chalgrove is as follows (note the author's comments in brackets):

> On Chalgrove Field, the Prince overtook a regiment of infantry, [the infantry and dragoons were a mile ahead of the cavalry] and here, among the standing corn, which covered a plain of several hundred acres, then as now, unenclosed, he drew up in order of battle. Gunter, now joining three troops of horse and one of dragoons who were advancing from Easington and Thame, over Golder Hill, came down among the enclosures facing the right of the Prince's line, along a hedge-row which still forms the boundary on that side of Chalgrove Field. [The precise location of where Parliament came to the boundary hedge has been identified.] The Prince with his life guards and some dragoons being in their front, [Nugent was unaware that dragoons are infantry and a race apart from the cavalry; they did not fight together] the fight began with several fierce charges. [This implies that the Royalists flew over the 20-foot-high hedge out of Chalgrove Field.] And now Colonel Neale [*sic*] and General Percy coming up, with the Prince's left wing, on their flank, Gunter was slain and his party gave way.[34]

John Hampden's monument, which Lord Nugent had raised, is a mile away across the fields. Nugent placed an advertisement in *The Aylesbury News* on 27 May 1843 for a dinner to take place on Chalgrove Field, 'at which John Hampden received his death wound and of the dedication of a monument to be unveiled in that place to the memory of Hampden'. The

---

29 BrL: TT, E 55 (19): *Two Letters*.
30 BrL: TT, E 55 (19): *Two Letters*.
31 Lester, 'Military and Political Importance', pp.34–35.
32 Nugent, *Some Memorials* (1832), vol. II, p.431.
33 Nugent, *Some Memorials* (1832), vol. II, p.431.
34 Nugent, *Some Memorials* (1832), vol. II, pp.432–33.

monument bears the inscription, 'WITHIN IN A FEW PACES OF THIS SPOT HE RECEIVED THE WOUND OF WHICH HE DIED'. 'One can't believe impossible things', Lewis Carroll wrote, but historians that accept Nugent's account that Hampden 'had lain that night in Watlington' failed to heed Carroll's advice.[35] Lord Macaulay was a renowned British historian and essayist who became a Whig political reformer and MP at the time that Nugent was a Lord of the Treasury. Nugent and Macaulay were extreme Whig reformers who were closely associated politically in demanding reform. Macaulay reviewed Lord Nugent's *Some Memorials* in glowing terms and reiterated the fictitious testament of Edward Clough's narrative referring to Hampden's death and funeral.[36] In 1847, Lord Nugent published *A Worthy Discourse between Colonel John Hampden and Colonel Oliver Cromwell*.[37]

It is supposedly 'A True and Faithful Relation' of Dr William Spurstow's 1647 publication that purported to be a verbatim account of a worthy discourse that was said to have taken place at Chequers on 11 June 1643. Lord Nugent's *A Worthy Discourse* was uncovered, after his death, as a forgery. The third edition of Lord Nugent's *Some Memorials*, published in 1854, four years after his death, is preceded with a *Memoir of Lord Nugent*. The memoir has, 'The discourse is supposed to have been overheard and reported by an Independent divine … It was one of those clever imitations of the political oratorical literature … Lord Nugent took great delight in the success with which he was able, by means of a copy elaborately stained with tobacco-juice, to pass it to his uncle, Mr Thomas Grenville'.[38] Nugent's oratorical literature in *A Worthy Discourse* is a continuation and embellishment of the fictitious Edward Clough's narrative published in *The Gentleman's Magazine* for May 1815.[39] *A Worthy Discourse*, *The History of the Rebellion*, *Memoirs of Prince Rupert* and Lord Nugent's *Some Memorials* are discredited accounts that form the basis of the twentieth and twenty-first centuries' authoritative interpretations of the Battle of Chalgrove. The fourth edition of Lord Nugent's *Some Memorials*, published 1860, has a memoir with the 'political oratorical literature' as found in the third edition.[40] The fifth edition, published in 1889, has a *Memoir of Lord Nugent*, which demotes Nugent from a historian to a novelist.[41]

---

35 Nugent, *Some Memorials* (1832), vol. II, p.431.

36 Lord Thomas Babington Macaulay, *Lord Macaulay's Essays and Lays of Ancient Rome* (Authorised edition, London: Longmans, Green and Co., 1885), pp.190–220.

37 Nugent, *Tract Entitled True and Faithful Relation of a Worthy Discourse*.

38 Lord George Nugent, *Some Memorials of John Hampden, His Party and His Times*, 3rd edn, revised, with a memoir of the writer (London: Chapman and Hall, 1854), p.lxvi.

39 BNA: 'Letter from Mr Urban, Stoneleigh, March 26', *The Gentleman's Magazine and Historical Chronicle*, vol. 85, part 1, 1815, pp.395–96.

40 Lord George Nugent, *Memorials of John Hampden, his party and his times*, 4th edn, with a memoir of the writer (London: H. G. Bohn, 1860).

41 Lord George Nugent, *Some Memorials of John Hampden, His Party and His Times*, 5th edn (London: George Bell and Sons, 1889).

True and faythfull Relationn of a worthye discourse, helde, June y̆ᵉ eleauenth, *in y̆ᵉ yeare of Grace* 1643, *betwene y̆ᵉ late* Colonell HAMPDEN, *Knighte of y̆ᵉ Shire for y̆ᵉ Countye of* Buckingham, *in y̆ᵉ p'sente Parliament, and* Colonell OLIUER CROMWEL, *Burgeſſe in y̆ᵉ ſame for y̆ᵉ Towne of* Cambridge.

Onn y̆ᵉ twentye fifth daye of *June*, 1643, I, *William Spurſtowe*, Miniſter of y̆ᵉ Worde, followed to y̆ᵉ Graue my moſte reuered friend and benefactor, Maſter *John Hampden*, who departed this life on y̆ᵉ 23ᵈ of y̆ᵉ ſayd moneth; Lorde of y̆ᵉ mannour of his name, and Colonell of foot in y̆ᵉ Armie of y̆ᵉ Earle of Eſſex, His

First page of *A Worthy Discourse*. (By the kind permission of the Bodleian Library)

Eliot Warburton (1810–1852) was renowned as a travel writer, having toured eastern Europe and the Middle East. He published *Zoe: An Episode of the Greek War* before embarking on *Memoirs of Prince Rupert, and the Cavaliers*. The publication *Memoirs of Prince Rupert* (1849) was compiled by condensing extracts of the Earl of Clarendon's *The History of the Rebellion* and Lord Nugent's *Some Memorials*. When Warburton undertook to write *Memoirs of Prince Rupert*, the credibility of the above publications was in question. Intertwined into the book's text is private correspondence, which volume I has an 'Alphabetical List of Writers'.[42] Following the list of writers is the statement 'The list comprises only the writers in Prince Rupert's own Correspondence, as preserved in the Benett Family'. Warburton's research for *Memoirs of Prince Rupert* used the notes reportedly of a Colonel Thomas Bennett from the English Civil War. It was reported in July 1646 at a Compounding sitting that a 'John Bennett of Pithouse' was compounded.[43] Thomas Bennett owned Pythouse in 1646.[44] The compound refers to (John) Thomas Bennett as 'a Trooper and in the Kings service in a Regiment of horse under the command of Colonel Strangewayes'.[45] The documents attributed to the Colonel were compiled possibly by his granddaughter Patience. She had married into the 'Benett' (one 'n') family and moved back into Pythouse, her grandfather's old residence. The reference in the archive clearly states, 'notes compiled towards a work on Prince Rupert … used by Warburton for his *Memoirs of Prince Rupert*'.[46] Warburton cited these papers variously as Prince Rupert's papers – 'Benett MS' and several times after as 'Prince Rupert's Diary' – to give gravitas to contentious items. Warburton cited 'Prince Rupert's Diary' many times, but this document does not exist and has never existed. Eliot Warburton's work as a historian is entirely discredited. Warburton reiterated Nugent's description of the Battle of Chalgrove near verbatim. He described Hampden's mortal wounding and his tortuous journey to Thame in the words of Edward Clough, but he cited a renamed *Some Memorials* as 'Lord Nugent's Life of Hampden'.[47] Warburton attributed and cited Lord Nugent himself as being the author of a passage out of Edward Clough's narrative that was said to have taken place by Hampden's bedside seven hours before he died.[48] Warburton's publication *Memoirs of Prince Rupert* is an excellent novel but cannot be taken as being historically accurate. 'Prince Rupert's Diary' is on record as a forgery but has been accepted in good faith by academia as being historically accurate.

---

42 Warburton, *Memoirs of Prince Rupert*, vol. I, p.473.
43 The National Archives (TNA) SP 23/185, f. 240.
44 Henry St George and Sampson Lennard, 'Bennett. [Harl. 1166, fo. 34ᵇ.]', in John P. Rylands (ed.), *The Visitation of the County of Dorset, Taken in the Year 1623* (London: Harleian Society, 1885), p.14.
45 TNA: SP 23/185, f. 240.
46 WSRO: 413/444 Personal 11.
47 Nugent, *Some Memorials* (1832), vol. II, pp.438–41.
48 Warburton, *Memoirs of Prince Rupert*, vol. II, p.208.

Professor Sir Charles Firth (1857–1936), the renowned nineteenth-century historian, wrote to *The Academy* on 2 and 9 November 1889.[49] In one letter, Firth cast doubt on the veracity of Clarendon's *The History of the Rebellion and Civil Wars in England*. Fifteen years later, Firth remarked that Clarendon's work was of 'treacherous foundation', his memory of 'very varying degrees of trustworthiness' and his accounts of the 'Army Plot' in early 1642 and attempted arrest of the five members 'are disingenuous and inaccurate'. Firth added that Clarendon '... cannot avoid relating these episodes, but he minimises their importance, mis-states their history, and conceals their connexion with the general policy of the king and the progress of the breach between king and parliament'.[50] In the other letter, Firth declared Edward Clough's narrative of Hampden's last days, found in *The Gentleman's Magazine* for May 1815, a nineteenth-century forgery.[51] What treasures of truth are there to be found in Sir Edward Hyde's private journal, which probably has his recollection of events written on the day in question?

Reverend Frederick George Lee DD (Doctor of Divinity) FSA (1832–1902) was born in Thame. He attended Lord William's School in Thame High Street, where John Hampden was schooled 200 years earlier. Lee was an antiquarian and great writer. He published *The History, Description, and Antiquities of the Prebendal Church of the Blessed Virgin Mary of Thame*, and within its pages is a tract referring to John Hampden.[52] His account of how the enemies came to be at Chalgrove is bizarre. Lee's style of writing can be described as inventive and opinionated. Lee was a contemporary of Mr William Smith, the gentleman who was present with Nugent at the exhumation. It was Smith who wrote the malicious letter to *The Times*, from which Lee modelled his account of the encounter at Chalgrove. Added into this mix was Nugent's account in *Some Memorials* and Edward Clough's narrative found in *The Gentleman's Magazine* for May 1815. Lee added to Clough's supposed eyewitness account and report of John Hampden's last words and instructions to Parliament, his last prayer being entirely different to Clough's. According to Lee, Dr William Spurstow, the chaplain of Hampden's regiment, 'fortified him in his political obstinacy and religious errors, and gave him what they termed "the Lord's Supper"'.

---

49 Conrad Russell, 'Hampden, John (1594–1643)', *Oxford Dictionary of National Biography* (2008), https://doi.org/10.1093/ref:odnb/12169.

50 Sir Charles Firth, 'Clarendon's "History of the Rebellion"', *The English Historical Review*, 19:73 (1904), pp.26, 37.

51 BNA: 'Letter from Mr Urban, Stoneleigh, March 26', *The Gentleman's Magazine and Historical Chronicle*, vol. 85, part 1, 1815, pp.395–96.

52 Frederick George Lee, *The History, Description, and Antiquities of the Prebendal Church of the Blessed Virgin Mary of Thame, in the County and Diocese of Oxford, Including a Transcript of All the Monumental Inscriptions Remaining Therein; Extracts from the Registers and Churchwardens' Books; Together with Divers Original Pedigrees, Copious Antiquarian, Architectural, Personal, and Genealogical Notes and Appendices, Relating to, and Illustrative of, the Town, its History, and Inhabitants: In Which is Included Some Account of the Abbey of Thame Park, the Grammar School, and the Ancient Chapelries of Towersey, Tettesworth, Sydenham, North Weston, and Rycott* (London: Mitchell and Hughes, 1883), column nos 538–43.

Clough's narrative invokes the first mention of Mr Ezekiel Browne and the circumstance of Hampden being taken to his house. Nugent added correctly of Hampden being taken to Thame but falsely that he 'was conducted to the house of one Mr Ezekiel Browne where, his wounds being dressed, the surgeons …', citing Clough as the source.

Lee's account of the wounded Hampden leaving the battlefield is that:

> … having ridden ten miles in intense pain, [Hampden] reached the Town of Thame. He rode straight for the Greyhound Inn, an old Hostel in the middle of Town on the north side of the street, which he had no doubt known well from boyhood. There his wounds were dressed by a local surgeon, Mr Ezekiel Browne, and there he died from the combined effects of the wound and the general shock to his system, on the 24th June.[53]

Lee added that the corpse was carried from the Market Place at Thame to Great Hampden and continued with Clough's narrative of muffled drums with arms reversed and singing the 90th Psalm as they reached the church. He then attacked those who had carried out the exhumation. Lee spoke erroneously of the vault being opened: lords of Great Hampden were buried in shallow graves in the chancel.

Reverend Lee should have read Numbers 32:23, which has, 'Behold if ye not do so, behold, ye have sinned against the Lord: and be sure your sin will find you out.' Lee's self-opinionated explanation of Hampden's last days allegedly in the Greyhound Inn is a deception unworthy of a man of the cloth; his act of corroborating Clough's fictitious document and Nugent's *A Worthy Discourse* and adding his fictional story of the Greyhound Inn is his sin that has been found out. In 1643, the Greyhound Inn was on the south side of High Street. In 1810, it is recorded that a Mr Wall moved the Greyhound Inn to the north side of High Street.[54]

A statue of John Hampden was raised in Market Square, Aylesbury, in 1911; it was here that Hampden mustered his regiment of Greencoats. One hundred years earlier, Lord Nugent became an MP and, from 1818–1832, served Aylesbury. Lord Nugent's contrived eulogy to John Hampden is encapsulated on the statue's column, with a plaque depicting his grand funeral. His coffin is shown being escorted to the door of St Mary Magdalene Church, Great Hampden, by his regiment and being received by Rector Robert Lenthall. Sir Charles Firth, regius professor of modern history at Oxford from 1904–1925, was evidently not consulted regarding the content of the plaque's validity. Hugh Ross Williamson published in 1933 a biography titled '*John Hampden: A Life*'.[55] Williamson was less than complimentary of Lord Nugent's work but used his interpretation to describe the events leading to the Battle of Chalgrove. John Drinkwater published *John Hampden's England* in 1933 and,

---

53 Lee, *History, Description, and Antiquities*, column nos 538–43.
54 Allan Hickman and David Bretherton, *Thame Inns Discovered II* (Thame: Daal Publishing, 2020), pp.21–22.
55 Hugh Ross Williamson, *John Hampden: A Life* (London: Hodder and Stoughton, 1933).

in the 'Notes', remarked, 'In writing this study, I have been constantly indebted to *Some Memorials of John Hampden his Party and his Times*, by George, Lord Nugent, published in 1831'.[56] In volume 38 of *Oxoniensia*, 'The Raid on Chinnor and the Fight at Chalgrove Field, June 17th and 18th, 1643', John Stevenson and Andrew Carter referred to Edward Clough's narrative without citing the source.[57] This article has, 'The alarm had also roused John Hampden, at Watlington'.[58] As stated earlier, Nugent's account that placed Hampden at Watlington on the day of the battle is entirely without foundation. Publications that reference Hampden being at Watlington on the morning of the battle reduce their writing's status to fiction.

Professor John Adair published *A Life of John Hampden, The Patriot, 1594–1643*, in which the selected bibliography cites John Drinkwater's *John Hampden's England*; Hugh Ross Williamson's *John Hampden*; W. Dunn Macray's 1888 edition of *The History of the Rebellion*; Lord Nugent's *Some Memorials* and Eliot Warburton's *Memoirs of Prince Rupert*.[59] Adair conjured John Hampden into the fray with obvious overtones to 'He instantly mounted' from Nugent's *Some Memorials*.[60] Adair wrote, 'Meanwhile Hampden and his borrowed troop, together with those of Major John Gunter and Captain James Sheffield'. Before Adair could finish writing *The Patriot*, the government announced that they had urgent business for him to attend that would take him out the country for an unspecified time. Chapter twelve, 'Chalgrove Fight', had to be written before Adair went away as the publisher's deadline was looming. Brigadier Peter Young had researched the Battle of Chalgrove for a book but was diverted to a greater prize, the Battle of Edgehill.[61] Adair, in conversation with the writer, admitted that research for chapter twelve was hurried in order to have his book ready for the publisher and had used Young's papers in order to finish his book. In debate with the writer about his research to counter English Heritage's downgrading of the Battle of Chalgrove, Adair acknowledged, 'you are probably right my boy, keep up the research'. After the publication of volume 80 of *Oxoniensia*, Adair, in email conversation, endorsed the writer's interpretation of the Battle of Chalgrove. English Heritage published a provisional register of battlefields that had a claim to being protected. English Heritage was minded to downgrade the Battle of Chalgrove Field to a skirmish. The provisional register cited John Stevenson and Andrew Carter's *Oxoniensia* article, John Adair's *The Patriot* and, with the exception of the *Late Beating Up*, English Heritage's interpretation of events based on Nugent. The Chalgrove Battle Group challenged English Heritage's interpretation, highlighting the impossibility of events posed by

---

56 John Drinkwater, *John Hampden's England* (London: Thornton Butterworth, 1933), p.11.
57 John Stevenson and Andrew Carter, 'The Raid on Chinnor and the Fight at Chalgrove Field, June 17th and 18th, 1643', *Oxoniensia*, 38 (1973), pp.346–56.
58 Stevenson and Carter, 'Raid on Chinnor', p.350.
59 Adair, *A Life of John Hampden*.
60 Nugent, *Some Memorials* (1832), vol. II, p.431.
61 Peter Young, 'National Army Museum: Unpublished papers, 9010-31-286: The Chalgrove Raid, 17–18 June, 1643', (Unpublished).

Nugent contained in the provisional register. The Chalgrove Battle Group sent a comprehensive report to an independent review panel that had been set up to adjudicate on such cases. The Chalgrove Battle Group's interpretation was accepted by the panel, which *English Heritage Battlefield Report: Chalgrove 1643* had to accommodate. The Chalgrove Battle Group's interpretation was accepted, but English Heritage did so in bad grace, preferring to restate, 'In strict terms of scale, Chalgrove Field was a skirmish … The fact that he was mortally wounded during the fight at Chalgrove may therefore be sufficient in itself to elevate the events at Chalgrove to a different plane'.[62] Evidence was presented to English Heritage that their *Battlefield Report: Chalgrove 1643* that had based its interpretation on Nugent was fundamentally flawed.

For nearly two centuries, academics have been aware that accounts of the English Civil War were subject to embellishment. In 1854, Lord Nugent was exposed as a fraud, a writer of novels rather than a historian. His work was vilified in 1854, 1860 and again in 1889 by the leading academic of the day, Sir Charles Firth. Sir Charles denounced Nugent as a fraud in an academic journal and further declared the Earl of Clarendon's *History of the Rebellion* to be of 'treacherous foundation'.[63] For over 100 years, Lord Nugent's account of the Battle of Chalgrove – backed by Clarendon's *The History of the Rebellion* – has been the accepted interpretation, its virtue endorsed by English Heritage. In volume 80 of *Oxoniensia* (2015), 'The Military and Political Importance of the Battle of Chalgrove (1643)' challenged the accepted interpretation of the battle.[64] The *JSAHR* published 'Clarendon and History: A Case Study of the Battle of Chalgrove, 18th June 1643'.[65] These articles put into the public domain that Clarendon's and Nugent's interpretations of the Battle of Chalgrove are based on false evidence. It is hoped that English Heritage will take note. *John Hampden and the Battle of Chalgrove* has explored Hampden's life and contribution to the historic record and revealed the detail of misinformation that went into *The History of Rebellion and Civil Wars in England* published in 1702. A comprehensive transcription and publication of the thousands of documents held in the Clarendon State Papers would be a massive task but one surely worth undertaking if John Hampden's true historical legacy as an eyewitness to events is to be appreciated.

---

62 English Heritage, *Battlefield Report: Chalgrove 1643*.
63 Sir Charles Firth, *The Academy*, 36 (9 November 1889).
64 Lester, 'Military and Political Importance', pp.27–39.
65 Lester, 'Clarendon and History', pp.134–51.

Appendix I

Book and Journal

Part One: *The History of the Rebellion* (1702–1704), Book VII, pp.202–203

This account of the Battle of Chalgrove is a compilation from several sources:

As soon as he returned, he made another proposition to the Prince for the attacking the Quarters near Thame; through which he had passed, when he came to Oxford, and so was well acquainted with the posture in which they were, and assured the Prince, that, if he went about it time enough, before there should be any alteration in their Quarters, which he believed the General would quickly make, the Enterprise would be worthy of it. The Prince was so well satisfied with what he had already done, that he resolved to conduct the next adventure himself, which he did very fortunately. They went out of the Ports of Oxford in the Evening upon a Saturday, and marched beyond all the Quarters as far as Wickham, and fell in there at the farther end of the Town towards London, from whence no Enemy was expected, and so no Guards were kept there. A Regiment of Horse, and of Foot, were lodged there; which were cut off, or taken Prisoners; and all the Horses and a good Booty brought away. From thence they marched backward to another Quarter, within less than two Miles of the General's own Quarters; where his Men lodged with the same security, they had done at Wickham, not expecting any Enemy that way; and so met with the fame fate the others had done; and were all killed, or made prisoners. Thus having performed, at least as much as they had proposed to do, and being laden with prisoners, and Booty, and the Sun being now rising, the prince thought it time to retire to Oxford, and gave orders to march accordingly with all convenient speed, till they should come to a Bridge which was yet two Miles from them, where he had appointed a Guard to attend, to favour their Retreat. But the Alarm had been brought to the Earl of Essex from all the Quarters, who quickly gathered those Troops together, which were nearest; and directed those to follow the Prince, and to entertain in Skirmishes, till Himself should come up with the Foot, and some other Troops; which he made all possible haste to do. So that when the Prince had passed a fair Plain, or Field, called Chalgrave [sic] Field, from whence he was to enter a Lane, which continued to the Bridge; the Enemies Horse were discovered marching after them with speed; and as they might easily overtake them in the Lane, so they must as easily have put them into great disorder. Therefore the Prince resolved to expect, and stand them upon the open Field, though his Horse were all tired, and the Sun was grown very hot, it being about eight of the clock in the Morning in June. He then directed, 'that the Guard of the Prisoners should make what hast they could to the Bridge', but that 'all the rest should return'; for some were entered the Lane: and so he placed himself and his Troops, as he thought fit, in that Field to receive the Enemy; which made more haste, and with less order than they should have done ; and being more in Number than the Prince, and consisting of many of the Principal Officers, who having been present with the Earl of Essex, when the Alarm came, stayed not for their own Troops, but joined with those who were ready in the pursuit as They thought, of a Flying Enemy, or such as would easily be arrested in their hasty retreat; and, having now overtaken them, meant to take revenge themselves for the damage they had received that Night, and Morning, before the General could come up to have a share in the Victory though his Troops were even in View. But the Prince entertained them so roughly, that though they charged very bravely and obstinately, being many of their best Officers, of which the chiefest falling, the rest shewed less Vigour, in a short time they broke, and fled, and were pursued till they came near the Earl of Essex's Body; which being a near a miles distance, and making a stand to receive their Flying Troops, and to be informed of their disaster, the Prince with his Troops hastened his retreat, and passed the Lane, and came safe to the Bridge before any of the Earls Forces came up; who found it then to no purpose to go farther, there being a good Guard of Foot, which had likewise lined both sides of the Hedges a good way in the Lane. Thus the Prince, about Noon, or shortly after, entered Oxford, with near two hundred Prisoners, seven Cornets of Horse, and four Ensigns of Foot, with most of the Men he carried from thence; few only having been killed in the Action, whereof some were of Name.

Part Two: Sir Edward Hyde's Private Journal (1641–1646)

This original manuscript is very different from Clarendon's *History*:

At the same time when the earl of Essex began his march from Reading, colonel Hurry, a Scotchman, who had served in that army from the beginning with great reputation, (as he was an excellent commander of horse,) till the difference that is before spoken of between the English and Scotch officers, (after which he laid down his commission, though, out of respect to the earl of Essex, he stayed sometime after with him as a volunteer, and now,) came to the King to Oxford, having before given notice to the earl of Brainford that he meant to do so. He came no sooner thither, than, to give proof that he brought his whole heart with him, he proposed to prince Rupert to wait on him to visit the enemy's quarters, and being well acquainted with their manner of lying and keeping their guards, undertook to be his guide to a quarter where they least expected : and the prince, willingly consenting to the proposition, drew out a strong party of one thousand horse and dragoons, which he commanded himself, and marched with colonel Hurry to a town four or five miles beyond the head quarter, where were a regiment of horse and a regiment of dragoons, and about daybreak fell upon them, and with little resistance , and no

APPENDIX I

loss of his own men, he killed and took the whole party, except some few, who hid themselves in holes or escaped by dark and untrodden paths. From thence, in his way back, according to purpose, he fell upon another village, where some horse and a regiment of foot were quartered, where he had the same success, and killed and took and dispersed them all. So he having fortunately performed all he had hoped, his highness hastened his retreat as fast as he could to Oxford, having appointed, a regiment of foot to attend him at a pass in the way of security. But the alarum had passed throughout all the enemy's quarters ; so that before the prince could reach the pass where his foot expected him, he found the enemy's whole army was drawn out, and a strong party of their horse, almost equal to his own number, so hard pressed him that, being then to enter a lane, they would disorder his rear before he could join with his foot, which were a mile before. He had very little time to deliberate, being even at the entrance to the lane. If he could have hoped to have retired in safety, he had no reason to venture to fight with a fresh party, excellently armed, and in number equal, his own being harassed and tired with near twenty miles' march and laden with spoil and prisoners, scarce a soldier without a led horse : but the necessity obliged him to stay ; and after a short consideration of the manner of doing it, directing as a convoy as was possible to guard the prisoners, and to hasten with all the unnecessary baggage and led horses, he resolved to keep the ground he had in the plain field, and after a short pause, to charge the party that advanced, lest the body might come up to them. And they came on amain, leaving it only in his election, by meeting them to have the reputation of charging them, or by standing still to be charged by them. Hereupon they quickly engaged in a sharp encounter, the best, fiercest, and longest maintained that hath been by the horse during the war ; for the party of Parliament consisted not of bare regiments and troops which usually marched together , but of prime gentlemen and officers of all their regiments, horse and foot, who being met at the head quarter, upon the alarum, and conceiving it easy to get between prince Rupert and Oxford, and not having their own charges ready to move, joined themselves as volunteers to those who were ready, till their regiment should come up ; and so, the first ranks of horse consisting of such men, the conflict was maintained some time with confidence. In the end, many falling and being hurt on both sides, the prince prevailed, the rebels being totally routed, and pursued till the gross of the army was discovered ;and then his highness, with the new prisoners he had taken, retired orderly to the pass where his foot and former purchase expected him ; and thence sending colonel Hurry to acquaint the King with the success, who knighted the messenger for his good service, returned, with near 200 prisoners, seven cornets of horse and four ensigns of foot, to Oxford. On the King's part in this action were lost, besides few common men, no officers of note, but some hurt : on the enemy's side, many of their best officers, more than in any battle they fought, and amongst them (which made the names of the rest less inquired after by the one and less lamented by the other) colonel Hambden, who was shot into the shoulder with a brace of pistol bullets, of which wound, with very sharp pain, he died within ten days, to as great a consternation of all that party as if their whole army had been defeated and cut off.[1]

---

1 BoL: MS. Clar. 112, f. 366: Sir Edward Hyde's Private Journal, 1641–1646; Hyde, *The History of the Rebellion* (1888), vol. III, pp.53–55, footnote 3 has the text of the original manuscript.

Appendix II

The Gentleman's Magazine and Historical Chronicle for May 1815

'THINKING that any particulars relative to that great Champion of English Liberty, the illustrious Hampden, would prove interesting to your Readers, I present to you the copy of a MS which has for many years been in of our family. Yours &c   A.'

'A true and faithful Narrative of the Death of Master Hampden, who was mortally wounded at Chalgrove Fight, Ann. Dom 1643 and on the 18th day of June.'

'Prince Rupert, perswaded thereunto by one Urrie, a Scottishman and malignant renegade, having, under the covertt of darkness, fallen upon defenseless Quarters at Wickenham, and cowardliwise put to the sword 57 of our men and three officers, carrying off with them one great gun, a quantitie of munitions, and other booty, with some prisoners, was retiring towards Oxford, when the alarum came to the Earl of Essex, who dispatched some horse with all speed to skirmish with and hinder the enemie, while he himself with the foot would cutt off their returne. Master Hampden volunteered his service with the horse, albeit he had a Colonelcie in a regiment of foot: he courageouslie advanced; and when the enemie bye this rough charge were on the point of being thrown into confusion, he received two carabine shott in his arme, which brake the bone; yet, being thus wounded, he would not presentlie leave the fielde, seeming regardless of paine and greate letting of bloode manfullie saying, "he would not onlie loose his arme, but lay downe his life in that good cause he was ingaged in." He was conducted to the house of Master Ezekiel Browne (a well-affected and godlie man, who afterwards did good service in our armie). He, contrarie to all opinion of skilfull Chirurgeons, appeared to have no hope of a recoverie from that hurt, and would so long as his strength sufficed, write directions for the vigorous prosecution of the warfare, which were bye special Messengers fowarded to the Parliament and these his letters, in the sober judgement of men, have, under God his providence, rescued these realms from the hands of wicked men, Abitophel-like, gave to a weake and credulous King that advice which has embroiled these kingdoms in present lamentable war. Being well nigh spent and labouring for breath, be uttered this praier, which I being present did presentlie commit to writing as well recollection served me. "O Lord God of Hosts, great is thy mercie, just and holie are thy dealings unto us sinnful men. Save me, O Lord, if it be thy good will, from the jaws of death : pardon my manifold transgressions : receive me to mercie. O Lord, save my bleeding Countrie have these in thine especiall keeping: confounde and level in the dust those who would rob the people of their libertie and lawful prerogative: let the King see his error: and turne the hearts of his evil counsillours from the maliee and wickedesse of their designes. Lord Jesu, receive my soule! Amen." After these his devout breathings he mournefullie uttered. "O Lord, save my Countrie! Oh Lord, be mercifull to …" Here his speech failed, and he fell back on the bed, and to the greate griefe of all good men, gave up the ghoste, after having with more than humane fortitude indured most cruel anguish for the space of 15 dayes. About seven houres afore his deathe he received the holie sacrament, after the manner sett forth by Law; saying, that though he could not away with the Gouvernance of the Church by Bishops, and utterlie did aborminate the scandalous lives of some Clergiemen, yet did he think its doctrine in the greater parte primitive, and conformable to God his worde, as in holie scriptures revealed. The whole Armie at his buriall followed, singing the 90th Psalme; and at their returne the 43rd; with ensignes furled and muffled drums their heads uncovered. Never were heard such piteous cryes at the deathe of one man as at Master Hambden's; trulie he was a wise and good man, who was bye all looked up to as the deliverer of his Countrie from Kinglie tyrannie and arbitrarie power. He had in all his a view not unto his own particular good, but that of the common weal; of integritie uncorrupted, of a good courage, and moste winning demeanour. In his young dayes he had entered too largelie into the vaine pastimes of the world, but was reclaimed, as I have heard him confess, by an inward call from the Lord, which enforced him to leave aside his pursuits. For his noble opposing of that unjust subsidie Ship-money, I need saye nothing, it being in the dailye converse of all men; but shall conclude this my narrative, hoping the Lord, of his marvelous mercie and loving kindness to us, will forward the good cause, and bring these our present troubles unto a happie and peaceable conclusion.'

'By me Edward Clough,
in the year of our Redemption
1643.'[1]

---

[1] BNA: 'Letter from Mr Urban, Stoneleigh, March 26', *The Gentleman's Magazine and Historical Chronicle*, vol. 85, part 1, 1815, pp.395–96.

Appendix III

The John Hampden Club (1812–1822)

The John Hampden Club was instituted on 20 April 1812, born out of the discontent of notable honourable worthies who were concerned at the corruption within Parliament. Pocket and rotten boroughs abounded, and seats were often willed to an interested party upon the death of an MP. As far back as 1793, a petition had been presented to the Commons calling for parliamentary reform, and this seems to have been the spur for likeminded reformers to meet.

The club formed in 1812 had a founding membership of 71 individuals who met under the chairmanship of Walter Fawkes at the Thatched House Tavern in St James'. The inaugural meeting started at 1:00 p.m. promptly. Membership was limited to those who owned £300 a year in land or were heirs to such an amount. They dined twice a year together on the second Saturdays in March and May, both at their own expense. Business commenced at 4:00 p.m., with dinner at 6:00 p.m. The membership fee was £2 a year. The first resolution stated, 'That a society be now instituted, which shall have for its object the securing to the people the free election of their Representatives in the Commons House of Parliament. That such society be called the Hampden Club.'[1] There was no reference to our John Hampden in any of their papers at this time, but Hampden's precept of 'no taxation without representation' was reiterated in the club's statement of 'taxation and representation are inseparably united; God hath joined them'.

The club published many wordy pamphlets over the years of its existence and presented the majority of these to Parliament. In 1816, a Mr Gedge of Bury St Edmunds proposed that a 'Hampden Gazette' or 'Britannia Revived' be published. But this seems to have never come to fruition. By 1819, the club had 'reformed' itself by dropping the money qualification for entry. Members attended from all over the country – Mr Fawkes, the original chairman, came from Farnley Hall in Yorkshire; Thomas Northmore, the secretary, came from Cleve in Devonshire; Major Cartwright from Brothertoft in Lincolnshire and

---

1   Cartwright, *Life and Correspondence*, vol. II, pp.24–25.

others from Reading, Herefordshire, Surrey and more. The Hampden Club's membership officers suffered at the hands of MPs, with legal action taken against them. Some were made bankrupt.

In 1816, the trust account of the Hampden Association at the Banking-House of Messrs. Spooner, Attwood and Co. of 29 Gracechurch Street amounted to '£202.0.0', but this amount slowly dwindled as membership decreased and fewer of those still belonging paid their membership dues. The club was wound up in 1822, with debts being paid by the remaining members.

These men kept the ideals of John Hampden alive and helped to bring about the first great Parliamentary Reform Bill of 1832.[2]

---

2   Cartwright, *Life and Correspondence*, vols I–II.

Appendix IV

The Pye Paper

In *Some Memorials of John Hampden, His Party and His Times*, Nugent described how 'He [John Hampden] was struck in the shoulder with two carabine balls' and how he had taken the information from a number of contemporary sources. He listed these sources in same the footnote preceding 'There is a groundless story told':

> These details have been taken from the account printed, by Leonard Lichfield, at the university press at Oxford, for the King; [commonly known as the *Late Beating Up*] also from *Mercurius Aulicus*, Lord Essex's *Two Letters*, from *The Parliament Scout*, from *A true Relation of a Great Fight between the King's Forces and the Parliament's at Chinnor, near Thame, &c Certaine Intelligences from Parts of the Kingdom*, printed for the Parliament in London.
>
> There is a groundless story told, upon the authority of a nameless paper, by Horace Walpole [Lord Orford, 1717–1797], and by Echard [1670–1730] of Hampden having received a wound from the bursting of one of his own pistols.
>
> All the contemporary accounts, diurnals, letters, and memoirs state the death as I [Nugent] have given them. In the Common-Place Book of Henry James Pye [1745–1813], late poet laureate, now in the possession of his son, [Henry John Pye, 1802–1884], the lineal descendant of Sir Robert Pye [d. 1701], son-in-law to Hampden, I [Nugent] find the following entry:-
>
> 'In the St. James Chronicle for the year 1761, there is an account of the death of Mr. Hampden, different from that given by Lord Clarendon. The account is, that Sir Robert Pye, being at supper at Farringdon House with two of the Harleys [Lord Oxford's family] and one of the Foleys, related the death of Hampden as follows:-'
>
> 'That, at Chalgrove Field, his pistol burst, and shattered his hand in a terrible manner; that, when dying, he sent for Sir Robert Pye, his son-in-law, and told him he was in some degree accessory to his death, as he had the pistols from him. Sir Robert assured him he bought them in France of an eminent maker, and tried them himself. It appeared, on examining the other pistol, that it was loaded to the top with several supernumerary charges, owing to the negligence of his servant.'
>
> 'Mr. [Henry James, 1745–1813] Pye adds these words, which discredit the whole of this anonymous account:-

APPENDIX IV

My father [Henry Pye, 1709–1766], on reading this account, sent to enquire of Baldwin, the printer of the paper, how he met with the anecdote, who informed him, that it was found written on a loose sheet of paper in a book that he, or some friend of his, bought out of Lord Oxford's family [the Harley's]. My father [Henry Pye, 1709–1766] always questioned the authenticity of it, as my grandfather [Henry Pye, 1683–1749] was bred up and lived with Sir Robert Pye till he was eighteen years old, and he never mentioned any such circumstance.'[1]

---

[1] Nugent, *Some Memorials* (1832), vol. II, pp.433–34.

Appendix V

Letter Published in *The Times* (28 July 1828)

'Narrative of the disinterment of the body of John Hampden, Esq., (commonly, called the 'Patriot') in Hampden Church, Bucks, on the 21st of July, 1828, to ascertain the cause of his death; some historians supposing that he was wounded in the shoulder by a shot from the enemy at the battle of Chalgrave-field [*sic*] June, 1643; others supposing that he was killed by the bursting of his own pistol, with which his son-in-law, Sir Robert Pye, had presented him.

Present on the occasion – The Right Hon. Lord Nugent, Counsellor Denman, the Rev. Mr. Brookes, Mr. Heron, Mr. Grace (Steward to the Right Hon. the Earl of Buckinghamshire), George Coventry, six other young gentlemen, with whose names I was not acquainted, 12 grave diggers and assistants, with the clerk of the parish.

The manner in which Mr. Hampden met his death had long been a disputed point in history.

Lord Clarendon, Rushworth, Ludlow, Noble, and others, severally state that at the Battle of Chalgrave-field* [*sic*] he was mortally wounded in the shoulder by a musket-ball that he lingered for several days, and expired in great agony.

Lord Clarendon says, that Hampden "being shot into the shoulder with a brace of bullets, which broke the bone, with-in three weeks after died with extraordinary pain, to as great a consternation of all that party as if their whole army had been defeated or cut off."

Sir Philip Warwick states that "Mr. Hampden received a hurt in his shoulder, whereof he died in three or four days after; for his blood in his temper was acrimonious, as the scurfe commonly on his face showed". In another place he observes, "One of the prisoners taken in the action said, that he was confident Mr. Hampden was hurt; for he saw him, contrary to his usual custom, ride off the field, before the action was finished, his head hanging down and his hands leaning upon his horse's neck."

What reliance can we place upon historians, when we see such contradictory statements? Lord Clarendon says, he lingered near three weeks* – Sir P. Warwick, that he died in three or four days; the former, that two bullets broke the shoulder-bone the latter, that he was only hurt in the shoulder. But the following is the most contradictory statement of all, equally worthy of credit, perhaps more so, as it was related by Sir Robert Pye, who married Hampden's eldest daughter:-

Two of the Harleys, and one of the Foleys, being at supper with Sir Robert Pye, at Farringdon-house, Berks., in their way to Herefordshire, Sir Robert Pye related the account of Hampden's death as follows:-

"That at the action of Chalgrave-field, his pistol burst, and shattered his hand in a terrible manner. He however rode off, and got to his quarters; but finding the wound mortal, he sent for Sir Robert Pye, then a colonel in the Parliament army, and who had married his eldest daughter, and told him, that he looked on him as in some degree accessory to his death, as the pistols were a present from him. Sir Robert assured him, that he brought them in Paris, of an eminent maker, and had proved them himself. It appeared, on examining the other pistol, that it was loaded to the muzzle with several supernumerary charges, owing to the carelessness of a servant, who was ordered to see the pistols were loaded every morning, which he did without drawing the former charge." – From Lord Oxford's papers.

In order to ascertain the real facts, application was made by Lord Nugent to the Earl of Buckinghamshire, [to whom the family estates have descended] that the coffin might be opened, and the body carefully examined.

The Earl, after due consideration, granted the request, which was confirmed by the rector, who politely tendered his assistance to further the inquiry.

It is remarkable, that so distinguished and opulent a family as that of Hampden should never have possessed a private vault for the interment of the respective branches of the family:- such, however, is not the case; they have, from a very early period, been buried in the chancel of the church, about four feet deep.

On the morning of the 21st July we all assembled in the church, and commenced the operation of opening the ground.

After examining the initials and dates on several leaden coffins, we came to the one in question, the plate of which was so corroded, that it crumbled and broke into small pieces on touching it. It was therefore impossible to ascertain the name of the individual that it contained.

The coffin had originally been enclosed in wood, covered with velvet, a small portion only of which was apparent, near the bottom at the left side, which was not the case with those of a later date, where the initials were distinct, and the lead more perfect and fresher in appearance. The register stated, that Hampden was interred on the 25th June, 1643, and an old document, still in existence, gives a curious and full account of the grand procession on the occasion; we were, therefore, pretty confident that this must be the one in question, having carefully examined all the others in succession.

It was lying under the western window, near the tablet erected by him, when living, to the memory of his beloved wife, whose virtues he extols in the most affectionate language. Without positive proof, it was reasonable to suppose that he would be interred near his adored partner, and this being found at her feet, it was unanimously agreed that the lid should be cut open to ascertain the fact, which proved afterwards that we were not mistaken.

The parish plumber descended, and commenced cutting across the coffin, then longitudinally, until the whole was sufficiently loosened to roll back, in order to lift off the wooden lid beneath, which was found in such good preservation, that it came off nearly entire. Beneath this was another lid of the same material, which was raised without materially giving way.

The coffin had originally been filled up with sawdust, which was found undisturbed, except the centre, where the abdomen had fallen in. The sawdust was then removed, and the process of examination commenced. Silence reigned. Not a whisper or breath was heard. Each stood on the tiptoe of expectation, awaiting the result as to what appearance the face would present when divested of its covering.

Lord Nugent descended into the grave, and first removed the outer cloth, which was firmly wrapped around the body, then the second, and a third – such care having been extended to preserve the body from the worm of corruption.

Here a very singular scene presented itself. No like whiteness, and showed the various windings of the blood vessels beneath the skin. The upper row of teeth were perfect, and those that remained in the under jaw, on being taken out and examined, were quite sound.

A little beard remained on the lower part of the chin, and the whiskers were strong, and somewhat lighter than his hair, which was a full auburn brown. The upper part of the bridge of the nose still remained elevated, the remainder had given way to the pressure of the cloths, which had been firmly bound round the head. The eyes were but slightly sunk in, and were covered with the same white film which characterised the general appearance of the face.

Finding that a difference of opinion existed as to the indentation in the left shoulder, where it was supposed he had been wounded, it was unanimously agreed upon to raise up the coffin altogether, and place it in the centre of the church, where a more accurate examination might take place.

The coffin was extremely heavy, but by elevating one end with a crow-bar, two strong ropes were adjusted under either end, and thus drawn up by 12 men in the most careful manner possible.

Being placed on a trestle, the first operation was to examine the arms, which nearly retained their original size, and presented a very muscular appearance.

On lifting up the right arm, we found it was dispossessed of its hand. We might therefore naturally conjecture that it had been amputated, as the bone presented a perfectly flat appearance, as if sawn off by some sharp instrument. On searching under the cloths, to our no small astonishment, we found the hand or rather a number of small bones enclosed in a separate cloth.

For about six inches up the arm the flesh had wasted away, being evidently smaller than the lower part of the left arm, to which the hand was very firmly united, and which presented no symptoms of decay further than the two bones of the fore finger loose. Even the nails remained entire, of which we saw no appearance in the cloth containing the remains of the right hand.

At this process of the investigation, we were perfectly satisfied that, independently of the result of any further examination, such a striking coincidence as the loss of the right hand would justify our belief in Sir Robert

Pye's statement to the Harleys, that his presentation pistol was the innocent cause of a wound which afterwards proved mortal. It was, however, possible, that at the same moment, in the heat of the action at Chalgrave [sic], when Colonel Hampden discharged his pistol at his adversary, that his adversary's ball might wound him in the shoulder; for he was soon after observed, as stated by Sir Phillip Warwick, "with his head hanging down, and his hands leaning upon horse's neck."

In order to corroborate or disprove the different statements relative to his having been wounded in the shoulder, a close examination of each took place.

The clavicle of the right shoulder was firmly united to the scapula, nor did there appear any contusion or indentation that evinced symptoms of any wound ever having been inflicted. The left shoulder, on the contrary, was smaller and sunken in, as if the clavicle had been displaced. To remove all doubts, it was adjudged necessary to remove the arms, which were amputated with a penknife.

The socket of the left arm was perfectly white and healthy, and the clavicle firmly united to the scapula, nor was there the least appearance of contusion or wound.

The socket of the right shoulder, on the contrary, was of a brownish cast, and the clavicle being found quite loose and disunited from the scapula, proved that dislocation had taken place. The bones, however, were quite perfect. Such dislocation, therefore, must have arisen, either from the force of a ball, or from Colonel Hampden having fallen from his horse, when he lost the power of holding the reins by reason of his hand having been so dreadfully shattered. The latter in all probability was the case, as it would be barely possible for a ball to pass through the shoulder without some fracture, either of the clavicle or scapula.

In order to examine the head and hair, the body was raised up and supported with a shovel; on removing the cloths which adhered firmly to the back of the head, we found the hair in a complete state of preservation. It was a dark auburn colour, and according to the custom of the times was very long, from five to six inches. It was drawn up and tied round at the top of the head with black thread or silk. The ends had the appearance of having been cut off. On the taking hold of the topknot, it soon gave way and came off like a wig.

Here a singular scene presented itself. The worm of corruption was busily employed, the skull in some places being perfectly bare, whilst in others the skin remained nearly entire, upon which we discovered a number of maggots and small red worms on the feed with great activity. This was the only spot where any symptoms of life was apparent, as if the brain contained a vital principle within it, which engendered its own destruction; otherwise, how can we account, after a lapse of nearly two centuries, in finding living creatures preying upon the seat of intellect, when they were nowhere else to be found, in no other part of the body. He was five feet nine inches in height, apparently of great muscular strength, of a vigorous and robust frame; forehead broad and high; the skull altogether well formed, such as one as the imagination would conceive capable of great exploits.

Here I close the narrative, one of singular interest to those who were eye-witnesses of the examination, which presented a scene so novel, so ghastly, but at the same time so full of moment, that it will ever prove a memorable event in the short era of our lives. We record to mind the virtuous actions of the deceased; his manly defense against the tyranny of the Star Chamber; his abandonment of every social and domestic tie for the glorious cause of freedom; and whilst we gazed upon his remains, remembered, that voice which was once raised on behalf of his country, had contributed in no small measure to pave the way for the blessings of liberty, which, but for his warning, might to this day have been withheld from an enlightened people.

* The battle of Chalgrave-field [sic] was fought on the 18th June, 1643. Mr. Hampden died on the 24th, and was buried on the 25th, as stated in the parish register. Sir W. Dugdale mentions several instances where persons of rank were interred the day after decease.'[1]

---

1 HL: Letter to *The Times* published 28 July 1828, Microfilm reel.

Appendix VI

Essex's *Two Letters*

TWO

LETTERS

FROM HIS

EXCELLENCIE

Robert Earl of

ESSEX

SIR

There being some of my Horse that had an Encounter with the Enemy yesterday being Sunday; I thought fit to give the House an Account of the Particulars of it, knowing how apt many are to mis-report things to our disadvantage.

 About two of the clock on Sunday morning the Enemy with about twelve hundred Horse and a great body of Dragoons fell into a Towne called *Porcham*, where one Troop of Horse (being Colonel *Morleys*) was Quartered, of which they took the greatest part, and from thence went not far to another Village called Chinner, where they beat up those of the new Bedfordshire Dragoons and took some of them Prisoners, and three of their Colours, and some Officers behaving themselves very well defending the Houses wherein they were; they set fire on the Town; these being out-Quarters, the Alarm came where Major *Gunter* lay with three Troops (*viz.*) his own, Captain *Sheffields* and, Captain *Crosses* whom he presently drew out and marched towards the Enemy; Colonel *Hampden* being abroad with *Sir Samuel Luke* and only one man and seeing Major *Gunters* Forces they did go along with them, Colonel *Dulbier* the Quarter-Master General did likewise come to them: with these they drew near the Enemy, and finding them marching away, kept still upon the rear for almost five miles. In this time there joined with them Captain *Sanders* Troop, and Captain *Buller*, with commanded men, which were sent to Chinner by *Sir Phillip Stapleton*, who had the watch here that at *Thame*, when he discovered the fire there, to know the occasion of it, he likewise sent one Troop of Dragoons under the command of Captain *Dundass*, who came up to them. There were likewise some few of Captain *Melves* Dragoons that came to them: at length our men pressed them to near, that being in a large pasture ground they drew up, and notwithstanding the inequality of the numbers, we having not above 300 Horse; our men charged them very gallantly, and slew divers of them; but while they were in fight, the Enemy being so very strong, kept a Body of horse for his reserve, and with that Body wheeled about and charged our men in the rear, so that being encompassed and overborne with multitude, they broke and fled, though it was not very far; For when I heard that our men marched in the rear of the Enemy, I sent to Sir *Phillip Stapleton* who presently Marched toward them with his Regiment; & though he came somewhat short of the Skirmish, yet seeing our men Retreat in disorder, he stopped them, caused them to draw into a Body with him, where they stood about an hour: Whereupon the Enemy marched away. In this Skirmish there were slain forty and five on both sides, whereof the greater part were theirs.

They carried off the bodies of divers persons of quality. On our side Major *Gunter* was killed, but some say he is prisoner and so hurt; a man of much courage and fidelity, his bravery engaging him, and his small party too far: Colonel *Hampden* put himself in Captain *Cross* his troop, where he charged with much courage, and was unfortunately shot through the shoulder. Sir *Samuel Luke* thrice taken prisoner, and fortunately rescued: Captain *Crosse* had his horse killed under him in the midst of the Enemy, and was mounted by one of his own men, who quitted his own horse to save his Captain.

Captain *Buller* was shot in the neck, who showed very much resolution in this fight, taking one prisoner he was shot. Monsieur *Dulbier* with Captain *Bosa* and Captain *Ennis*, did likewise carry themselves very well. We likewise lost two colours, *viz;* Major *Gunters* and Captain *Sheffields*; no prisoners of quality were taken by the Enemy, but Captain *Sheffields* Brother. Prince *Rupert* was there in person, and the Renagado *Hurry*. We took prisoner one of the Earl of Berks sons, Captain *Gardener*, the late Recorders son of London, and Captain *Smith*, with some others of quality and divers prisoners.

Sir, this is the true Relation of what passed in this business. I rest;

Your assured Friend

ESSEX

Thame. 19. June 1643.

Appendix VII

James Otis (alias John Hampden)

'"Long before [the Battle of] Lexington, James Otis' fight for civil liberties gave heart to the rebel cause ..." The article states that Otis was a Mass. delegate to the Stamp Act Congress in New York in 1765, where he had "the satisfaction of seeing his constitutional doctrine of no taxation without representation embodied by that body".

Although far more moderate on the Stamp Act issue than either Patrick Henry or Daniel Dulaney, Otis plucked up his courage and under the pseudonym "John Hampden" published in the Boston press a sweeping denial of Parliament's right to tax the colonies.

People of Boston as well as their kinfolk in western Mass. may then have become well aware of Otis' 18th century articles. Possibly Otis was quoting the "Patriot" John Hampden, as well as using his name.

In western Mass. when the county names were selected, they continued to identify with the English patriot whose cause Otis championed.

In our area of Maine, an influx of settlers from southern New England moved here, in some cases for land granted in exchange for services rendered in the Revolutionary War. It was called "The Great Migration." Here in Hampden lived an aide to General George Washington, and who was involved directly with the "Boston Tea Party." Other veterans' services are listed in the town records.'

Courtesy of Alice Hawes – Chair of the John Hampden Society – Hampden, Maine, Est. 1794.[1]

---

1   Morris, "'Then and There'", pp.36–39.

Appendix VIII

The Sydney Morning Herald

'No. 16. – JOHN HAMPDEN DISINTERRED : Or, Lord Nugent and Lord Denman, Chief Justice of the King's Bench, as Resurrectionists.

A German physician of the nineteenth century collected, with unweariable industry, all the facts which he could find recorded those concerning the human body in its changes after death, and published them in a most curious volume, which he entitled De Miraculis Mortuorum. In this book are related many extraordinary and ghastly circumstances ; but whoever will turn to the *Gentleman's Magazine* for August, 1828, will find none more appalling than the hideous facts which were revealed to these noble body lifters within "the dread abode" of John Hampden. This narrative is said to have been compiled either by or under the direction of Lord Nugent, who about thirty years ago published a work, in two volumes, which he called the "*Some Memorials of John Hampden, his Party, and his Times.*"

Now, it so happened, that on a certain Sunday in June, to wit, the 18th, 1643, which was the second year of the Civil War, Hampden was mortally wounded in a skirmish with Prince Rupert's troops on Chalgrove-field, near Thame; which was the scene of his school-boy life.

"It is a tradition", Lord Nugent writes "that he was first seen moving in the direction of his father-in law's house, at Pyrton. There he had in youth married the first wife of his love (for he was twice married), and thither he would have gone to die ; but Rupert's cavalry were covering the plain between. Turning his horse, therefore, he rode back across the grounds of Haseley, on his way to Thame. At the brook which divides the parishes he paused awhile, but it being impossible for him, in his wounded state, to remount if he had alighted to turn his horse over, he suddenly summoned his strength, clapped spurs, and cleared the leap."

These circumstances his biographer has collected from tradition. He reached Thame in great pain and almost fainting, and there, at the house of one Ezekiel Brown, and on the anniversary of his wedding, he expired, after six days of cruel suffering. While his strength sufficed it was employed in despatching letters of counsel to Parliament, whose affairs were at that time in a most unprosperous state ; when it failed, he disposed himself religiously for death.

APPENDIX VIII

His death is ascribed here to a wound in his shoulder, "with two carabine balls, which, breaking the bone, entered the body;" and in a note Lord Nugent repeats the tradition, which he discredits, that he died from the bursting of his own pistol. To determine this point, however, at least three or four years before the publication of his memorials, Lord Nugent had obtained permission to disinter the body of Hampden for the purpose of ascertaining the cause of his death.

This seems to have been an object with him, in deference to that vague feeling which cannot be easily shaken off, which connects such catastrophes in individuals with what among Christian people is designated by the name of a special Providence, and which the heathen world more exactly shadowed forth under the name and idea of an avenging deity that followed upon men's actions, as Nemesis ; under which apprehension his friends and party were more anxious to attribute his misfortune to casual and extraneous accident than to the immediate results of his personal conduct. Be this, however, as it may, the vault was opened ; there stood by the noble lord himself; there was also there Mr. Counsellor Denman, afterwards Thomas Lord Denman, with several other persons; and the leaden coffin having been cut open, and the lids of two inner ones raised, Lord Nugent descended into the grave, and himself unrolled the cere cloths. An indentation was observed on the left shoulder ; and as there was a difference of opinion concerning it, the coffin was raised up, and placed on trestles in the middle of the church, that a more accurate examination might be made. It was then found that the left shoulder had been dislocated, but that there was no fracture, and this, therefore, was accounted for by supposing that he had fallen from his horse when wounded, for the right hand had been amputated, and the remains of its bones were found inclosed in a separate cere cloth ; the flesh of that arm had wasted away for about six inches up, being evidently smaller than that of the left arm. The spectators were then perfectly satisfied that the tradition preserved in one branch of the family was true, and that his own pistol bursting had shattered the hand and occasioned his death.

It is now time to state another hypothesis of the cause of Hampden's death. If he fell from his horse on receiving the injury in his hand, and dislocated his left shoulder, it seems incredible that he should have been able to regain his saddle. But he might have lost his seat, and sustained his second injury at the brook, whence he proceeded on foot fainting to Thame.

"Whether the motive was sufficient to justify this violation of the grave, and disturbance of the dead, and the cutting the arms off with a penknife, to remove all doubt," may be questioned, and possibly some natural repugnance may have induced Lord Nugent (if the narrative be a true one, and of that no doubt has been entertained) to omit all mention of it in his book ; but there seems no reason why the tradition, which the examination had verified, should have been represented as unfounded, if such an examination actually took place. The farther results of the scrutiny are yet to be told.

When Lord Nugent descended into the grave he first removed the outer cloth, which was firmly wrapped round the body, then the second, and a third-such care having been extended to preserve the body from the worm of corruption. Here a very singular scene presented itself. No regular features were apparent, although the face retained a death-like whiteness, and showed the various windings of the blood vessels beneath the skin. The teeth of the upper row were perfect, and those that remained in the lower jaw, on being taken out and examined, were quite sound. A little beard remained on the lower part of the chin, and the whiskers were strong, and somewhat lighter than his hair, which was a full auburn brown. The upper part of the bridge of the nose was still elevated, the remainder had given way to the pressure of the cloth, which had been firmly bound round the head. The eyes were but slightly sunk in, and were covered with the same white film which characterised the general appearance of the face.

This was ghastly enough for persons who were neither accustomed to act as resurrectionists, nor had gone through a course of experiments like Frankenstein in his laboratory when he manufactured his monster. But in order to examine the head and hair, the body was raised up and supported with a shovel ; on removing the cloths which adhered firmly to the back of the head the hair was found in a complete state of preservation. It was a dark auburn colour, and according to the custom of the times, was very long-from five to six inches. It was drawn up, and tied round at the top of the head, with black thread or silk. The ends had the appearance of having been cut off. And now opens upon us the most hideous fact that has ever yet been revealed by the grave! On taking hold of the top-knot it soon gave way, and came off like a wig. Here a singular scene presented itself; the worm of corruption was busily employed, the skull in some places being perfectly bare, whilst in others, the skin remained perfectly entire, upon which might be seen a number of maggots and small red worms on the feed with great activity. This was the only spot where any symptom of life was apparent, as if the brain contained a vital principle within it, which engendered its own corruption ; otherwise how can it be explained that, after a lapse of more than two centuries, living creatures should be found preying upon the seat of intellect, when they were nowhere else to be found in any other part of the body?'[1]

---

1 British Newspaper Archive (BNA) *Sydney Morning Herald*, 22 October 1861, p.2.

Appendix IX

Collected Letters of Private Correspondence

Item 1 – Buckinghamshire Archives (BA) D/MH 39/88: Letter fragment from Dr James Grace to the Earl of Buckinghamshire, March 1828

Lord Nugent has not been at Hampden nor have I received any intimation from his Lordship of such intention. I will immediately write to him and inform him of your Lordship's wishes, also accompany him whenever he may be disposed to visit Hampden …

Item 2 – Buckinghamshire Archives (BA) D/MH 39/84: Letter from Dr James Grace to the Earl of Buckinghamshire, 5 April 1828

Princes Risborough,
April 5th 1828,

My Lord,
In consequence of the letter I wrote to Lord Nugent by your Lordship's desire he appointed for the purpose of looking over the papers and memorandums likely to afford his Lordship any information related to The Patriot John Hampden but as your Lordship anticipated we found very few papers to repay his search: Lord Nugent however selected a few which pleased him. The Dean of Killaloe's account of the Portrait of John Hampden is one. The old Pedigree of the Hampden Family, and a Memorandum of your Lordship's Family of Sir Miles Hobart in the reign of Chas. 1st. these were the only papers lord Nugent wished for a second perusal and I have at his request agreed to copy them for his Lordship. Lord Nugent inquired if the pavement of the church was going to be taken up and re-laid and he begs to be informed when that takes place and depends on finding the grave of the Patriot and would very much like to look into the vault if he fails in finding any inscription when the floor is removed and if your Lordship would sanction it: he asked me if I thought you would consent to it should

he make application for that purpose. Before I commence the operation on the greenhouse to convert it into a residence for Robertson; I should like to know how much your Lordship is willing to expend for this purpose, not that I should make a point of expending a certain sum whether it be necessary or not but that it makes a very material difference in the expense how the thing is done. In consideration of Robertson having no family and only his wife during this state of things, it is not necessary to make two bedrooms but to make one comfortable living room and one bedroom, the expense of which will be about 20.00 whereas on the other hand and as I expect this will not satisfy Mr. Robertson and that he expects a parlour, as well as a kitchen and two bedrooms, which will cause the present building to be so pulled to pieces in order to get room and height for this purpose that it will be very much like building it up now except that it will not require bricks-the latter alteration which I don't think necessary cannot most certainly be completed for no smaller a sum as 60.00. I mention these particulars that your Lordship may not be deceived not only in the expense, but to show the difference of expense in the manner which it is to be done-I shall therefore be glad to know how much your Lordship will positively allow for this alteration and I will only spend whatever.

I remain my Lord,
Your Lordship's most faithful,
Servant,
J. Grace

Item 3 – Buckinghamshire Archives (BA) D/MH 39/87: Letter fragment from Dr James Grace to the Earl of Buckinghamshire, early June 1828

… write to you on this subject, to say that he [the archdeacon] has discovered the entry of the burial of John Hampden in an old register proving beyond doubt the circumstance of his being buried at Hampden. I hope your Lordship will be pleased with the appearance of the church, altogether which looks very neat, the altar cloth is not quite as plain as it should have been, but Mr Brooks has taken upon himself to reconcile your Lordship to the alterations which I should have not chosen myself.

I remain my Lord,
Your Lordship's most faithful,
Servant,
J. Grace

Item 4 – British Newspaper Archive (BNA) 'Rector Brookses copy of a Letter from James Grace, Esq., Land Steward to the Earl of Buckinghamshire and Churchwarden of Great Hampden, to Lord Nugent. Risborough dated June 17, 1828', *Derby Mercury***, Wednesday, 21 January 1863**

Risborough June 17, 1828,

My Lord,
I went to Hampden the next morning after your Lordship's last visit there intending to prevent the floor being laid over the grave containing the coffin which you wished opened; on my arrival there I found that Mr. Brooks had workmen to fill up the grave and proceed with the floor, all of which I found done. I however, lost no time communicating your Lordship's wishes to Lord Buckinghamshire, telling him the scruples Mr. Brooks had with regard to his consenting to the opening of the coffin, to which I have since had a reply, and the result is that Lord Buckinghamshire wishes by all means that the coffin should be opened and examined. I have not had an opportunity of seeing Mr. Brooks, scarcely, since I had the pleasure of meeting your Lordship, so as to have any conversation with him on the subject; perhaps you would write to him as his consent is the only thing necessary. It is true that the floor must be disarranged again, but this must have been the case if we had proceeded the time we intended for I think it would have been impossible to have examined the coffin properly or satisfactorily without taking up the floor. As Lord B has so strongly intimated his wishes in the matter. I apprehend Mr. Brooks will no longer hesitate about it, provided he is put to no additional expense in setting to right the floor after the examination has taken place.

I remain, my Lord, your Lordship's obdt. Servant. J. GRACE

Item 5 – British Newspaper Archive (BNA) 'Correspondence sent by Lord Nugent 27 June 1828 to Mr. G W Brooks, the Rector at Great Hampden at the time of the exhumation', *Derby Mercury***, Wednesday, 21 January 1863**

From Lord Nugent to the Rev. G. W. Brooks. 27th June 1828

Lord Nugent presents his compliments to Mr. Brooks. He received the enclosed letter from Mr. James Grace, in consequence of an application made at Lord N.'s request to Lord Buckinghamshire for his consent that the lid of the coffin might be raised which Lord Nugent has reason to believe contains the bones of John Hampden. Lord Nugent has particular reasons for being anxious to ascertain whether John Hampden was buried in the chancel of Great Hampden Church. And has no doubt, with Mr. Brooks's leave, of being able to ascertain whether that coffin contains his remains or not, as in case of that coffin being his the skeleton will be found with the shoulder broken. If Mr. Brooks will be kind enough to give his consent to the lid being raised no examination would be necessary, or desired, excepting the looking at the shoulder which may be done without touching the remains or in any way disturbing them. And the lid and floor might be instantly replaced. In case of Mr. Brook not withholding his consent, Lord Nugent would be glad that he should be present at the opening, in order that he might be satisfied that no disturbance of the bones should take place. Lord Nugent will scarcely be able conveniently to come down to Hampden till Saturday, the 19th, or Monday, the 21st of July. If Mr. Brook would have the kindness to fix one of those two days for him he should feel extremely obliged. Mr. Brook's would probably think it desirable in order that no idle persons should be present in the church that the examination should take place in the morning, and that nothing should be said about the intention to anybody but Mr. James Grace. Mr. Brooks would confer a great obligation on Lord Nugent by meeting his wishes in these particulars, to which he trusts he will feel no objection since the announcement of Lord Buckinghamshire's consent and wishes. 31, Park Street, Grosvenor square, June 27, 1828.

Item 6 – Extract from Buckinghamshire Archives (BA) AR 62/92 (Box File) A6: Letter from Dr James Grace to Earl of Buckinghamshire, Union Club, Cockspur Street, London, 22 July 1828

The leaden coffin has been opened, but not satisfactory proof obtained that the body contained in it, was that of the Patriot. Lord Nugent attended, accompanied by Mr. Denman & they went away under the impression that they had discovered a fracture in the collar bone, but on Mr. Norris's examination it proved to be no such thing, and he reported all the bones to be in a perfect state. The body was in a fine state of preservation enclosed with a considerable quantity of wrapping within three coffins, one of lead. The flesh and muscles not much wasted & the face plump & must have had nearly the same appearance as when buried. There was a large quantity of hair in good preservation. Mr. Norris supposes the body has been buried upwards of two hundred years & would have remained as much longer without being disturbed. There is a description on the stone over the grave to William Hampden Esq. and it is probable that this must be the same person. It is extraordinary that no trace can be discovered of the body of the Patriot which can only be accounted by his not being buried in lead and consequently gone completely to decay.

I remain my Lord
Your Lordship's faithful servant
J. Grace.

Item 7 – <BL_000052_18630121_042_0008.pdf>. *Derby Mercury*, **Derbyshire, England, Wednesday, 21 January 1863**

These letters with other additional evidence collected on the spot after a most searching investigation of all the circumstances, and a special parochial visitation, held in the church, satisfied the Bishop and Arch-deacon whose kindness ever after I can never forget, and whose letters to me upon leaving I treasure up with no ordinary feelings of pride and gratitude. It not necessary, it is to be hoped, for me to go through all the revolting details of the statement in question, nor will it be expected that I should remember circumstantially, with freshness of yesterday, incidents which happened between 30 and 40 years ago. My impression is, as I have stated, that the body was examined by Mr. J. Norris, the surgeon, of Princes. Risborough, on the same day that it was disinterred, because I distinctly recollect giving orders to the clerk, before leaving the church, to have the coffin immediately closed and put into the grave. Those who know me, know perfectly well, how foreign it would be to my nature to show disrespect either to the living or the dead — the particulars mentioned did not take place (if they took place at all) with my sanction or in my presence. And it would be a dishonour the memory of such noblemen as Lord Nugent and Lord Denman to mention even their names in connection with the alleged desecration. They were men, it is well known who were proverbially humane, of the keenest sensibilities, and the most enlarged philanthropy; with minds cast in no common mould, and hearts such as rarely beat in human breasts, and who would not have permitted such things much less have participated in them.

I have the honour to be Sir,
your obedient Servant,
Aston-on-Trent, Jan. 17, 1863 G. W. Brooks

Item 8 – Buckinghamshire Archives (BA) D/MH 39/86, Transcript 11: Letter from Dr James Grace to Richard Cumberland at the Exchequer, Palace Yard, London, 9 August 1828

Richard Cumberland Esq.
Exchequer,
Palace Yard,
London.

Dear Sir,
Princes Risborough
9th August 1828

I have not seen the account given in the Times Newspaper relative to the disinterment of John Hampden, but the several other accounts I have seen in other papers have been all incorrect. The fact is that Lord Nugent instead of waiting for Mr. Norris to examine the arm and shoulder bones, satisfied himself with his own examination and went away with a fancied idea that both were fractured. The coffin remained in the chancel till the next morning, when Mr. Norris examined the skeleton and pronounced it in a perfect state at least as far as related to the fracture in the arms and shoulder on opening the leaden coffin we found two others of wood not much decayed, the body was curiously enclosed in several linen wrappers parts of which were preserved so as to tear as you would a piece of cloth. The upper part of the body as far as the breast was very beautifully preserved, and I think must have had nearly the same appearances as when first interred except the colour which was chocolate, the face large and plump, the eyes not much sunk, the nose (not an aquiline one) very perfect and the cartilage not gone when first opened the teeth and mouth good the hair long and fine of a dark auburn and tied with a string close behind the head and spread over the back part so as to form a kind of nightcap. The arms and shoulders were very large and muscular the body had the appearance of having died at about from 40 to 50 years of age without much previous illness, he must have been a corpulent man at the time of his decease, the breasts were very large and full and had every appearance of a fat man. I saw nothing like a fracture of either hands or shoulders, nor was there any dislocation.

The account you saw describing the hand as being found in a separate bag (which on being examined proved to have been sawn off) was altogether incorrect, it might have been separated at the wrist by the action of moving the body from its position. There certainly was no fracture or anything of the kind and although separated at the wrist was not from a wound or by amputation – my opinion of this at the time of the disinterment was fully corroborated by Mr. Norris when he examined it afterwards the legs and lower parts of the body were not examined that part of the coffin was filled with sawdust. There was nothing appeared in the examination which could in any way prove, or so make it even supposable that the body was that of The Patriot on the contrary, if the prints and portraits we have seen of him can give one any idea of his person the features of this which could be seen perfectly were of a different character altogether. Instead of that high nose and thin visage which I have always pictured the Patriot to have had, this was a short nose and fat round face and Mr. Norris thinks it much older than the Patriot's time, and would he says if not disturbed have remained as much longer the same state. I think it not unlikely that it was Mr. William Hampden as the coffin was immediately under the stone bearing his Inscription upon it. In my last letter from Lord Buckinghamshire he mentions the 20th August for coming to Hampden.

I remain Dr Sir
Yours very faithfully
James Grace.

Item 9 – Buckinghamshire Archives (BA) D/MH 39/85: Letter from Dr James Grace to the Earl of Buckinghamshire, 19 August 1828

Prince's Risborough,
August 19 1828

My Lord,
I am glad to find that your Lordship found no further difficulty in getting the Cheque on Proceeds exchanged. The account given in the Times Newspaper relative to the disinterment of the Patriot was I suppose authorised by Lord Nugent as the person who noted down the particulars did so by his Lordships direction, and was brought down for the purpose. The statement was altogether incorrect. I daresay Lord Nugent imagined that the hand was separated from the body and that it must have been so buried, but when Mr. Norris examined the arm and shoulder bones the hand although separated at the wrist was not by a fractured wound, or by amputation, in all probability it was done by the action of moving the body from its position. Mr. Norris assures me that all the bones and joints of the arm and shoulders were in a perfect state.

 The fingers of that hand were also disjointed as though the bones were fractured, and it is not more surprising that the wrist should be disjointed as well. I attribute this from the circumstance of the right side of the inner coffins being decayed near the position of the right hand than any other parts. I don't believe the account of the hand being wrapped in a separate bag. I saw no difference in the situation of the two hands. The covering of the right hand might be decayed from the same cause as the hand itself, but I saw nothing to justify the idea of its being originally buried separately from the body. I never heard that any of the Hampden family was buried in this manner, but it is not very likely that such circumstance if so, should be handed down to the present period.

 There was nothing appeared in the course of the examination which could in any way prove or make it even probable that the body was that of the Patriot; on the contrary the features which could be distinctly seen, were instead of the high nose, and thin face which the print portraits of the Patriot represent, this had instead more a fat round face.

 Butt will write to your Lordship tomorrow but I fear his account of the partridges will not be favourable, the late rains have been very destructive to the young coveys and there is the appearance of a bad season for birds.

 The service at Hampden Church on the 31st of this month will be in the afternoon 1/2 past two unless any alteration should be made by Mr. Brooks if there should be I will appraise your Lordship.

Mrs. Birr did receive a letter some time ago from your Lordship

I am my Lord your Lordship's
most faithful servant.
J. A. Grace

Item 10 – British Library (BrL) Hampden Papers 38986, f. 266: Letter sent from a Mr Trudal informing the lord of the Manor House of Aylesbury of his findings at Hampden House

MANOR HOUSE AYLESBURY WEDNESDAY 31 ST AUGUST 1859.

Dear Sir,
I have been working according to your directions at Hampden, and I have been lucky enough to trace out and to get from an intelligent eye witness a description of the body and the appearance it presented at exhumation. It has been written for me by a Mr. Robertson who was the Scotch gardener and favourite factotum of the late Earl of Buckinghamshire – Hampden's descendant and he tells me that the picture of the Patriot at Hampden used to hang unknown unnoticed on the best staircase, in that the first time he went up it afterwards this portrait which confronted – and appeared to be looking at him – was immediately recognised by him as that of the jawes, face and figure which was so disgracefully mutilated by gentlemen who ought to have known better. And on the arrival of his Master from France Mr. Robertson communicated his strong impression that this unknown portrait was that of the Patriot – It was immediately taken down and examined and under a piece of canvas was found inscribed the name John Hampden – the date 1640. And the history of the Picture, Robertson says that the face of the corpse was perfectly entire except the gristly part of the nose had sunk from the pressure of the cere cloths. I shall give the description in full and as nearly as I can in my informants words whose account differs somewhat from that published by Lord Nugent. And the charming incident of the recognition of the Portrait has never yet been printed – I have also been enstrusted with the Parish Register, which contains some curious remarks and entries and all this is woven up with a sort of family sketch of John Hampden and his mother. The learned old Clergyman Egeon asked when do you leave England and when do you return? I shall be glad to send you the article when it is finished before I venture to let Mr. Hewin see it. I am going to put all the rest into a strong jelly of concentration and to strike out a great quantity – I am afraid I am bothering you, but I could not help telling you about Robertson's information – The Tories are going to give a piece of plate to Bule!! Will you be in England the end of September or beginning of October. We shall be able to see our friends then. Mr. Wentworth is coming down to look up the people. It is such a pity that he can't speak – but no more can Smith. Bernard is the Orator among us now and enjoys the honours of this work. Your friend Mr. Lccman appears to advantage in the pamphlet business, *The Pomfret*. Each dear Sir your much obliged.

H. E. Trudal
I saw the Ropes at the Connel's the other day and Mary looks more like a gypsy than ever!

Item 11 – British Library (BrL) MS Egerton 2646, f. 293: Rob. Goodwin's letter to Sir Thomas Barrington sent from Thame, 26 June 1643

To my highly honoured Colonell Sir Thomas Barrington att his House in Queene Streete, London,
I Present,
Honoured Sir,

You shall understand that this present Monday morning, being the 26 of June, we received the sad tidings of Colonel Hamdens death; he died on Saturday night last; it being to all honest men a cause of much reluctation and sorrow this day likewise was read in the howse a proclamation which came from Oxford, granting pardon to all members of either howse that would come in to Oxford within ten daies excepting out of that pardon only 5 Lords and 13 Commoners the Earles of Essex Warwick Manchester Stamford and my Lord Say and Seale; Sir John Hotham, Sir Ar: Haselrigg, Sir ffran: Popham, Sir Ed: Hungerford, Sir Hen: Lindloc??, Mr Pym, Mr Strode, Mr Natha: Fiennes, Mr Alex: Popham, Mr Hamden, My Lord Major Colonel Mann the proclamation did seeme to anihilate this Parliament; the Lords voted that they would maintaine this Parliament with their lives and sent it downe at the conference; and do fixed a declaration might be sett forth concerning this proclamation; our howse did concur; my Lord General is yet at Tame; but we had this day an intimation given us by Mr Pym that he would goe forward upon some designe tomorrow : some commanders in the armie doe refuse the Covenant, I wish the number be not many; I cannot write you any good newes our forces at Leister have taken some of their Commanders ; my Lord Fairfax is in great want of horse ; the Queene advanceth: the last night the Cavaliers plundered Wickham and tooke a troope of my Lo: Generals horse; and this City tooke an alarum upon it and were up in armes all night: Colonel Martin's regiment is to goe downe to the armie with all convenient speede: there is nothing yet done in your Committee since you want although I pressed it for the other armies which concerns Essex I will doe anything you shall command: I have nothing else for the present thus in hast my humble service being presented to your selfe and my Ladie I take my leave and with ease rest

June 26 1643   Yours to Serve you

I beseech you present my
service to Sir John and
his Ladie and all the rest
of the Ladies./ Rob: Goodwin

Item 12 – British Library (BrL) MS Egerton 2646, f. 285: Letter by Will Hales to Sir Thomas Barrington, 22 June 1643, sent from Thame

June 22 1643
To the right honourable Sir Tho Barrington Knt and Baronet
These in haste

Sir,
I have but little news as yet but daily there are greater expectations as from the Lord General and likewise from the front??
    Sir Will Wallor gives in his letters hope of doing good service. The Lord General I hear intends to march today from Thame. The king is yet at Oxford the Queen at Newark, Sir John McDunn is put in Captain Hotham his place and Captain Hotham is prisoner at Nottingham Castle and it is with you that Sir John Hotham is found. Sir William Fairfax writes they hope ?????? to be able to go into the House of Lords and to the House of Commons about another motion(?) with the King, but it was laid by for the present. The house this day was about the excise (?) and an ordnance(?) for the finance ????????? Wallor and the ??? will come to ???? the worst news. I know is that Colonel Hampden is in great danger ????? on you this day to him,

I have scribbled you to long,

I remain yours at the throne of grace, Will Hale

I delivered your letter to Mr Pim and that to Mr Goodwin, who intends to write by the week.

Appendix X

Boulogne and the Brookses: The Life of Reverend G. W. Brooks

John Brooks (the son of George Brooks the Banker and founder of the family's fortunes) was baptized at Great Hampden, Bucks, October 1776.

The reason for his parents' being there must have much to do with the business of the Viscounts Hampden whom George Brooks had been agent for in Mayfair. John Brooks married Harriet Sophia Egerton on 1 January 1801 at St Margaret's Westminster, her first cousin the Revd Francis Henry Egerton (later last Earl of Bridgewater and notable eccentric) officiating. But the Egerton's were not the only aristocratic relations John Brooks acquired. His new sister-in-law Audrey was married to a French aristocrat called Édouard Mouron de Réty. How they met we can only speculate, but most probably he was in England to escape the Revolution.

Notes

1) F. H. W. Sheppard (ed.), *Survey of London* Vol XL, The Grosvenor London, 1980 p.191. Estate in Mayfair, Part II, The Buildings, tells us that the 1st Viscount Hampden found a house at 60 Green Street Mayfair for 'his agent and banker, George Brooks'. Viscount Hampden was a Trevor and George Brooks had begun his career by holding numerous offices under Bishop Trevor of Durham.

2) John Brooks was 35 and his wife 10 years younger. Audrey Mouron was her elder by 4 years, being born 15 February 1762 (Brooks/Egerton family tree in my possession, where Mouron is bluntly described as 'A Foreigner'). Audrey and Harriet Sophia were daughters of Col Charles Egerton, who served in the 4th Regiment of Foot (Army Lists) and transferred to the East India Company's service to become Governor of Bombay and disastrous commander of the Company's troops at Wargaon in 1779 (East India Co Minutes, Home & Misc. 143, pp.339 *et seq*.) He retired to Bath, dying there in 1793. He left £200 a year to each of his daughters (Will at the Public Record Office PROB Il 1223 Dodwell 312)

9) 'The 3rd and last Viscount Hampden died in 1824. The Viscounts had inherited Hampden under the Will of John Hampden died 1754. That same Will devised the estates, on the extinction of that branch and the Viscounty, [sic] to the descendants of Sir Henry Hobart who became Earls of Buckinghamshire. Thus in 1824 the 5th Earl inherited Hampden Estates and the gift of the living (GEC The Complete Peerage, Vol II p.440 (Buckinghamshire)

George William Brooks' Early Life
Meanwhile John and Harriet Sophia Brooks second son George William Brooks had been born on 28 February 1803 at 4.O'clock in the afternoon at his parents' house on John Street, Bedford Row. He had four brothers and a sister. He was baptized at St Andrew's Holborn on 12 May by the Revd Arthur Bold, his sponsors being Mrs Smith of Chiswick, John William Earl of Bridgewater, and the Revd Francis Drake of Beverley. The note copied from a family Bible which gives us this information also tells us that he was 'inoculated with vaccine matter in August 1803, and had the disorder very satisfactorily & favourably'. Along with his brothers he 'had the Measles in July 1808 at Hastings'. He was educated at Westminster 1816–1818 and on 25 June 1821 matriculated at Christ Church Oxford. He took his BA in 1825 and later became ordained. For some reason he did not take his MA till 1857. In 1827 he became Rector of Great Kimble and Great Hampden, Bucks., probably through the Hampden connection.

Appendix XI

The *Late Beating Up*

> HIS HIGHNESSE
> PRINCE RUPERTS
> LATE BEATING UP THE
> REBELS QUARTERS
> At Post-comb & Chinner
> In Oxford Shire.
> And his Victory in Chalgrove Field,
> on Sunday morning, June 18th 1643.[1]

Since the Earl of Essex late drawing down his Army unto *Tame,* nothing of moment hath been offered at, untill Saturday June 17th. 1643. Upon which day, we had the Alarm of a strong Partee of about 2500 Horse & Foot, sent out to beat up the Kings Out-Quarters. Their design was for *Islip,* within 5 miles of *Oxford*. There, at that time the most valiant Sir *Arthur Asten*, Sergeant-Major General of the Kings *Horse Forces*, lay quartered.: Lieutenant-General *Wilmot* lying not far off at *Bletchington*. To whom the Sergeant-Major sending these vigilant chieftains by their espialls [spies] getting time enough, that the rebels were approaching, made show presently upon the Hill, how ready they were to bid them welcome. Thither, one after another, were drawn the horse Regiments of the Prince of *Wales,* of Mr. *Henry Percy,* General of the Ordnance; with Sir *Arthur Astons* own, and some 150 Dragooners of my Lord *Wentworth*, and others. The Rebels perceiving such a Body of resistants and that they were still increasing; drew back a little down into *Beckley Park*: making *halt* there, and falling to make fires, throughout all their Guards and Regiments. But otherwise bethinking themselves after a while, they all drew off, and marched away back again to their old Quarters. Thus was that design of theirs lost utterly.

    The Earl of *Essex* having by this alarm begun the courtesy, his *Highness* Prince *Rupert* would not be long behind hand with him. And to put the affront the homer [i.e. Rupert], resolved that very day to march quite through the

---

1   Bodleian Library, ref. Wood 376 (14).

middle of the Quarters: even to the very farthest of them towards *London*, beyond & besides *Tame*, the Earls head-quarter.

For this purpose, on the same Saturday *June* 17th.. 1643 about 4 in the afternoon his *Highness* drew out of *Oxford*: crossing the river *Charwell* [River Thame] at *Chiselhampton-Bridge*. His strength was near **2000** men: whereof about 1000. Horse under 3. Regiments. Those namely, of his *Highness* the Prince of *Wales*, commanded by Sergeant-Major *Daniel*: his *Highness's* own Regiment, commanded by Lieutenant Colonel *O' Neale*; to which was added his *Highness's* fair Troop of *Lifeguards;* commanded by Sir *Richard Crane*. The third and last Regiment was General *Percyes*, by himself commanded. Of *Dragooners*, marched some 350. under my Lord *Wentworth* their Sergeant-Major General, drawn altogether out of his Lordships own Troop, Prince *Rupert's* Regiment, Sir *Robert Howard's*, and Colonel *Washington's* Regiment, commanded by Colonel *Innes*. Of Foot, there were betwixt 400. and 500. *commanded* men without *Colours*: and Colonel *Lunsford* had the leading of them. The *van* of this greater *Partee*, was a lesser *Partee* commanded by Sergeant Major *Legge*: made up of the Prince of *Wales* his Regiment , with 100 other *commanded* Horse; and some 50. *Dragooners,* under *Lieutenant-Colonel Lisle*. These marched like a *forlorn hope*, a distance before the greater *Partee*. With this little Army, without any |*Ordnance*, after some *Halts* on purpose by the way; by one a clock next morning, was the Prince advanced as high as over against *Tetsworth*, and upon the right hand of it. Thereabouts, by the highways side had the Rebels a strong Guard, both of *Horse* and *Foot* or *Dragooners*. Here our *Partee* being discovered by their *Sentinel*, we were saluted with his Pistol first, & Carbine immediately after: and by and by as we marched along, with several shots more from their *main-guard*; where some of ours discovered many light-matches. But the Prince would have none of these answered: for his design being to advance farther, he would neither lose time, nor by shooting give the Alarm to other Quarters of the Rebels. However, from this time forward they had the Alarm, and warning by it throughout all their Quarters to draw together to confront the *Prince*, either in his advancing or returning.

By 3 in the morning, we had reached *Postcomb*, a Hamlet belonging to *Lewknor* parish. There lay a Horse Quarter of Rebels: who having some little time to mount, whilst our Dragooners at the streets end alighted; those only in some of the nearer houses were surprised. Some Pistols, with other Horsemen's Arms and Horses were here taken: together with 9 Prisoners, and one Cornet of Colonel *Morleys of Sussex*, as we were informed. This town was beyond *Tame*, and upon the south of it.

Hence after half an hour, his *Highness* advanced somewhat towards the *left*, along under the ledge of hills, not far from *Stokenchurch*, and the Villages in the bottom. Before 5 in the morning; were we got to *Chinner,* some 4 miles beyond *Tame:* being the very farthest of the Rebels Quarters towards *London*. The Town was presently entered by Sergeant-Major *Legg* and his Partee, and by & by surrounded by the rest of the *Princes* Forces. Within it lay some 200 Dragooners of Sir *Samuel Luke's Bedfordshire* Regiment: under their Sergeant-Major *Edwards*. These, though but new levied men, yet had already actually appeared in Rebellion: as being part of that strong *Partee,* which the day before had marched out against *Islip*. These all weary and new come into the Quarters, were taken sleepers in the Barns and Houses. Diverse were killed as they bustled up: and others, that upon the Alarm, had already gotten themselves to their Arms. Some Captains and Officers (as we were told) getting into a house at the Towns end, would needs there stand upon their Guard: shooting at the *Prince* and his company out at the windows. Upon which the house being fired by a Soldier, diverse of them running out on the backside, were there shot by our Foot and Dragooners. Our men report that they killed some 50 or more in all of them: eight of which they say were slain in one Barn. Which number alone amounts to more than some of the Rebels will confess, who say they buried but 5 in all *Chinner*. Prisoners we brought away about Sixscore: so that very few of all that were Quartered there, escaped. Almost all their Horses and Armes were taken, with three of Sir *Samuel Luke's* Dragoon Cornets. Their *Field* or Ground was *black*, with 1, 2, 3, 4, or 5 *Bibles* bost and bufft, depainted in them.

Parting from this town, we missed narrowly, and but half an hour, of Twenty one thousand pound then coming to the Earl of *Essex:* but the conductors hearing of the Alarm, drove the Carts into the wood, and so we missed it.

This Action having taken up about some hour and halfs time, His *Highness* commanded away to Horse, bending His march homewards all along under the ledge of hills to the South and South-westward. But yet on purpose with so slow a march, that the Rebels (if they pleased) might have leisure to confront Him. And so it happened: news being brought us betwixt 7 and 8 a clock, that a body of the Rebels were discovered in the village hard upon the left hand of us. Presently whereupon some half score of their Scouts were discovered upon the sides of the *Becon-hill*, beyond the Village. After a little farther march, the *Princes* own Regiment, and General *Percyes* being in the rear, and at that time over-marched by the *Princes* Troop of *Life-guard*, the Rebels Horse fell upon their rear; skirmishing lightly with them for a while. It would seem by my Lord of *Essex* Letter, that these Rebels were Major *Gunter*, with his own Troop, Captain *Sheffield*'s & Captain *Crosse*'s Troops, with Colonel *Dulbeir*, their Quarter-Master-General. These being once or twice faced by General *Percy*, and Lieutenan*t* Colonel *O'Neale*, they so far retreated, that ours had time to recover up to the *Prince*, and V*an* of the Army. His *Highness* was now making *halt* in *Chalgrove* cornfield: about a mile & half short of *Chiselhampton Bridge*. Just at this time (being now about 9 a clock) we discerned several great Bodies of the Rebels Horse and Dragooners, coming down *Golder-hill* towards us; from *Esington* and *Tame*: who (together with those that had before skirmished with our Rear) drew down to the bottom of a great Close, or Pasture: ordering themselves there among trees beyond a great hedge, which parted that Close from our Field. My Lord of *Essex's* Relation, here mentions Captain *Sanders* Troop, and Captain *Buller* with 50 commanded men; Captain *Dundasses* Troop of Dragooners, with some few of Colonel *Melves*. But surely these were not all their Forces. His *Highness* perceiving this great Body, took care first of all how to secure the *pass* over *Chiselhampton Bridge* for making good the Retreat to us; least other enemies as yet undiscovered, might cut it off from us. For this purpose Colonel *Lunsford*, & Colonel *Washington* being sent with all the *Foot* to lye on both ends the bridge; the *Princes* next design was to line the hedges along the Lanes that led thither. For this purpose, my Lord *Wentworth* and his Lieutenant-Colonel Mr. *John Russell*, were sent before hand with the *Dragooners*: for his *Highness* well hoped the Rebels might be trained into that Ambush. The better to entice them on, the *Prince* with Horse made show of a Retreat: whereupon the Rebels advanced cheerfully: doubling their march for eagerness, and coming up close to us. Then we discerned them to be eight Cornets of *Horse*, besides about 100 commanded *Horse*, and as many *Dragooners* of Colonel *Mills* (*Melves*, my Lords Relation writes him) his Regiment; now led by Captain *Middleton*. We were now parted by a hedge, close to the midst whereof the Rebels brought on their Dragooners: and to the end of it came their *Forlorn hope* of horse. Their whole Body of 8 Cornets faced the *Princes Regiment* and Troop of *Lifeguards,* and made a Front so much too large for the *Princes* Regiment, that two Troops were faine to be drawn out of the Prince *of Wales* Regiment, to make our Front even with the enemy. And this was their Order. Besides which, they had left a *Reserve* of 3 Cornets in the Close aforesaid among the trees by *Wapsgrove House*, and two Troops more higher up the hill, they were in sight of one another, by 9 a clock in the morning.

The *Princes* battalions were thus ordered. His *Highness's* own Regiment, with the Lifeguards on the right hand of it, had the *middle-ward*: the Prince of *Wales* his Regiment making the *Left -wing*, and Mr. *Percy's* having the *Right*. Both these Regiments were at first intended for *Reserves*: though presently they engaged themselves in the encounter. It was diverse of the Commanders counsels, that the *Prince* should continue on the retreat, and so draw the Rebels into the Ambush, but his *Highness's* judgement overswayed that ; for that (saith he) the Rebels being so near us, may bring our Rear into confusion, before we can recover to our ambush. Yea (saith he) their insolency is not to be endured. This said, His *Highness* facing all about, set spurs to His Horse, and first of all (in the very face of the Dragooners) leapt the hedge that parted us from the Rebels. The *Captain*, and rest of His Troop of *Lifeguards* (everyman as they could) jumbled over after him: and as about 15 were gotten over, the *Prince* presently drew them up into a Front, till the rest could recover up to him. At this the Rebels Dragooners that lined the hedge, fled: having hurt and slain some of ours with their first volley. Meantime Lieutenant-Colonel *O'neale* having passed with the *Princes* Regiment beyond the end of the hedge on the left hand, had begun the encounter with 8 Troops of Rebels. These having before seen ours facing about, took themselves off their speed presently, and made a fair stand till ours advanced up to charge them. So that they being first in order, gave us their first Volley of Carbines and Pistols at a distance, as ours were advancing: yea they had time for their second Pistols, ere ours could charge them. The hottest of their charge fell upon Captain *Martins*, and Captain *Gardiner's* Troops, in Prince *Ruperts* Regiment: and indeed the whole Regiment endured the chief shock of it. To say the truth; they stood our first charge of Pistols and Swords, better then the Rebels have ever yet done, since their first beating at *Worcester*; especially those of their *Right-wing*: for their *Left* gave it over sooner: for that the *Prince* with his *Lifeguards*, with Sword and Pistol charging them home upon the *Flank*, (not wheeling about upon their Rear, as the *London Relation* tells it) put them in rout at the first encounter. By this time also was General *Percy* with some Troops of his Regiment fallen upon that *Flank*, and followed upon the execution. As on the other wing did Major *Daniel* with the *Prince of Wales* his Regiment: so that now were the Rebels wholly routed. Some of ours affirm, how they over-heard *Dulbiere* (who brought up some of the Rebels first Horse) upon sight of the *Princes* order and dividing of his *Wings*, to call out to his People *to retreat, least they were hemmed in by us.*

The Rebels now flying to their *Reserve* of three *Colours* in the Close by *Wapsgrove* house, were pursued by ours in execution all the way thither: who now (as they could) there *rallying*, gave occasion to the defeat of those three *Troops* also. So that all now being in confusion, were pursued by ours a full mile and quarter (as the neighbours say) from the place of the first encounter. These all fled back again over *Golder hill* to *Esington*: and so far Sir *Phillip Stapleton* with his Regiment was not yet come. And if he stopped and drew the *Retreaters* up into a body, and made a stand for an hour with them, (as the *London Relation* tells us) it was surely behind and beyond the great hill where ours could not discern them. Yea plainly our two Prisoners since their return affirm, that it was two miles from the place of fight ere he met them, nor yet could he stay the Parliamentiers from running. Before this, and in time of the fight, some three *Cornets* of them were observed to wheel abouts; as if they intended either to get betwixt us and *Chiselhampton bridge*, or to charge us upon the rear. Which being observed by Lieutenant Colonel *O'neale*, he borrowed two Troops of General *Percy's* Regiment, and made out after them: which they perceiving, turned bridles about, and made haste back again to their fellows.

In the encounter, one daring fellow bare himself hard upon the *Prince*, and had the honour to die by His Pistol. One great commander was shot by Mr. *Percy*, thought to be Sergeant-Major *Gunter*; who that day commanded the Earl of *Essex* own Regiment. Colonel *Urrey* that day charged in the very left hand of the front of the Prince of *Wales* his Regiment: where being engaged, and known, he was offered quarter: but he brought off himself by his sword cheaper, then they would have ransomed him. Lieutenant Colonel *O'neale* offering quarter to a proper young Gentleman, was reproached by him, for which he died in the very act of discourtesy, as well as of Rebellion. Sergeant-Major *Legge's* courage having engaged him too far among the Rebels so long, became their Prisoner, till themselves were Routed. The same mischance (and some slight wounds) had Sergeant-Major *Daniel*, by the fall of his Horse but being re-mounted, he in pursuit required it upon his adversaries, he having before that shot dead a *Cornet* of the Rebels, recovered the honour to the Prince of *Wales*. His troop, henceforth again to bear a Cornet which (having heretofore in fight at *Hopton* Heath lost their own) it seems by Law of Arms they might not bear, till some of theirs again in fight had won a Colour from the Rebels. The Earl of *Essex* had notice by some of his, of a Gentleman charging in the head of Prince *Rupert's* Regiment, who fought like a Lion; who by the description of his Person, was judged to be Sir *Thomas Dallison*. In brief, all our *Commanders* and *Officers*, with the Soldiers generally, behaved themselves valiantly: though such be their modesty, that the *Writer* must learn what each man did from the report of others. Some of our *Troopers* (both they and their Horses being overtired with several days hard and long duty) could not, indeed, advance so forwardly as their fellows: which was one of the two reasons, the Rebels could no further be pursued by the residue of our *Troopers*. Plainly our Horses were too much tired generally. But the main reason indeed was the temper and discretion both of the Commanders and the Soldiers, they had learned by *Edge hill*, not to pursue too far: so that now contenting themselves to have routed the Rebels, they were seen to rally themselves again into order handsomely, and suddenly in their ground.

Thus (by the help of God only) without the assistance of our own Foot or Dragooners were the Rebels Horseman and Dragooners, utterly defeated, by the *Prince* and His *Horsemen*. Diverse of the their Commanders were slain upon the place: of whom (that we yet know) Sergeant-Major *Gunter* was the chiefest. The number of the slain, we cannot yet learn: only we hear that 33 (say some, 29 say others) were buried in *Chalgrove:* which doubtless were killed in that field. And 15 more in *Esington* that were slain in the pursuit: in which fewer more being deadly wounded, died as they were carrying towards *Tame*. But to reckon up the slain by the number of burials, is no sure way of coming by the truth: for that diverse of these *Brownists* and *Anabaptists* refuse to have their Soldiers buried, otherwise then they do their Horses. My Lord of *Essex* Letter says, there were but 45 killed on both sides: the most of which were the Kings. But surely none of his men could assure his Lordship of that, because they left us masters of the field, and leisure, by that, to survey the dead bodies. But neither did we rely upon our own account, but more upon the number brought in by the Country people, where the dead were buried; now the reason why we killed no more was, partly because diverse of the Rebels had red scarves like ours, and by following them, were Mr. *Howard*, and Captain *Gardner* unawares engaged and taken.

The chief of the wounded men was Colonel *Hampden*, and he supposed to be the chief or second man, to whom this Rebellion and these miseries are much to be imputed. He put him self under Captain *Cross's* Troop, says my Lords letter: and was unfortunately shot through the shoulder. So we heard to, and that the anguish of it had put him into a fever, of which he is since dead. 'Tis wished his fellow Rebels would take notice of the first parts of Gods judgements towards him. How that he received this wound in the very same *Chalgrove* Field, where August 15 1642 himself had sent together a power of *Redcoats*, which he procured to be sent from *London*, with 200 *Buckinghamshire* men (all under his own and Colonel *Goodwins* command) for the taking of the Earl of *Berkshire*, Sir John *Curson*, Mr. *Branthwaite*, Mr. *Hone*, and other Justices, then sitting (not upon the *Commission of Array*, but) upon settling the peace of the County at Sir *Robert Dormer's* house at *Ascot*. These forces (I hear) did Mr *Hampden* then send by his man *William Lidall*, into this *Chalgove Field* (himself being not far of) by which those parts of the County were first of all disturbed. Captain *Buller* was also shot in the neck, says my Lord of *Essex* Letter, who coming that day into my Lords

Chamber at *Tame*, told him openly in the hearing of our two Prisoners, *'That he would not give a fig for all his Lordships Horse.'*

Ten other sorely wounded men, were brought into Mr. *Stevens* house in *Esington*; who being there dressed, they pressed his Cart to carry them to their Quarter. In the field were found dangerously wounded, and at first left for dead, Mr. *Sheffield* a son of the Earl of *Mulgraves*; this day a Cornet of the Earl of *Essex*, with one Captain *Berkeley*, a *Scottishman*, both these by the *Princes* courtesy, were left near the place to be dressed; each promising upon the word and *Parole* of a Soldier, to become true Prisoners, which whether they forgot or no, I know not. Sure it is, that on *Monday* night, they excused themselves by their soreness and disability, to come away hither in Sir *Lewis Dives* his Coach, on purpose sent for them which notwithstanding they were next morning fetched away by their own party. These brake *Chalgrove Cross*, and so home again.

Observed it is by the Country People, that most of the Rebels slain and wounded men, were hurt upon their backs. Of prisoners taken in this last encounter, we brought away but eleven into *Oxford*, Cornet *Sanders* and some others being still kept at *Abingdon*. We took two Orange *Cornets* of the Earl of *Essex* own Regiment, belonging to Major *Gunter*, and Captain *Sheffield*. The *Word* upon one of these *Cornets* was *Cave adsum*: thought to belong to the Earl's own Troop of Lifeguards. On the Kings party, were slain some 10 or 12 and some of them through mistake by our People. The reason of the mistake being for want of Scarves, or their not having the word readily. Of wounded men, I observed some 16 or 20 to be dressed by our Surgeons: The man of most note among them was Captain *Jackson* of Prince *Charles* His Regiment: to whom Prince Rupert gave this honourable testimony, that he behaved himself bravely. Now though it be seldom seen, that the vanquished men carry off any Prisoners of the Victors: yet two Gentlemen of note of the Kings Party by mistaking of their Colours, fell in among them; namely, Mr. *Henry Howard* son to the Earl of *Berkshire*: & Captain *Thomas Gardiner*, of Prince *Rupert's* Regiment, both which are since exchanged for Sergeant-Major *Edwards*. The *London* Relation says they have Captain *Smith* also whom we know nothing.

Prince *Rupert* upon the return of His People from the pursuit, kept the field about half an hour: expecting whether the Rebels would make head again: but perceiving no more adversaries, the victorious *Prince* retired his Troops over *Chiselhampton* bridge leisurely. There having ordered Mr. *Percy* with his Horse Regiment, and Colonel *Washington* with his Dragooners for that night to quarter near the *pass*, and to send out strong *patrols* or *rounds* for scouting all along the River Charwell: His Highness by two a clock came safely back into *Oxford*. He had sent the news of all before by Colonel Urrey whom the King presently Knighted. The report of these *two* Victories, were so much the welcomer to His Majesty, for that he had heard the Prince have been engaged.

The Lord of Hosts be praised, that giveth victory to his anointed: and by it vouch safe. He to give the blessing of PEACE unto his People.

Bibliography

Archival Sources

Bodleian Library (BoL)
249: E, 128, no. 33: *Abingdons and Ailisburies Present Miseries*, 19 December 1642
Clarendon State Papers – Repositories 7567, Biographical and Historical
Map (R) C17:49 60: John Badcock's map of Pyrton, 1835
MS. Clar. 112, f. 366: Sir Edward Hyde's Private Journal, 1641–1646
MS. Eng. Hist. c. 53: Parliamentary scout reports of Royalist forces at Rycote, 14 June 1643 during the first English Civil War, fol. 46r. – fol. 47r., 16 June 1643
MS. Tanner 62/1B, fols. 233, 240
Wood 376 (14): *His Highnesse Prince Ruperts Late Beating Up of the Rebels Quarters at Post-comb & Chinner in Oxford Shire. And his Victory in Chalgrove Field on Sunday morning, June 18th 1643. Where unto is added Sr John Urries Expedition to West-Wickham the Sunday after : June 25. 1643*

British History Online (BHO)
Journal of the House of Lords, vol. 5, 1642–1643
Journal of the House of Lords, vol. 20, 25 May 1717, 'Earl of Oxford and E. Mortimer impeached'

British Library (BrL)
Hampden Papers 38986, f. 266: Letter sent from a Mr Trudal informing the lord of the Manor House of Aylesbury of his findings at Hampden House (see Appendix IX, Item 10, for text)
MS Egerton 2643, f. 7: Col. John Hampden's last known letter, 9 June 1643, from Stokenchurch, Oxon, to Sir Thomas Barrington
MS Egerton 2646, f. 259: Grey of Werke, Letter sent from Nettlebed, Oxon, 7 June 1643
MS Egerton 2646, f. 263: Letter from the Earl of Essex, 'For my worthy friends the Gentlemen Householders and other well affected in the County of Essex', Stokenchurch, 9 June 1643
MS Egerton 2646, f. 285: Letter by Will Hales to Sir Thomas Barrington, 22 June 1643, sent from Thame (see Appendix IX, Item 12, for text)
MS Egerton 2646, f. 289: Letter from the Earl of Essex to Sir Thomas Barrington, 24 June 1643
MS Egerton 2646, f. 293: Rob. Goodwin's letter to Sir Thomas Barrington sent from Thame, 26 June 1643 (see Appendix IX, Item 11, for text)

British Library (BrL): Thomason Tracts (TT)
E 55 (11): *A True Relation of a Gret fight between the Kings forces and the Parliaments at Chinner neer Tame on Saturday last*
E 55 (19): Second letter of *Two Letters* from the Earl of Essex, 'For my worthy friends the Deputy Lieutenants of Essex', Stokenchurch, 9 June 1643

BIBLIOGRAPHY

E 55 (19): *Two Letters from his Excellencie Robert Earl of Essex. The one unto the Speaker of the House of Commons; relating the true state of the late skirmish at Chinner, between a party of the King's and Parliament's Forces, on the Sabbath day the 19 June 1643. With the number of such persons as was taken and slain on both sides. The other to the well affected of the County of Essex*

E 64 (3): *The Earle of Essex His Letter to Master Speaker,* 9 July 1643

E 96 (10): *The Parliament Scout, Communicating His Intelligence to the Kingdome,* From Tuesday the 20. June, to Tuesday the 27. of June 1643, no. 1

E 114 (25): *A True and Perfect Relation of the first and victorious skirmish*

E 126 (9): *Good and Joyfull Newes out of Buckinghamshire, Being an exact relation of a battle stricken between Prince Robert and Sir William Balforth, Lieut-General to his Excellency the Earl of Essex, near Aylesbury, in this County on Tuesday last, 1 Nov' when the said Sir William obtained a happy and glorious Victory* (London: Francis Wright, 1642)

E 245 (36): *Mercurius Aulicus Communicating the Intelligence and affaires of the Court, to the rest of the Kingdom,* The five and twentieth week

British Newspaper Archive (BNA)

BL_000052_18630121_042_0008.pdf. *Derby Mercury,* Derbyshire, England, Wednesday, 21 January 1863 (see Appendix IX, Item 7, for text)

'Correspondence sent by Lord Nugent 27 June 1828 to Mr. G W Brooks, the Rector at Great Hampden at the time of the exhumation', *Derby Mercury,* Wednesday, 21 January 1863 (see Appendix IX, Item 5, for text)

'Letter to Mr Urban, Stoneleigh, March 26', *The Gentleman's Magazine and Historical Chronicle*, vol. 85, part 1, 1815, pp.395–96 (see Appendix II for text)

'Rector Brookses copy of a Letter from James Grace, Esq., Land Steward to the Earl of Buckinghamshire and Churchwarden of Great Hampden, to Lord Nugent. Risborough dated June 17, 1828', *Derby Mercury,* Wednesday, 21 January 1863 (see Appendix IX, Item 4, for text)

Sydney Morning Herald, 22 October 1861, p.2 (see Appendix VIII for text)

Buckinghamshire Archives (BA)

AR 62/92 Box A4: *Hampden Magna: Tombs' Location in the Chancel of St Mary Magdalene, Great Hampden (1663–1675)*

AR 62/92 (Box File) A6: Letter from Dr James Grace to Earl of Buckinghamshire, Union Club, Cockspur Street, London, 22 July 1828 (see Appendix IX, Item 6, for text)

D/MH 39/84: Letter from Dr James Grace to the Earl of Buckinghamshire, 5 April 1828 (see Appendix IX, Item 2, for text)

D/MH 39/85: Letter from Dr James Grace to the Earl of Buckinghamshire, 19 August 1828 (see Appendix IX, Item 9, for text)

D/MH 39/86, Transcript 11: Letter from Dr James Grace to Richard Cumberland at the Exchequer, Palace Yard, London, 9 August 1828 (see Appendix IX, Item 8, for text)

D/MH 39/87: Letter fragment from Dr James Grace to the Earl of Buckinghamshire, early June 1828 (see Appendix IX, Item 3, for text)

D/MH 39/88: Letter fragment from Dr James Grace to the Earl of Buckinghamshire, March 1828 (see Appendix IX, Item 1, for text)

D/MH Trans 11: *The Gentleman's Magazine* 6 June 1829, Letter signed by P.Q.

D/MH Trans 11: *The Gentleman's Magazine* Sept 1828, pp.199–200, Letter by J. De Alta Ripa

PR 90/1/1: Great Hampden Register of Baptisms and Burials, 1557–1812, Microfilm

Clergy of the Church of England Database (CCEd)
ID 8618

Hatfield Library (HL)
Letter to *The Times* published 28 July 1828, Microfilm reel (see Appendix V for text)

Lambeth Archive (LA)
Stanley and W. F. Harradence (eds), '[visit] No 4 June 10th 1893 (Led by) Mr G. H. Lindsay-Renton – Great Hampden, Halton and Wendover', in *Upper Norwood Athenaeum: An Account of the Winter Meetings and Summer Excursions of 1892–3* (Privately published, n.d. [1893]), pp.47–54

Massachusetts Historical Society (MHS)
The Annotated Newspapers of Harbottle Dorr, Jr.

Oxfordshire History Centre (OHC)
Magd. Coll. MP/1/77: William Webb map 1612 – Golder Manor Estate
Ordnance Survey, Epoch1, sheet XLVI.4 (1881), 1:5,000, North East of Chalgrove
PAR 279/9/M5/1: *History of Watlington 1816*

The National Archives (TNA)
SP 23/185, f. 240
SP 28/1C, f. 226
SP 28/1D Part 2, f. 477
SP 28/2B, ff. 321–24
SP 28/7, f. 395
SP 28/7, f. 438
SP 28/7, f. 440
SP 28/39, ff. 571r –72
SP 28/140 Part 6
SP 28/143, unfold
SP 28/252 Part 1

Wiltshire and Swindon Record Office (WSRO)
413/444 Personal 11

Newspapers and Periodicals

Bucks Advertiser and Aylesbury News
Bucks Herald
Chester Courant
Cork Constitution
Dublin Evening Mail
Hampshire Advertiser
London Courier and Evening Gazette
Morning Post
St. James Chronicle
The Aylesbury News

The Chronicle
The Gentleman's Magazine and Historical Chronicle
The London Magazine
The Times
Westmoreland Gazette

Online References

Lester, Derek, *Parslow's Military Chest: An Urban Legend Resolved, Find Out Why Colonel John Hampden's Regiment's Pay was Given to the Landlord of the Hare and Hounds* (Chalgrove Battle Group, 2018, Flipbook), <https://johnhampdensregiment.org.uk/parslowschest/#p=1>

Lester, Derek, *Time and Places in the 'Late Beating Up' Compared with the Essex Letters in Chronological Order* (Chalgrove Battle Group, 2023, Flipbook), <https://johnhampdensregiment.org.uk/Time%20and%20place/mobile/index.html#p=1>

Lester, Derek (ed.), *Hampden Magna: Tomb's Location in the Chancel of St Mary Magdalene, Great Hampden: Hampden Family Tombs in Hartwell Church and St Andrew's Church, East Hagbourne* (Chalgrove Battle Group, 2017, Flipbook), <https://johnhampdensregiment.org.uk/hampdenmagna/index.html#p=1>

Lester, Derek (ed.), *His Highnesse Prince Ruperts Late Beating Up the Rebels Quarters at Post-comb & Chinner in Oxford Shire. And his Victory in Chalgrove Field, on Sunday morning, June 18th 1643. Whereunto is added Sr John Urries Expedition to West-Wickham the Sunday after : June 25. 1643* (Chalgrove Battle Group, 2018, Flipbook), <https://johnhampdensregiment.org.uk/LateBeatingUp/#p=1>. See Appendix XI for full text.

Lester, Derek (ed.), *History of Watlington 1816* (Chalgrove Battle Group, 2018, Flipbook), <https://johnhampdensregiment.org.uk/how/#p=1>

Lester, Derek (ed.), *Two Letters from his Excellencie Robert Earl of Essex: The One unto the Speaker of the House of Commons; Relating the True State of the Skirmish at Chinner, Between a Party of the Kings and Parliaments Forces on the Sabbath Day the 19 of June, 1643, with the Number of Such Persons as was Taken and Slain on Both Sides. The Other to the Well Affected of the County of Essex* (Chalgrove Battle Group, 2018, Flipbook), <https://johnhampdensregiment.org.uk/EssexLetters/#p=1>

Lester, Derek and Gill, *The Controversy of John Hampden's Death* (Chalgrove Battle Group, 2000, Flipbook), <https://johnhampdensregiment.org.uk/Controversy/index.html#p=1>

Lester, Derek and Gill (eds), *Hampden's Monument Unveiled* (Chalgrove Battle Group, 2006, Flipbook), <https://johnhampdensregiment.org.uk/unveiled/#p=1>

Printed Primary Sources

Cartwright, John, *The Life and Correspondence of Major Cartwright* (London: Henry Colburn, 1826), vols I–II

Gardiner, Samuel R. (ed.), *The Constitutional Documents of the Puritan Revolution, 1625–1660* (Oxford: Clarendon Press, 1906)

Green, Mary Anne Everett (ed.), *Letters of Queen Henrietta Maria, Including Her Private Correspondence with Charles the First. Collected from the Public Archives and Private Libraries of France and England* (London: Richard Bentley, 1857)

Hyde, Edward, *The History of the Rebellion and Civil Wars in England* (Oxford: Printed at Theater, 1702–1704), vols I–III

Hyde, Edward, *The History of the Rebellion and Civil Wars in England* (Oxford: Printed at Theater, 1717), vols I–VII

Hyde, Edward, *The History of the Rebellion and Civil Wars in England* (Oxford: Clarendon Press, 1826), vols I–VIII

Hyde, Edward, *The History of the Rebellion and Civil Wars in England*, 1969 edn (Oxford: Clarendon Press, 1888), vols I–VI

Hyde, Edward, *The Life of Edward Earl of Clarendon, Lord High Chancellor of England and Chancellor of the University of Oxford. Containing, 1. An Account of the Chancellor's Life from his Birth to the Restoration in 1660. II. A Continuation of the same, and of his History of the Grand Rebellion, from the Restoration to his Banishment in 1667* (Oxford: Clarendon Printing-House, 1759), vols I–III

Ludlow, Edmund, *Memoirs of Edmund Ludlow Esq; Lieutenant General of the Horse, Commander in Chief of the forces in Ireland, one of the Council of State, and a Member of the Parliament which began on November 3, 1640* (Switzerland: Printed at Vivay in the Canton of Bern, 1698), vols I–II

Noble, Mark, *Memoirs of Several Persons and Families, Who, by Females Are Allied To, or Descended From, the Protectorate-House of Cromwell, Chiefly Collected From Original Papers and Records: To Which Is Added, a Catalogue of Such Persons Who Were Raised to Honors or Great Employments by the Cromwells; With the Lives of Many of Them* (Birmingham: Pearson and Rollason, 1784), vol. II

Nugent, Lord George, *Memorials of John Hampden, his party and his times*, 4th edn, with a memoir of the writer (London: H. G. Bohn, 1860)

Nugent, Lord George, *Some Memorials of John Hampden, His Party and His Times* (London: John Murray, 1832), vols I–II

Nugent, Lord George, *Some Memorials of John Hampden, His Party and His Times*, 3rd edn, revised, with a memoir of the writer (London: Chapman and Hall, 1854)

Nugent, Lord George, *Some Memorials of John Hampden, His Party and His Times*, 5th edn (London: George Bell and Sons, 1889)

Nugent, Lord George, *Tract Entitled True and Faithful Relation of a Worthy Discourse, Between ye late Colonel Hampden and Colonel Oliver Cromwell held June ye Eleventh, in ye Yeare of Grace 1643* (London: Chapman and Hall, 1847)

Philip, I. G. (ed.), *Journal of Sir Samuel Luke: Scoutmaster to the Earl of Essex* (Oxford: Oxfordshire Record Society, 1947, 1950, 1952–1953), vols I–III

St George, Henry, and Lennard, Sampson, 'Bennett. [Harl. 1166, fo. 34b.]', in John P. Rylands (ed.), *The Visitation of the County of Dorset, Taken in the Year 1623* (London: Harleian Society, 1885), p.14

Toynbee, Margaret (ed.), *The Papers of Captain Henry Stevens, Waggon-Master-General to King Charles I* (Oxford: Oxfordshire Record Society, 1961)

Warburton, Eliot, *Memoirs of Prince Rupert, and the Cavaliers. Including their Private Correspondence, Now First Published from the Original Manuscripts* (London: Bentley, 1849), vols I–III

Warwick, Sir Philip, *Memoires of the reigne of King Charles I. With a Continuation to the Happy Restauration of King Charles II* (London: Ri. Chiswell, 1701)

Whitelocke, Bulstrode, *Memorials of the English Affairs: Or, An Historical Account of What Passed from the Beginning of the Reign of Charles the First, to King Charles the Second his Happy Restauration Containing the Publick Transactions, Civil and Military: Together with the Private Considerations and Secrets of the Cabinet* (Oxford: University Press, 1853)

Secondary Sources

Adair, John, *A Life of John Hampden, The Patriot, 1594–1643* (London: Macdonald and Jane's, 1976)

Bailey, Roy, 'The Funeral of John Hampden', *The Patriot*, 79 (2014), pp.1–2

Barrès-Baker, M. C., *The Siege of Reading, April 1643: The Failure of the Earl of Essex's 1643 Spring Offensive* (Ottawa: eBooksLib, 2004)

'Battle of Chalgrove 1643', *Historic England*, <https://historicengland.org.uk/listing/the-list/list-entry/1000006>, accessed 18 Feb. 2023

Beckett, Ian F. W., *Wanton Troopers: Buckinghamshire in the Civil Wars, 1640–1660* (Barnsley: Pen and Sword, 2015)

Burns, Eric, *Infamous Scribblers: The Founding Fathers and the Rowdy Beginnings of American Journalism* (New York: Public Affairs, 2006)

Claus, Patricia W., *Conscience is my Crown: A Family's Heroic Witness in an Age of Intolerance* (Leominster: Gracewing, 2017)

'Declaratory Act', *Wikipedia*, <https://en.wikipedia.org/wiki/Declaratory_Act>, accessed 18 Feb. 2023

De la Torre Bueno, J. R., 'Francesco Redi and the Spontaneous Generation of Life (Note on a New 17th Century Accession to the Library)', *The Brooklyn Museum Quarterly*, 12:1 (1925), pp.24–26. <https://www.jstor.org/stable/26459525>

Dickinson, H. T., *Walpole and the Whig Supremacy* (Aylesbury: Hazell, Watson and Viney, 1973)

Drinkwater, John, *John Hampden's England* (London: Thornton Butterworth, 1933)

Echard, Laurence, *The History of England. From the First Entrance of Julius Cæsar and the Romans, To the Conclusion of the Reign of King James the Second, and the Establishment of King William and Queen Mary upon the Throne, in the Year 1688* (London: Jacob Tonson, 1707–1720), vols I–III and an Appendix of Errata

English Heritage, *English Heritage Battlefield Report: Chalgrove 1643: Chalgrove Field (18 June 1643)* (Swindon: English Heritage, 1995)

Firth, Sir Charles, 'Clarendon's "History of the Rebellion"', *The English Historical Review*, 19:73 (1904), pp.26–54

Firth, Sir Charles, 'The Journal of Prince Rupert's Marches, 5 Sept. 1642 to 4 July 1646', *The English Historical Review*, 13:52 (1898), pp.729–41

Firth, Sir Charles, *The Academy*, 36 (2 November 1889)

Firth, Sir Charles, *The Academy*, 36 (9 November 1889)

Forster, John, *The Debates on the Grand Remonstrance, November and December, 1641. With an Introductory Essay on English Freedom under Plantagenet & Tudor Sovereigns* (London: John Murray, 1860)

Gardiner, Samuel R., *History of the Great Civil War, 1642–1649* (New York: Longmans, Green and Co., 1888), vols I–IV

Gardiner, Samuel R., *History of the Great Civil War, 1642–1649* (New York: Longmans, Green and Co., 1893), vols I–IV

'George Hobart-Hampden, 5th Earl of Buckinghamshire', *Wikipedia*, <https://en.wikipedia.org/wiki/George_Hobart-Hampden,_5th_Earl_of_Buckinghamshire>, accessed 18 Feb. 2023

Gibbs, Robert, *Buckinghamshire: A History of Aylesbury with Its Borough and Hundreds, the Hamlet of Walton, and the Electoral Division* (Aylesbury: Bucks Advertiser and Aylesbury News, 1885)

Gibbs, Robert, *Buckinghamshire: A Record of Local Occurrences and General Events, Chronologically Arranged* (Aylesbury: Bucks Advertiser and Aylesbury News, 1882), vol. IV

Harris, William, *An Historical and Critical Account of the Lives and Writings of James I. and Charles I. and of the Lives of Oliver Cromwell and Charles II. after the Manner of Mr. Bayle. From Original Writers and State-Papers* (London: G. Woodfall, 1814), vol. III

Hickman, Allan, and Bretherton, David, *Thame Inns Discovered II* (Thame: Daal Publishing, 2020)

Hill, Brian W., *Robert Harley: Speaker, Secretary of State and Premier Minister* (New Haven, CT: Yale University Press, 1988)

Hooper, Paul, *John Hampden in the Short Parliament, 1640* (London: John Hampden Society, 2007)

Huggett, Jane, *The Shaking of the Sheets Spotted: Death 1350–1660* (Bristol: Stuart Press, 1997)

Jansson, Maija, 'Shared Memory: John Hampden, New World and Old', *Journal for Eighteenth-Century Studies*, 32:2 (2009), pp.157–71

Lee, Frederick George, *The History, Description, and Antiquities of the Prebendal Church of the Blessed Virgin Mary of Thame, in the County and Diocese of Oxford, Including a Transcript of All the Monumental Inscriptions Remaining Therein; Extracts from the Registers and Churchwardens' Books; Together with Divers Original Pedigrees, Copious Antiquarian, Architectural, Personal, and Genealogical Notes and Appendices, Relating to, and Illustrative of, the Town, its History, and Inhabitants: In Which is Included Some Account of the Abbey of Thame Park, the Grammar School, and the Ancient Chapelries of Towersey, Tettesworth, Sydenham, North Weston, and Rycott* (London: Mitchell and Hughes, 1883)

Lester, Derek, 'Clarendon and History: A Case Study of the Battle of Chalgrove, 18th June 1643', *Journal of the Society for Army Historical Research*, 99:397 (2021), pp.134–51

Lester, Derek, and Blackshaw, Gill, *The Controversy of John Hampden's Death* (Oxford: Parchment Press, 2000)

Lester, Derek and Gill, 'The Military and Political Importance of the Battle of Chalgrove (1643)', *Oxoniensia*, 80 (2015), 27–39. <https://johnhampdensregiment.org.uk/oxoniensia/#p=1>

Lipscomb, George, *The History and Antiquities of the County of Buckingham* (London: J. & W. Robins, 1847), vol II

Macaulay, Lord Thomas Babington, *Lord Macaulay's Essays and Lays of Ancient Rome* (authorised edition, London: Longmans, Green and Co., 1885)

Morris, Richard B., '"Then and There the Child Independence was Born"', *American Heritage: The Magazine of History*, 13:2 (1962), pp.36–39 (see Appendix VII for text)

Newton, Arthur P., *The Colonising Activities of the English Puritans: The Last Phase of the Elizabethan Struggle with Spain* (New Haven, CT: Yale University Press, 1914)

Peachey, Stuart, and Turton, Alan, *Old Robin's Foot: Equipping and Campaigns of Essex's Infantry, 1642–1645* (Leigh-on-Sea: Partizan Press, 1987)

Porter, Stephen, and Marsh, Simon, *The Battle for London* (Stroud: Amberley Publishing, 2010)

Roberts, Keith, and Turner, Graham, *First Newbury 1643: The Turning Point* (Oxford: Osprey Publishing 2003)

Russell, Conrad, 'Hampden, John (1594–1643)', *Oxford Dictionary of National Biography* (2008), <https://doi.org/10.1093/ref:odnb/12169>

Sabine, Lorenzo, *The American Loyalists: Or, Biographical Sketches of Adherents to the British Crown in the War of the Revolution; Alphabetically Arranged; with a Preliminary Historical Essay* (Boston: Thurston, Torry and Co., 1847)

Scott, Christopher L., Turton, Alan, and Gruber von Arni, Eric, *Edgehill: The Battle Reinterpreted* (Barnsley: Pen and Sword, 2004)

Steane, John, *Medieval Bridges in Oxfordshire* (Oxford: Oxfordshire Council and Vale and Downland Museum, 1997)

Stevenson, John, and Carter, Andrew, 'The Raid on Chinnor and the Fight at Chalgrove Field, June 17th and 18th, 1643', *Oxoniensia*, 38 (1973), pp.346–56

Townley, Simon (ed.), *A History of the County of Oxford: Volume XVIII: Benson, Ewelme, and the Chilterns (Ewelme Hundred)* (Woodbridge: Boydell and Brewer, 2016)

Turton, Alan, *The Chief Strength of the Army: Essex's Horse (1642–1645)* (Leigh-on-Sea: Partizan Press, *c.* 1988)

Williams, Ann, *Domesday Book* (London: Folio Society, 2003), vols I–III

Williamson, Hugh Ross, *John Hampden: A Life* (London: Hodder and Stoughton, 1933)

Young, Peter, *Edgehill 1642: The Campaign and the Battle*, 2nd edn (Moreton-in-Marsh: Windrush Press, 1998)

Zeepvat, Bob, 'Battles and Burials at Holman's Bridge: Fact or Fiction?', *Records of Buckinghamshire*, 54 (2014), pp.135–41

Unpublished Works

Family tree of an unbroken line of Barbadian Hampden's 1645–1950 who returned to England in early 1800s (Private Collection, unpublished)

Lawrence, Norman, 'Notes on The Pye Family as written by Norman Lawrence (a descendant of the Pyes) in his unpublished *History of the Pye Family*, held by his son. Included is *The Pye Family of Faringdon – Historiette 1613–1813*, not attributed [Note by Norman Lawrence – Possibly by Samuel James Arnold, son-in-law to H. J. Pye (1745–1813)]', (unpublished)

Lawrence, Norman, *Of Royal Descent The Pye Family – Of Most Honourable and Ancient Extraction* (Private Collection, unpublished)

MacLaughlin, Eve, *Compiled Genealogy of Hampdens from 1066–1824* (unpublished)

Pearson, Michael J., *The History of a Regiment of Foot in the Earl of Essex's Army, 1642–1645*. 1997. Unpublished. University of Wales, Certificate in Local History

Young, Peter, 'National Army Museum: Unpublished papers, 9010-31-286: The Chalgrove Raid, 17–18 June, 1643', (unpublished)